Industrial Economics

Industrial Economics

By

N. Mani

Professor and Head,
Postgraduate and Research Department of Economics,
Erode Arts and Science College, Erode, Tamil Nadu

New Century Publications
New Delhi, India

NEW CENTURY PUBLICATIONS
74, Ansari Road, Ground Floor,
Daryaganj,
New Delhi – 110 002 (India)

Tel.: 011-4101 7798; 4358 7398; 98117 88655
E-mail: info@newcenturypublications.com
www.newcenturypublications.com

Editorial office:
4800 / 24, Bharat Ram Road,
Ansari Road, Daryaganj,
New Delhi – 110 002

First Published: **2021**

ISBN: **978-81-7708-531-0**

Published by New Century Publications and printed at Milan Enterprises, New Delhi

Designs: Patch Creative Unit, New Delhi

PRINTED IN INDIA

About the Book

Industrialization, being the significant determinant of economic development, has become the focus of economic policy for most countries of the world. Industrial growth contributes to the welfare of an economy by creating new occupations and hence new job opportunities. It is also associated with improvement in infrastructural facilities like transport and communications. In the wake of liberalization, privatization and openness wave sweeping across the world, emerging economies are paying greater attention to industrialization of their respective economies.

Industrial economics is the study of firms, industries, and markets. In the context of decision-making, industrial economics helps to understand such issues such as the levels at which capacity, output, and prices are set. Industrial economics also gives insights into how firms organize their activities with the main objective of profit maximisation.

There is also an international dimension to industrial economics: firms have the option to source inputs from and sell their products to foreign countries. Globalization has led to the growth of transnational (or multinational) corporations which operate in many parts of the world. Companies which operate in more than one country face different regulatory and tax regimes. Cross-border mergers and acquisitions (M&As) are becoming popular as transnational corporations take advantage of widespread liberalisation and deregulation to gain market shares, consolidate operations, improve efficiency and dilute the costs associated with investing in research and development and information technology. Although formation of regional groupings have been the prime movers of the bulk of the cross-border M&As in the developed world, M&As have also emerged as the preferred mode of foreign direct investment (FDI) inflows to the developing countries.

This book provides an understanding of the various problems and situations faced by the present and prospective entrepreneurs in setting-up/expanding their industrial units. It underscores the significance of industrialization and how modern economies are ensuring it. It explains and examines various issues involved in the process of industrialization in a lucid, cogent and analytical manner. It would connect teachers and students of the subject to the basic concepts, components and processes of industrial economics.

The book contains 25 chapters which have been organized into 2 parts.

Part I (chapters 1 to 18) is titled Basics of Industrial Economics. It provides conceptual and analytical clarification as regards forms of business organization, location of industry, types of market, production, cost and revenue functions of a firm, industrial productivity and efficiency, trade marks and patents, mergers and acquisitions (M&As), special economic zones (SEZs) and technology parks, entrepreneurship and innovations, industry and internet, industrial pollution and various other topics related to the subject.

Part II (chapters 19 to 25) is titled Industrialization in India. It explains and examines Indian industry in historical perspective, important laws to regulate industry and business, public sector enterprises (PSEs), micro, small and medium enterprises (MSMEs), industrial finance, recent initiatives for industrial development and ease of doing business in India.

About the Author

Dr. N. Mani is presently Head of the Postgraduate and Research Department of Economics, Erode Arts and Science College, Erode, Tamil Nadu. He holds M.A., M.Phil. and Ph.D. degrees from Bharathiar University, Coimbatore. Specializing in development economics, he has 30 years of teaching experience to postgraduate and undergraduate classes. He successfully completed 2 major research projects sponsored by the University Grants Commission (UGC), New Delhi. He is currently engaged in a research project sponsored by Indian Council of Social Science Research (ICSSR), New Delhi.

Dr. Mani has published 12 books and written several papers on varied subjects in reputed journals and dailies. He is also the former President of Tamil Nadu Science Forum and was organizing secretary of the National Children Science Congress, 2006. He has also organised more than 10 state, national and international level seminars, conferences and workshops. He has successfully guided and supervised the works of 6 Ph.D. and 14 M.Phil. scholars. He is a member of various academic bodies including Indian Society of Labour Economics and Indian Society of Agricultural Economics.

Contents

Part I: Basics of Industrial Economics

Part II: Industrialization in India

Preface

Industrial revolution started in the middle of the 18th century in Britain and gradually spread to other European countries. It was the transition to new manufacturing processes in Europe in the period from about 1760 onwards. This transition included going from hand production methods to machines, new chemical manufacturing and iron production processes, the increasing use of steam power and water power, the development of machine tools and the rise of the mechanized factory system. Industrial revolution also led to an unprecedented rise in urbanization. In short, industrial revolution marked a major turning point in history as almost every aspect of daily life was influenced in one way or the other.

In the wake of liberalization, privatization and openness wave sweeping across the world, emerging economies are paying greater attention to industrialization of their respective economies. A well-performing industrial sector plays an important role in poverty mitigation, unemployment reduction, trade promotion, exchange of goods and services, increased gross domestic product (GDP) and per capital income. Industrialization, being the significant determinant of economic development, has become the focus of economic policy for most countries of the world. Industrial growth contributes to the welfare of an economy by creating new occupations and hence new job opportunities. It is also associated with improvement in infrastructural facilities like transport and communications.

Industrial economics is the study of firms, industries, and markets. It looks at firms of all sizes. When analyzing decision-making at the levels of the individual firm and industry, industrial economics helps to understand such issues as the levels at which capacity, output, and prices are set. Industrial economics also gives insights into how firms organize their activities with the main objective of profit maximization.

One of the key issues in industrial economics is the type of market in which a particular firm operates. The number of buyers and sellers, and the nature of the product traded are important characteristics of market structure. Perfect competition and monopoly are the two extreme market situations. In between these two extremes lie a number of other market structures such as monopolistic competition, oligopoly and duopoly. All these in-between market structures are collectively called imperfect competition. Production and pricing decisions of a firm are conditioned by the type of market in which it operates.

There is also an international dimension to industrial economics. Firms have the option to source inputs from and sell their products to foreign countries. Globalization has led to the growth of transnational (or multinational) corporations which operate in many parts of the world. Companies which operate in more than one country face different regulatory and tax regimes.

Cross-border mergers and acquisitions (M&As) are becoming popular as transnational corporations take advantage of widespread liberalisation and deregulation in an effort to gain market shares, consolidate operations, improve efficiency and dilute the cost associated with investing in research and development and information technology. Although formation of regional groupings have been the prime movers of the bulk of the cross-border M&As in the developed world, M&As have also emerged as the preferred mode of foreign direct investment (FDI) inflows to the developing countries.

A country has to grapple with various issues in framing a suitable industrial policy for the country. These, *inter alia*, include the following.

1. Determination of the Relative Roles of Public and Private Sectors.
2. Relative Emphasis on Consumer Goods and Capital Goods Industries.
3. Relative Roles of Large and Small-scale Industries.
4. Location Policy for Industries.
5. Concentrated versus Broad-based Entrepreneurship.
6. Licensing Policy, Procedures, Rules and Regulations to Control Industrial Activities.
7. Role of Foreign Investment in Domestic Industrialization.

A well-performing industrial sector plays an important role in poverty mitigation, unemployment reduction, trade promotion, exchange of goods and services, increased gross domestic product (GDP) and per capital income. Industrialization, being the significant determinant of economic development, has become the focus of economic policy for most countries of the world. Industrial growth contributes to the welfare of an economy by creating new occupations and hence new job opportunities. It is also associated with improvement in infrastructural facilities like transport and communications.

In the wake of liberalization, privatization and openness wave sweeping across the world, emerging economies are paying greater attention to industrialization of their respective economies.

Industrial economics is the study of firms, industries, and markets. It looks at firms of all sizes. When analyzing decision-making at the levels of the individual firm and industry, industrial economics helps to understand such issues as the levels at which capacity, output, and prices are set. Industrial economics also gives insights into how firms organize their activities with the main objective of profit maximisation.

The book would connect teachers and students to the basic concepts, components and processes of industrial economics.

Erode
August 2021

N. Mani

Explanation of Select Terms Related to Industrial Economics

Agglomeration: It means area concentration of industrial activity which often provides firms with collective benefits that they would not enjoy in an isolated location. These collective benefits take the form of external economies or agglomeration. The advantages of a new firm locating among other firms engaged in the same activity include a pool of labour with particular skills and special educational institutions geared to the needs of the particular industry, both of which reduce the cost of training workers. Firms may also join together to develop a research institute, a marketing organization, and other collective facilities that individual manufacturers would be unable to provide for themselves.

Alfred Weber's Theory of Industrial Location: Alfred Weber, a German economist, enunciated a systematic theory of industrial location in 1909. Weber's theory of location is purely deductive in its approach. He formulated a theory of industrial location according to which an industry is located where the transportation costs of raw materials and final products are minimum.

Backward and Forward Linkages: Backward linkages occur when finished goods of a firm are used in the manufacturing process of another firm. Backward linkage is extremely common because so much of the activity in any region is producing for and oriented to the regional market. Forward linkages occur when a firm produces raw materials or intermediate products that are used in the manufacture of finished goods by another firm. This means that an impact of change is transmitted to an activity further along in the sequence of operations. Large food processing industry can develop linkages with agricultural producers, transporters and packaging suppliers. The agro-related industry has probably the most significant linkages.

Bilateral Monopoly: It is a market structure where there is one buyer and one seller. If the inhabitants in the above example form a trade union and deal with the owner of the sugar mill collectively, it will be a case of bilateral monopoly.

Co-operative: A co-operative is an organization that a group of individuals owns and runs to meet a common goal. These owners work together to operate the business, and they share the profits and other benefits. In a co-operative, the membership is voluntary. Anybody having a common interest is free to join a co-operative society. The member can also leave the society anytime after giving proper notice. In a co-operative society, the principle of *one-man, one vote* is adopted. A member has only one vote irrespective of the number of shares held by him. Thus, a co-operative society is run on democratic principles. A co-operative society is required to be registered with the relevant authority.

Corporate Governance: What constitutes corporate governance has been a subject of intense debate throughout the world with no concise, universally agreed upon, defined parameters. However, the concept has evolved in different ways in recent years depending upon the prevailing economic system. As per some of the well-accepted definitions, corporate governance refers to: (a) the system by which business corporations are directed and controlled and (b) structure through which the company objectives are set, means of attaining those objectives and monitoring the performance.

Corporate Social Responsibility (CSR): Corporate social responsibility (also called corporate conscience, corporate citizenship, social performance, sustainable responsible business) is a form of corporate self-regulation integrated into a business model. CSR policy functions as a built-in, self-regulating mechanism whereby a business monitors and ensures its active compliance with the spirit of the law, ethical standards, and international norms. In some models, a firm's implementation of CSR goes beyond compliance and engages in "actions that appear to further some social good, beyond the interests of the firm and that which is required by law". CSR is a process with the aim to embrace responsibility for the company's actions and encourage a positive impact through its activities on the environment, consumers, employees, communities, stakeholders and all other members of the public sphere who may also be considered as stakeholders.

Duopoly: Duopoly is a market situation characterised by two sellers and many buyers as, for example, two firms selling identical spring water. Duopoly is the simplest and special case of oligopoly. Since in duopoly there are only two producers, any price or output change by one is bound to affect the other significantly.

Entrepreneur: An entrepreneur is an individual who organizes and operates a business or businesses, taking on financial risk to do so. The entrepreneur is commonly seen as an innovator of new ideas, and business processes. Management skill and strong team building abilities are often perceived as essential leadership attributes for successful entrepreneurs. Leadership, management ability, and team-building are considered to be the essential qualities of an entrepreneur.

Entrepreneurship: In political economics, entrepreneurship is the quality of being an entrepreneur, i.e. one who *undertakes an enterprise*. The term puts emphasis on the risk and effort taken by individuals who both own and manage a business, and on the innovations resulting from their pursuit of economic success. Entrepreneurship in this sense may result in new organizations or may be part of revitalizing mature organizations in response to a perceived opportunity. The most obvious form of entrepreneurship is that of starting new businesses (referred as a start-up company). In recent years, the term has been extended to include social and political forms of entrepreneurial activity. When entrepreneurship is describing activities within a firm or large organization it is referred to as intra-preneurship and may include corporate venturing, when large entities spin-off organizations.

Environmental Pollution: It can be defined as an undesirable change in the physical, chemical, or biological characteristics of the air, water or land that can harmfully affect health, survival or activities of human beings or other living organisms. Pollution refers essentially to a process by which a resource is rendered unfit for some beneficial use. Of the various kinds of pollution (air, water, land, noise, radiation and odour) that affect the quality of life in India, water pollution is by far the most serious in its implications for the health and well-being of the people.

Foreign Direct Investment (FDI): FDI is the outcome of the mutual interests of multinational firms and host countries. According to the International Monetary Fund (IMF), FDI is defined as "investment that is made to acquire a lasting interest in an enterprise operating in an economy other than that of the investor. The investor's purpose is to have an effective voice in the management of the enterprise". The essence of FDI is the transmission to the host country of a package of capital, managerial, skill and technical knowledge. FDI is generally a form of long-term international capital movement, made for the purpose of productive activity and accompanied by the intention of managerial control or participation in the management of a foreign firm.

Geographical Indication: A geographical indication identifies agricultural or natural or manufactured goods as originating or manufactured in the territory of a country or region or locality in that territory, where a given quality, reputation or other characteristic of such goods is essentially attributable towards geographical origin and in case where such goods are manufactured goods one of the activities of either the production or a processing of preparation of the goods concerned takes place in such territory, region, or locality as the case may be.

Globalisation: Globalisation implies widening and deepening integration with the *globe*, i.e. with people and processes abroad. The trend towards the evolution of a global society is generally thought of in economic terms and in terms of the consequences of the revolution in communication technologies. There is undoubtedly much greater economic integration among the nations of the world today. Globalisation is widely seen as the most important factor that could influence economies of nations the world over in the 21st century. The rapid advancement in information technology and communications has made it not just possible but absolutely essential for economies of the world to adapt or fall by the wayside. More changes can be expected in the business scenario specifically in terms of openness, adaptiveness and responsiveness.

Human Resources Development (HRD): HRD aims at improving human resources. HRD is concerned with the development of competencies and effectiveness of people working in the organization. The design of HRD system should strengthens corporate planning, production processes, marketing strategies, and budgeting and finance. Different roles in an organization should be integrated using different mechanisms, e.g. manpower planning inputs should be available to line managers so that they can do career planning. A systematic way to monitor the progress and to identify the level of effectiveness of the system is required.

Human Resources Management (HRM): HRM relates to formulation of strategies by business entities concerning selection, training and rewarding of their personnel. The subject has assumed added significance in the wake of liberalization and globalization trends sweeping across the world. In the face of intense competition unleashed by market-oriented reforms, firms are vying with each other to acquire competitive advantage to prosper in business and in many cases to survive in business. Every possible strategy is being applied to achieve the explicit and implicit objectives of the firm. HRM has emerged as an important ingredient of the policy mix to score points over the existing and potential competitors.

Industrial Clusters: Industrial clusters occur when many industries are located close to each other and share the benefits of their closeness. It is widely observed that industrial clusters play a significant role in successful industrial development in both developed and developing countries. They are also seen as drivers of national competitiveness and growth. In many developing countries, micro and small enterprises dominate the industrial clusters. They tend to be successful because they have the capacity to improve the quality of their products and to develop new marketing channels. As these enterprises are labour-intensive, they are expected to contribute to poverty alleviation by raising employment opportunities.

Industrial Design: A design refers only to the features of shape, configuration, pattern, ornamentations, composition of colour or line or a combination thereof, applied to any article, whether two or three dimensional or in both forms by any industrial process or means which in the finished article, appeal to and are judged solely by the eye.

Industrial Economics: Industrial economics is the study of firms, industries, and markets. It looks at firms of all sizes. When analyzing decision-making at the levels of the individual firm and industry, industrial economics helps to understand such issues as the levels at which capacity, output, and prices are set. Industrial economics also gives insights into how firms organize their activities with the main objective of profit maximisation.

Industrial Productivity: It is a measurement of the efficiency of production. Basically, it is the relationship between the amount of output and the amount of inputs used to produce goods. In other words, it is the ratio of output to input: Productivity = output ÷ input.

Industrial Revolution: Industrial revolution started in the middle of the 18th century in Britain and gradually spread to other European countries. It was the transition to new manufacturing processes in Europe in the period from about 1760 onwards. This transition included going from hand production methods to machines, new chemical manufacturing and iron production processes, the increasing use of steam power and water power, the development of machine tools and the rise of the mechanized factory system. Industrial revolution also led to an unprecedented rise in urbanization.

Infrastructure: Infrastructure is generally defined as the physical framework of facilities through which goods and services are provided to the public. Its linkages to the economy are multiple and complex, because it affects production and consumption directly, creates positive and negative spill over effects (externalities), and involves large flows of expenditure. In economic literature, infrastructure is popular by the name *overhead capital* which represents basic services without which primary, secondary and tertiary productive activities cannot function. Generically, infrastructure has the following distinct components: energy, transport, telecommunications, information technology, irrigation facilities etc.

Innovation: Innovation is a process whereby people or groups of people with an entrepreneurial mindset (organizations, enterprises) develop new ideas or absorb and adapt existing ones. Together with institutions and policies that affect their behaviour and performance, they create new products, processes, and forms of organization. Innovation is not only about scientists in laboratories, theoretical science, or new discoveries. It is about building the capacity to find solutions to practical everyday development problems. So, an innovative economy is marked by ideas for new products or new ways of doing things and transforming them into profitable products or activities.

Input-Output Analysis: Input-output analysis, attributed to American economist Wassily Loentief, deals with general equilibrium situation in the empirical study of production. It has three distinctive features: (a) it deals almost exclusively with production, (b) it is concerned with empirical investigations, and (c) it is related to general equilibrium phenomenon.

Intellectual Property Rights (IPRs): IPRs refer to the legal ownership by a person or business of an invention/discovery attached to particular product or process which protects the owner against unauthorized copying or imitation. The Agreement establishing the World Trade Organization (WTO) contains, *inter alia*, an Agreement on Trade-related Aspects of Intellectual Property Rights (TRIPS). TRIPS Agreement, which came into effect on January 1, 1995, is to date the most comprehensive multilateral agreement on intellectual property. TRIPS provides, among others, for norms and standards in respect of following areas of intellectual property: trademarks, patents, industrial designs, and geographical indications.

Internet Marketing: New forms of marketing also use the internet and are therefore called *internet marketing* or more generally *e-marketing*, *online marketing*, *digital marketing*. Internet marketing is sometimes considered to be broad in scope, because it not only refers to marketing on the internet, but also includes marketing done via e-mail, wireless media as well as driving audience from traditional marketing methods like radio and billboard to internet properties or landing page.

Joint Stock Company: A joint stock company or simply a company may be defined as a voluntary association of persons having separate legal existence, perpetual succession and a common seal. There must be a group of persons who voluntarily agree to form a company. Once formed the company becomes a separate legal entity with a distinct name of its own. Its existence is not affected by change of members. It must have a seal to be imprinted on documents whenever required. The capital of a company consists of transferable shares, and members have limited liability. A large company may employ thousands of people. A company is considered by law to be a unique entity, separate from those who own it. A company can be taxed, sued and enter into contractual agreements. A company has a life of its own and does not dissolve when ownership changes.

Law of Diminishing Returns: The law of diminishing returns states that if increasing quantities of a variable factor (labour) are applied to a given quantity of fixed factor (land), the marginal product of the variable factor will eventually decline. Historically, the law of diminishing returns is associated with agricultural operations, with land being the fixed factor and labour the variable factor. However, this law holds good for all those productive activities where increasing quantities of a variable factor are applied to a given quantity of a fixed factor.

Law of Returns to Scale: This law pertains to production situation under which all factors of production can be increased in a given proportion. By assuming that all factors are variable, the law deals with long-run variations in output. Only two factors of production, viz. labour and capital are taken into account. There are three dimensions of returns to scale. 1. Increasing Returns to Scale: This is a situation where if factors are increased in a given proportion, output increases in a greater proportion. For example, if labour and capital are doubled, output is more than doubled. 2. Constant Returns to Scale: This case refers to that situation where if factors are increased in a given proportion, the output also increases in the same proportion. 3. Decreasing Returns to Scale: If factors of production are increased in a given proportion and output increases in a smaller proportion, it will be a situation of decreasing returns.

Location of Industry: It refers to establishment of an industry or cluster of industries in a particular location or region due to availability of cheap factors of production, transport and infrastructural facilities, demand incentives, raw materials etc. These are some of the factors which attract entrepreneurs to set up their plants in a particular area. Once the process starts, it has a tendency to accelerate. A series of location factors influence the location patterns of various individual industries during their respective periods of evolution. No single location factor on its own absolutely determines or clearly indicates the right location of a given industry. Among the principal factors enumerated by the theorists, transportation costs in general, and those of finished products in particular, seem decisive in the choice of the location of most industrial plants.

Logistics: It refers to a series of services and activities, such as transportation, warehousing, and brokerage, that help to move goods and establish supply chains across and within borders. Logistics organizes the movement of goods through a network of activities and services operating at global, regional, and local scale. Efficient logistics connects people and firms to markets and opportunities and helps achieve higher levels of productivity and welfare.

Make in India Campaign: *Make in India* is an initiative of the Government of India to encourage multinational, as well as domestic, companies to manufacture their products in India. It was launched by Prime Minister Narendra Modi on September 25, 2014. The objective is to make India as the top destination globally for foreign direct investment.

Mergers and Acquisitions (M&A): M&A is a general term used to describe the consolidation of companies or assets through various types of financial transactions, including mergers, acquisitions, consolidations, purchase of assets, and management acquisitions. Collectively, M&A are transactions in which the ownership of companies or other business organizations is transferred or consolidated with other entities. As an aspect of strategic management, M&A can allow enterprises to grow and change the nature of their business or competitive position.

Monopolistic Competition: Perfect competition and monopoly are two extreme market situations. In the real world, most firms operate under intermediate market structures like oligopoly, duopoly and monopolistic competition. These intermediate market structures are collectively called *imperfect competition*. Monopolistic competition is the most representative example of *imperfect competition*.

Monopoly: Monopoly is a market situation characterised by one seller and many buyers. It is the opposite extreme of perfect competition. Being the sole seller, a monopolist has the power to influence the market price. Unlike a competitive firm, a monopolist firm is a price-setter, not a price-taker. Since a monopolist is the only producer of his product, the distinction between a firm and the industry vanishes.

Monopsony: It is a market situation where there is only one buyer but the number of sellers is very large. For example, owner of a sugar mill in a remote area is the only buyer of the labour services of the inhabitants of that area.

Oligopoly: It is a market structure characterised by few sellers and many buyers. An oligopoly is an industry comprising only a few competing firms. These firms are strong rivals constantly watching jealously each other's decisions and reacting accordingly. This type of market structure is frequently observed in real life as, for example, car manufacturers.

Partnership: In a partnership, two or more people share ownership of a single business. More specifically, partnership is an association of persons who agree to combine their financial resources and managerial abilities to run a business and share profits in an agreed ratio. The law does not distinguish between the business and its owners. The partners generally have a legal agreement (called *partnership deed*) that establishes, *inter alia*, how decisions will be made, how profits will be shared, how disputes will be resolved, and what steps will be taken to dissolve the partnership in case things go sour. In other words, a partnership deed lays down the terms and conditions of partnership and the rights, duties and obligations of partners.

Patent: A patent is granted for an invention which is a new product or process, that meets conditions of novelty, non-obviousness and industrial use. Inventive step is the feature(s) of the invention that involves technical advance as compared to existing knowledge and that makes the invention not obvious to a person skilled in the art. Industrial use means that the invention is capable of being made or used in an industry.

Perfect Competition: It is a market situation marked by a large number of buyers and sellers so that no individual buyer or seller can influence the market price. A firm is a price-taker, i.e. it must accept the price ruling in the market. All the firms in a competitive market sell homogeneous product. Firms enjoy freedom of entry into and freedom of exit from the industry. Moreover, buyers and sellers are well informed about market conditions.

Production Function: A production function explains the technological relationship between inputs and output: $P = f(F_1, F_2, ...F_n)$. In this equation, P is the quantity of production and $F_1, F_2, ...F_n$ are the quantities of different factors of production.

Sargent Florence's Theory of Industrial Location: According to this theory, geographical location of an industry is not as important as the distribution of occupied population. It advocates that occupational distribution of population should be the main and primary factor for taking into consideration the location of an industry. It is based on inductive analysis and while explaining location of an industry it takes into consideration co-efficient of localisation.

Sole Proprietorship: Sole proprietorship (also called single ownership) is a form of business that is owned, managed and controlled by an individual. He has to arrange capital for the business and he alone is responsible for its management. He is therefore, entitled to the profits and has to bear the loss of business. However, he can take the help of his family members and also make use of the services of others such as a manager and other employees. Small factories and shops are often found to be sole proprietorship organizations. It is the simplest and most easily formed business organization. This is because not much legal formality is required to establish it. Sole proprietorship has one owner who makes all of the business decisions, and there is no distinction between the business and the owner. Some typical examples of sole proprietorship include grocery shops, fruit and vegetables marts, tea stalls, beauty parlours and wellness centres and personal businesses of doctors, teachers, artists, consultants and other self-employed business owners who operate on a solo basis.

Special Economic Zones (SEZs): SEZs are geographical regions in a country subject to economic laws which are liberal than typical economic laws of that country. The word *special* mainly means special economic system and policies. A SEZ can be deemed as a *foreign territory* for the purposes of trade operations, duties and tariffs. Units in SEZs enjoy lot of fiscal pampering. SEZs are self-contained islands providing high-quality infrastructural facilities. SEZs offer industrial, residential and commercial areas with developed plots/pre-built factories, power, telecommunications, water supply, sewerage and drainage, and educational and medical facilities.

Stand-up India Scheme: Scheduled castes (SCs) and scheduled tribes (STs) entrepreneurs are beginning to show great promise in starting and running successful business enterprises. Stand-up India scheme was announced by Prime Minister Narendra Modi in his address to the nation from the ramparts of Red Fort on August 15, 2015. The scheme was launched on April 5, 2016. The scheme caters to promoting entrepreneurship amongst women, SCs and STs categories, i.e. those sections of the population facing significant hurdles due to lack of advice/mentorship as well as inadequate and delayed credit. The scheme intends to leverage the institutional credit structure to reach out to these underserved sectors of the population in starting green-field enterprises. It caters to both ready and trainee borrowers.

Start-up India Initiative: Launched on January 16, 2016, Start-up India is a flagship initiative of the Government of India, intended to build a strong eco-system for nurturing innovation and Start-ups in the country that will drive sustainable economic growth and generate large scale employment opportunities. The Government through this initiative aims to empower Start-ups to grow through innovation and design.

Start-up: A start-up company (or simply a start-up) is an entrepreneurial venture which is typically a newly emerged, fast-growing business that aims to meet a marketplace need by developing a viable business model around an innovative product, service, process or a platform. A start-up is usually a company designed to effectively develop and validate a scalable business model. Start-ups have high rates of failure, but the minority of successes includes companies that have become large and influential. Although there are start-ups created in all types of businesses, and all over the world, some locations and business sectors are particularly associated with start-up companies. The internet bubble of the late 1990s was associated with huge numbers of internet start-up companies, some selling the technology to provide internet access, others using the internet to provide services. Most of this start-up activity was located in the most well-known start-up ecosystem—Silicon Valley, an area of northern California renowned for the high level of start-up company activity.

Sustainable Development: The concept of sustainable development is inextricably linked with environment protection. It is a strategy for improving the quality of human life while living within the carrying capacity of supporting eco system. Sustainable development is that which meets the needs of the present without compromising the ability of future generations.

Technology Park: The ultimate objective of a technology park is to provide an environment that will enable the localization of various tech-related companies. It is a development that brings together office spaces, residential areas, and retail developments in order to enhance the operations of tech corporations, thereby providing various benefits and economies of scale to each individual business entity. Technology parks are able to perfectly integrate row houses, residential complexes, villas, as well as low-rise and high-rise apartments with commercial and convenience establishments, clubs and resorts, and various facilities that make living and working as comfortable as possible. All of these amenities are ideally supposed to help in attracting investors and to promote the setting up of various businesses, ensuring that they get all they need to thrive and reach their operating objectives.

Trademark: A trademark means a mark capable of being represented graphically and which is capable of distinguishing the goods or services of one undertaking from those of other undertakings. A trade mark can be a device, brand, heading, label ticket name, packaging, sign, word, letter, number, drawing, picture, emblem, colour or combination of colours, shape of goods, signature or a combination thereof.

William Launhardt's Location Triangle Model: The analysis of William Launhardt provided the basis for the theory of industrial location. It was his contention that the decision to locate in a particular place would be based on transport costs of raw materials, inputs, finished goods etc. Using a simple model called the *location triangle* and the concept of ton-mileage, Launhardt suggested that as bulky products incur high transportation costs, the profits of finished goods should make these costs worthwhile; If not, a rational manufacturer would opt to relocate, always seeking the point of least transportation costs.

World Bank's Doing Business Report: *Doing Business Report* is a flagship annual publication of the World Bank. It looks at domestic small and medium-sized companies and measures the regulations applying to them through their life cycle. Doing business captures several important dimensions of the regulatory environment as it applies to local firms. The purpose of *Doing Business Report* is to provide objective data for use by governments in designing sound business regulatory policies and to encourage research on the important dimensions of the regulatory environment for firms.

Abbreviations/Acronyms

AC	Average cost
ACF	Average cost of funds
AP	Average product
B2B	Business-to-business
B2C	Business-to-consumers
BOO	Build-own-operate
BOT	Build-operate-transfer
BPO	Business process outsourcing
BRAP	Business reform action plan
CCI	Competition Commission of India
CPSEs	Central public sector enterprises
CSR	Corporate social responsibility
DCF	Discounted cash flow
DFIs	Development finance institutions
DIPP	Department of Industrial Policy and Promotion
ECB	External commercial borrowing
EDIs	Entrepreneurship development institutes
EDPs	Entrepreneurship development programmes
EIA	Environmental impact assessment
EMAS	Eco-management and audit scheme
EPZ	Export processing zone
EV	Enterprise value
EV/sales	Enterprise-value-to-sales ratio
FDI	Foreign direct investment
G2B	Government-to-business
GPD	Gross domestic product
HRD	Human resource development
HRM	Human resources management
IBBI	Insolvency and Bankruptcy Board of India
IBC	Insolvency and Bankruptcy Code
IPO	Initial public offering
IPRs	Intellectual property rights
IT	Information technology
JV	Joint venture
JVC	Joint venture company
LLP	Limited liability partnership
M&As	Mergers and acquisitions
MC	Marginal cost
MFP	Multi-factor productivity
MNCs	Multinational corporations

MP	Marginal product
MSMEs	Micro, small and medium enterprises
MVP	Minimum viable product
NGOs	Non-governmental organizations
OECD	Organization for Economic Co-operation and Development
P/E Ratio	Price-earnings ratio
PPP	Public-private-partnership
RBV	Resource-based-view
SEZs	Special economic zones
SNA	System of National Accounts
SPV	Special purpose vehicle
SRI	Socially responsible investment
STPs	Software technology parks
TBL	Triple bottom line
TC	Total cost
TFC	Total fixed cost
TFP	Total factor productivity
TNCs	Transnational corporations
TP	Total product
TRIPS	Agreement on trade-related aspects of intellectual property rights
TVC	Total variable cost
UNEP-F1	United Nations Environment Programme-Finance Initiative
UNO	United Nations Organization
WACC	Weighted average costs of capital
WIPO	World Intellectual Property Organization
WTO	World Trade Organization

Part I
Basics of Industrial Economics

1

Industrial Economics: An Introduction

A well-performing industrial sector plays an important role in poverty mitigation, unemployment reduction, trade promotion, exchange of goods and services, increased gross domestic product (GDP) and per capital income. Industrialization, being the significant determinant of economic development, has become the focus of economic policy for most countries of the world. Industrial growth contributes to the welfare of an economy by creating new occupations and hence new job opportunities. It is also associated with improvement in infrastructural facilities like transport and communications.

1.1 Meaning and Scope of Industrial Economics

In the wake of liberalization, privatization and openness wave sweeping across the world, emerging economies are paying greater attention to industrialization of their respective economies.

Industrial economics is the study of firms, industries, and markets. It looks at firms of all sizes. When analyzing decision-making at the levels of the individual firm and industry, industrial economics helps to understand such issues as the levels at which capacity, output, and prices are set. Industrial economics also gives insights into how firms organize their activities with the main objective of profit maximisation.

One of the key issues in industrial economics is the type of market in which a particular firm operates. The number of buyers and sellers, and the nature of the product traded are important characteristics of market structure. Perfect competition and monopoly are the two extreme market situations. In between these two extremes lie a number of other market structures such as monopolistic competition, oligopoly and duopoly. All these in-between market structures are collectively called imperfect competition. Production and pricing decisions of a firm are conditioned by the type of market in which it operates.

There is also an international dimension to industrial economics: firms have the option to source inputs from and sell their products to foreign countries. Globalization has led to the growth of transnational (or multinational) corporations which operate in many parts of the world. Companies which operate in more than one country face different regulatory and tax regimes.

Cross-border mergers and acquisitions (M&As) are becoming popular as transnational corporations take advantage of widespread liberalisation and deregulation in an effort to gain market shares, consolidate operations, improve efficiency and dilute the cost associated with investing in research and development and information technology. Although formation of regional groupings have been the prime movers of the bulk of the cross-border M&As in the developed world, M&As have also emerged as the preferred mode of foreign direct investment (FDI) inflows to the developing countries.

1.2 Industrial Revolution

Industrial revolution started in the middle of the 18th century in Britain and gradually spread to other European countries. It was the transition to new manufacturing processes in Europe in the period from about 1760 onwards. This transition included going from hand production methods to machines, new chemical manufacturing and iron production processes, the increasing use of steam power and water power, the development of machine tools and the rise of the mechanized factory system. Industrial revolution also led to an unprecedented rise in urbanization.

Textiles were the dominant industry of the industrial revolution in terms of employment, value of output and capital invested. The textile industry was also the first to use modern production methods.

Many of the technological innovations had origins in Britain which became the world's leading commercial nation, controlling a global trading empire with colonies in North America, the Caribbean, and the Indian subcontinent through the activities of the East India Company. The development of trade and the rise of business were among the major causes of the industrial revolution.

Industrial revolution marked a major turning point in history as almost every aspect of daily life was influenced in one way or the other. In particular, average income and population began to exhibit unprecedented sustained growth. The most important effect of the industrial revolution was that the standard of living for the general population in the western world began to increase consistently for the first time in history.

Industrial revolution in any country implies the onset of fundamental changes in the structure of its economy, particularly redeployment of resources away from agriculture. Each industrial revolution contains the following essential ingredients:

1. Shift from primary production to secondary and tertiary production.
2. Shift from family-based subsistence units of production to the impersonal capitalistic form of enterprise.
3. Use of machines and modern technology.
4. Use of new raw materials which are either more efficient or less scarce.
5. Opening up of national and international markets for goods and factors of production.

1.3 Issues in Industrialization

A country has to grapple with various issues in framing a suitable industrial policy for the country. These, *inter alia*, include the following.

1.3.1 Determination of the Relative Roles of Public and Private Sectors: Industrial policy should clearly mention the responsibility of the government in the matter of promoting, assisting and regulating the development of industry in the national interest. In other words, the fields for the public and private sectors need to be demarcated. For example, in India, the Industrial Policy Resolution of 1948 envisaged a mixed economy for the country. It declared that public sector would play an effective and dominant role in the future economic development of India. This role was to be particularly significant in the establishment and development of heavy and basic industries. Certain crucial sectors for industrial development were reserved for Government initiative.

1.3.2 Relative Emphasis on Consumer Goods and Capital Goods Industries: Consumer goods (or consumption goods) are purchased and used by households. They have no future productive use. Contrarily, capital goods include machines, tools and implements which are purchased by manufacturers for producing other goods. The relative emphasis on the production of these two categories of goods has implications for the rate of growth of the economy.

1.3.3 Relative Roles of Large and Small-scale Industries: Apart from large-scale industries, micro, small and medium enterprises (MSMEs) also play an important role in the economic and social development of a country. MSMEs are the nursery for entrepreneurship, often driven by the individual creativity and innovation, with a significant contribution in the country's gross domestic product (GDP), manufacturing output, exports and employment generation.

1.3.4 Location Policy for Industries: There are various economic and social criteria to determine location of industries. Economic criteria include availability of raw materials, nearness to market and infrastructural facilities. These may be available in already developed areas. Social criteria include employment opportunities and laying of social and economic overheads in backward areas.

1.3.5 Concentrated versus Broad-based Entrepreneurship: Industrial policy must ensure the dispersal of ownership and avoid the growth of economic concentration and of monopolies.

1.3.6 Licensing Policy, Procedures, Rules and Regulations to Control Industrial Activities: Government has to put in place a variety of legislations and rules which are aimed at controlling and regulating the industrial activities in the economy. Necessary legislative framework is necessary for implementing the industrial policy and to enable the government to direct investment into desired channels of industrial activity through the mechanism of licensing keeping with national development objectives.

1.3.7 Role of Foreign Investment in Domestic Industrialization: Foreign direct investment (FDI) is an important source of non-debt finance and hence a factor in the economic development of a country. Apart from supplementing domestic investment, it brings with it internationally available technologies, managerial skills and practices, and new employment opportunities.

1.4 Classification of Industries

Economic activities can be classified in a variety of ways. In general, all economic activities are broadly divided into three categories:
1. Primary sector (agriculture and allied activities).
2. Secondary sector (industrial activities).
3. Tertiary sector (services sector).

Industries are part of the secondary sector which converts raw material into finished goods which are more valuable to society.

Industry   classification organizes   companies   into industrial groupings   based   on similar production processes, similar products, or similar behaviour in financial markets.

1.4.1 Raw Material-based Classification:

1. **Agro-based Industries:** These industries use <u>plants</u> and animal-based products as their raw materials as, for example, food processing, vegetable oil, cotton textile, dairy products, and leather industries.
2. **Mineral-based Industries:** Mineral-based industries are based on mining and use mineral <u>ore</u> as raw material as, for example, aluminium industry.
3. **Marine-based Industries:** Marine-based industries use raw materials from sea as, for example, fish oil.
4. **Forest-based Industries:** These industries use raw materials from the forest as, for example, paper, pharmaceutical, and furniture.

1.4.2 Size-based Classification: Size of industries is measured by amount of investment, number of employees and the value of goods produced.

1. **Cottage Industries:** These are generally artisan-based, located mostly in rural and semi-urban areas. These industries use local skills and resources and sell their products locally. These enterprises involve lower levels of investment in machinery and provide largely part-time employment. In India, they are spread throughout the country and include such activities as handlooms, *khadi*, sericulture, coir, *bidi*-making, embroidery, knitting, wood-carving and other handicrafts.
2. **Small and Medium Industries:** Such industries use power-driven machines and possess some technological sophistication. The market for these industries is relatively wide and quite often includes export market. These industries are generally located close to or in the urban areas including large industrial centres. Their products include hosiery goods, ready-made garments, motor-parts, electronics, sports goods, rubber goods, and engineering goods.
3. **Large-scale Industries:** In these industries, capital invested is large and advanced technology is in used as, for example, automobiles and steel industries.

1.4.3 Ownership-based Classification:

1. **Private Sector Industries:** Private industries are businesses that are owned and operated by an individual or group of individuals.
2. **Public Sector Industries:** Public industries are owned and managed by the government as, for example, Steel Authority of India.
3. **Joint Sector Industries:** These industries are jointly operated by the government and individuals as, for example, Maruti Udyog.
4. **Co-operative Sector Industries:** Co-operative industries are operated by the suppliers, producers or workers as, for example, Amul India.

1.5 Industrial Clusters

Industrial clusters occur when many industries are located close to each other and share the benefits of their closeness. It is widely observed that industrial clusters play a significant role in successful industrial development in both developed and developing countries. They are also seen as drivers of national competitiveness and growth. In many developing countries, micro and small enterprises dominate the industrial clusters. They tend to be successful because they have the capacity to improve the quality of their products and to develop new marketing channels. As these enterprises are labour-intensive, they are expected to contribute to poverty alleviation by raising employment opportunities.

1.5.1 What is an Industrial Cluster? Traditionally, clustering refers to the process in which geographically proximate producers, suppliers, buyers, and other actors develop and intensify collaboration with mutually beneficial effects. In its most advanced form, a cluster can be defined as a geographically proximate group of interconnected enterprises and associated institutions in a particular field, linked by commonality and complementarity. Thus, a cluster may include suppliers of inputs, or extend downstream to regular buyers or exporters, government institutions, business associations, providers of business services, and agencies that support clustered enterprises in such fields as product development, production process improvement, technology, marketing information and vocational training.

1.5.2 Potential Benefits of a Cluster: A growing body of literature in both advanced as well as developing countries suggests that the collocation of enterprises in clusters is aimed at securing some of the following benefits:

1. Reduction in transaction costs.
2. Innovation and technological development arising from local interactions (knowledge externalities and spillovers).
3. Reduced costs through learning by imitation and emulation.
4. Localised external economies such as specialized labour market, specialization through increased local division of labour and existence of competent specialized suppliers.
5. Advantages related to being customer-driven organization and product diversification.
6. Joint action of local producers—cooperation among enterprises or groups of firms joining forces in business associations or consortia—that would *inter alia* enable the cooperating units collectively to reap the economies of both scale and scope to the extent they work as complementary and mutually supportive producers.

A vast majority of the empirical studies have found that clustered enterprises show a higher innovative capacity than isolated firms. Such clusters open up efficiency gains which individual enterprises rarely attain. These efficiency gains are due to the competitive advantage derived from local external economies and joint action. This is true not only in developed countries but also in developing countries. As a result, clusters are now common in a wide range of countries and sectors. In addition, they have helped small enterprises to overcome well-known growth and marketing constraints. However, the growth experiences have been diverse. At one extreme, there are artisanal clusters with little dynamism and low innovative capacity. At the other extreme, there are clusters with deepening inter-firm division of labour, enhanced competitiveness and international market penetration.

Isolated enterprises generally face additional constraints in the era of liberalization and globalization that require products with higher quality, larger production quantities, and regular supply. This restricts their ability to improve efficiency and productivity and also to adapt and be flexible in changing market conditions including difficulties associated with economies of scale. Thus, clusters can be a powerful means for overcoming these constraints and succeeding in an ever more competitive market environment.

1.5.3 Determinants of Cluster Development: The critical factors that explain growth and competitiveness of clustered enterprises are local external economies (incidental benefits producers provide for each other) and consciously pursued joint action (industrial networks or collective action).

Whether or not a cluster becomes an integrated part of an economic system and contributes to economic growth depends on the type of cluster (sectoral location), geography (physical location), institutional landscape, external (macroeconomic) environment, and whether or not the combination of all these factors is conducive to learning.

Research on industrial clusters provides evidence on the following conditions for successful industrial clusters: (a) infrastructure, (b) institutional framework (legal system, participatory actors, coordination among actors etc.), and (c) government support in terms of laws, taxation and finance. Among these conditions, the role of government is particularly emphasized. It is well known that in developing countries market mechanisms for fostering development does not function well due to regulations, bureaucracy and existing legal framework. In addition, there is no proper market for capital or human resources. Hence, the government must complement market mechanism and address the conditions to foster industrial clusters.

Historically, the best known examples are the Italian industrial districts and similar examples in other developed countries where clusters of small enterprises have broken into international markets. Recent research on industrial clusters has documented some notable success stories of small enterprises growing fast and competing in export markets. Some such examples are the following: furniture (Indonesia), towels (Turkey), jewellery (Thailand), computers (Taiwan), and shoes (Brazil).

In India, in recent times, a new and modern coir cluster has emerged in Pollachi in Tamil Nadu. Ahmedabad, Bangalore, Delhi and Mumbai have a strong presence in readymade garments. In cotton hosiery, Tiruppur accounts for more than 80 percent of the country's exports; so is the situation of Ludhiana in woollen hosiery and knitwear. Surat, Jaipur and Tiruchirappalli have clusters of gems and jewellery mainly for exports. Leather and leather products are concentrated in Agra, Chennai, Howrah and Kanpur. A number of handicraft clusters can be found in many parts of the country. To this list may be added the less well-known agro-processing and agro-industry clusters in many parts of the country such as those based on spices, bamboo, rubber and fruits.

1.6 Globalization and Industrial Development

The 1990s witnessed a paradigm shift towards market-oriented economic policies and a careful dismantling of obstacles in its wake. Globalization has resulted in the creation of a new business framework.

1.6.1 Meaning and Impact of Globalization: Globalization implies widening and deepening integration with the *globe*, i.e. with people and processes abroad. The trend towards the evolution of a global society is generally thought of in economic terms and in terms of the consequences of the revolution in communication technologies. There is undoubtedly much greater economic integration among the nations of the world today. Globalization is widely seen as the most important factor that could influence economies of nations the world over in the 21st century. The rapid advancement in information technology and communications has made it not just possible but absolutely essential for economies of the world to adapt or fall by the wayside. More changes can be expected in the business scenario specifically in terms of openness, adaptiveness and responsiveness.

1.6.2 Growth of Transnational Corporations: Globalization has resulted in the growing concentration and monopolisation of economic resources and power by transnational corporations and by global financial firms and funds. This process has been termed transnationalisation, in which fewer and fewer transnational corporations are gaining a large and rapidly increasing proportion of world economic resources, production and market shares. Where a multinational company used to dominate the market of a single product, a big transnational company (TNC) now typically produces or trades in an increasing multitude of products, services and sectors. Through mergers and acquisitions, fewer and fewer of these TNCs now control a larger and larger share of the global market, whether in commodities, manufactures or services.

1.6.3 Globalization of National Economic Policies: Globalization process has led to globalization of national policies and policy-making mechanism. National policies (including industrial policy) that until recently were determined by the government and people within a country have increasingly come under the influence of international agencies and processes or by big private corporations and economic/financial players. This has led to the narrowed ability of governments and people to make choices from options in economic, social and cultural policies.

Most developing countries have seen their independent policy-making mechanism capacity eroded, and have to adopt policies influenced by other entities, which may on balance be detrimental to the countries concerned. The developed countries, where the major economic players reside, and which also control the processes and policies of international economic agencies, are better able to maintain control over their own national policies as well as determine the policies and practices of international institutions and the global system. However, it is also true that the large corporations have taken over a large part of decision-making even in the developed countries, at the expense of the power of the state or political and social leaders.

1.6.4 Flexible Production Processes: Globalization of the economies across the world has changed the notions of manufacturing, productivity and competitiveness. Flexible production processes and structures are being increasingly put in place to compete in very dynamic markets where product life is very short and discerning customers with higher purchasing power and more differentiated and international tastes are demanding much more product variety, higher quality and greater value for money. The new production systems are increasingly moving to the network form of enterprises, each contributing to the production and distribution according to their respective core competencies. Therefore, competitiveness now requires the ability to constantly take the most advantageous position or niche in the rapidly changing market environment.

1.6.5 Globalization and Developing Countries: The issue that concerns developing countries is how they can ensure greater participation of the weaker economies in the global process and what needs to be done to ensure that the course of globalization benefits more people in more countries. The uneven and unequal nature of the present globalization is manifested in the fast growing gap between the rich and poor people of the world and between developed and developing countries; and by the large differences among nations in the distribution of gains and losses.

This imbalance leads to polarisation between countries and groups that gain, and the many countries and groups in society that lose out or are marginalised. Globalization, polarisation, wealth concentration and marginalisation are therefore linked through the same process. In this process, investment resources, growth and modern technology are focused on a few countries, mainly in North America, Europe, Japan and a few East Asian countries. A majority of developing countries are excluded from the process, or are participating in it in marginal ways.

Although the developed world is in a dominant position and has been prepared to use this to further their control of the global economy, the developing countries have not done well in organising themselves to co-ordinate on substantial policy and negotiating positions. The developed countries, on the other hand, are well-organised within their own countries, with well-staffed departments dealing with international trade and finance, and with university academics and private and quasi government think tanks helping to obtain information and map policies and strategies. They also have well-organised associations and lobbies associated with their corporations and financial institutions, which have great influence over the government departments.

On the positive side, globalization has compelled developing countries to improve overall economic management, and make their economies efficient. To get a share of global capital and technology, developing countries have to upgrade their social and economic institutions through administrative, legislative and legal reforms. The quality of governance has to improve to encourage productivity and efficiency. Political stability has to be established.

Globalization has helped the smaller, emerging economies gain access to world markets, emergent technologies and collaborations. This has also given them a window to the developed world and helped them understand the significant role of globalization as an instrument, which could be utilised not just to achieve economic efficiency, but also eradicate poverty.

1.6.6 Future of Globalization: Globalization is an irreversible trend and developing economies are also inevitably involved in the process. Developed countries should, therefore, carefully consider how to restructure the world trading system to accommodate developing economies, by enabling them to benefit from globalization while minimising external shocks. The World Trade Organization (WTO) should work more effectively, through an enlargement of waiver clauses which recognise the weaker position of developing countries.

Despite distortions and aberrations, globalization is a reality. Developments in information and communication technologies are unifying markets and people, cutting across barriers of space and time. At the end of the day, one has to understand and accept that globalization is the stratagem for the new millennium. Every country, developed and developing, has to accept this and formulate their economies around it.

The socio-economically disadvantaged are yet to benefit from globalization. The challenge to overcome the scourge of poverty remains a daunting task. The support of the poor for reforms and their involvement in the development process can be achieved only if they start benefiting from government policies. It is necessary to ensure that the poor and the deprived have a greater stake in economic reforms than at present for mobilising their enthusiastic participation in the development process. Economic reforms must be guided by compassion and distributive justice. Improvement of living conditions of the poorest and the weakest sections of society should be high priority areas of welfare and development programmes/schemes of the government.

1.7 Input-Output Analysis

Input-output analysis, attributed to American economist Wassily Loentief, deals with general equilibrium situation in the empirical study of production. It has three distinctive features: (a) it deals almost exclusively with production, (b) it is concerned with empirical investigations, and (c) it is related to general equilibrium phenomenon.

Input-output analysis examines the interdependence of the production plans and activities of the various industries which constitute an economy. This interdependence arises because each industry employs the outputs of other industries, and its own output in turn is used by other industries. For example, steel is used to make railway wagons and railway wagons are in turn used to transport steel.

An input-output transaction matrix is a framework of data which provides a detailed information on how the final demand for output is related to the requirements placed on individual industries. It thus, highlights the interdependence of various economic sectors (industries) in the production of final output for the economy as a whole.

It is an array of rows and columns forming a square matrix. For each industry, the row displays the credit side of the production account, i.e. sales to other industries plus sales to final users. The column for the industry displays the debit side, i.e. purchase of materials and services from other industries plus purchases of factor services and non-factor charges. For each industry, the sum of row items equals the sum of the column items. Thus, for each industry total output produced equals the total inputs (including the non-factor charges). It should be noted that in the input-output transaction matrix the productive units of an economy are grouped into separate clusters to form a certain number of industries. Since in these groups all the productive units are covered, input-output transaction matrix encompasses all the productive activity within an economy.

There are various uses of input-output analysis to solve real world problems. It can be used in predicting future production requirements if demand estimates are available. It can be used for economic planning, including problems of backward areas of a country.

Moreover, it provides useful information for national income accounting.

There are two important assumptions of input-output analysis. Firstly, no two commodities are produced jointly. In other words, each industry produces only one homogeneous output. Secondly, in any productive process all inputs are employed in rigidly fixed proportions and the use of these inputs expands in proportion with the level of output. This is a special case of an assumption of constant returns to scale. Input-output analysis requires the solution of a set of N simultaneous linear equations in N variables.

2

Forms of Business Organizations and Start-ups

After identifying the business in any field, it is necessary then to have a legal entity to be known in the market. The legal entity can be in any form of a business organization. In other words, one of the first decisions a prospective entrepreneur is required to make is how his business will be structured. He needs to know the advantages and disadvantages of each of the different forms of business organization to make sure that he makes the right decision for his new business. All businesses must adopt some legal configuration that defines the rights and liabilities of participants in the ownership, control, personal liability, lifespan and financial structure of the business. This is a big decision that has long-term implications.

Starting a business involves making many important decisions, especially in terms of selecting the right type of business structure. Broadly speaking, there are the following 4 forms of business organization.

1. Sole proprietorship
2. Partnership
3. Joint stock company
4. Co-operative society

Meaning, features, advantages and disadvantages of each of these organizations are discussed below.

2.1 Sole Proprietorship

The vast majority of small businesses start out as sole proprietorships. These businesses usually are owned by one individual who has day-to-day responsibility for running the business.

2.1.1 Meaning and Features: Sole proprietorship (also called single ownership) is a form of business that is owned, managed and controlled by an individual. He has to arrange capital for the business and he alone is responsible for its management. He is therefore, entitled to the profits and has to bear the loss of business. However, he can take the help of his family members and also make use of the services of others such as a manager and other employees. Small factories and shops are often found to be sole proprietorship organizations. It is the simplest and most easily formed business organization. This is because not much legal formality is required to establish it. Sole proprietorship has one owner who makes all of the business decisions, and there is no distinction between the business and the owner.

Some typical examples of sole proprietorship include grocery shops, fruit and vegetables marts, tea stalls, beauty parlours and wellness centres and personal businesses of doctors, teachers, artists, consultants and other self-employed business owners who operate on a solo basis.

2.1.2 Advantages: These can be listed as under:

A. Easy to Establish: A single proprietorship business is easy to form because no legal formalities are involved in setting up this type of organization. It is not governed by any specific law. It is simply required to comply with the rules and regulations laid down by public authorities for business activities.

B. Total Control of Business: As the sole owner of the business, the proprietor has full control of business decisions and spending. He takes all the decisions relating to business which makes functioning of the business simple and easy. He can also bring about changes in the size and nature of activity. He keeps all the business secrets only to himself.

C. Sole Beneficiary of Profits: Sole proprietor is the only person to whom the profits belong. There is a direct relation between work and reward. This motivates him to work hard and bear the risks of business.

D. Low Start-up Costs: The costs of starting and maintaining a sole proprietorship are much less than other business structures. It is the easiest and least expensive form of ownership to organize.

E. No Public Disclosure Required: A sole proprietor is not required to file annual reports or other financial statements with public authorities.

F. Minimum Government Regulations: The government does not interfere with the working of sole proprietorship organizations. However, they have to comply with the general laws and rules laid down by government.

2.1.3 Disadvantages: These can be as follows:

A. Unlimited Liability: Sole proprietor is personally responsible for all business debts and actions under this business structure. If anything adverse happens in the business, owner's personal assets are put at risk. The sole proprietor has to bear the losses and is responsible for the liabilities of the business. If the business assets are not sufficient to meet the liabilities, he may also have to sell his personal property for that purpose.

B. Limitation of Resources: The sole proprietor of a business is generally at a disadvantage in raising sufficient capital. His own capital may be limited and his personal assets may also be insufficient for raising loans against their security. This reduces the scope of business expansion. He may have to acquire loans at high rate of interest. Investors typically favour companies when lending money because they know that those businesses have strong financial records and other forms of security.

C. Carelessness in Managing Funds: Since he is not required to keep financial statements, a sole proprietor runs the risk of becoming too relaxed when managing his monetary and other resources.

D. Limitation of Management Skills: A sole proprietor may not be able to manage the business efficiently as he is not likely to have necessary skills regarding all aspects of the business. This poses difficulties in the growth of business also.

E. Lack of Continuity: A sole proprietary organization suffers from lack of continuity. If the owner is sick this may cause temporary closure of business. The business may be permanently closed in the event of the death of the owner.

2.2 Partnership

A partnership is a business set up between two or more individuals. It can be between family members, friends or colleagues.

2.2.1 Meaning and Features: In a partnership, two or more people share ownership of a single business. More specifically, partnership is an association of persons who agree to combine their financial resources and managerial abilities to run a business and share profits in an agreed ratio.

The law does not distinguish between the business and its owners. The partners generally have a legal agreement (called *partnership deed*) that establishes, *inter alia*, how decisions will be made, how profits will be shared, how disputes will be resolved, and what steps will be taken to dissolve the partnership in case things go sour. In other words, a partnership deed lays down the terms and conditions of partnership and the rights, duties and obligations of partners.

A partner is jointly and individually liable for other actions of other partners. Business can suffer if the detailed partnership agreement is not in place. Partnership is formed on the basis of an agreement between two or more persons to carry on business. It does not arise out of the operation of law.

A partnership can be formed only on the basis of a business activity. Its business may include any trade, industry or profession. In a partnership firm, partners are entitled to share the profits and bear the losses, if any.

Every partner has a right to take part in the running of the business. However, it is not necessary for all partners to participate in the day-to-day activities of the business. Even if partnership business is run by some partners, the consent of all other partners is necessary for taking important decisions.

No partner can transfer his share in partnership to any other person. He may, however, do so with the consent of all other partners.

To form a partnership firm, it is not compulsory to register it. However, if the partners so decide, it may be registered with the relevant authority. The partnership firm continues at the pleasure of the partners. Legally, a partnership comes to an end if any partner dies, retires or becomes insolvent. However, if the remaining partners agree to work together under the original firm's name, the firm will not be dissolved and will continue its business after settling the claim of the outgoing partner.

Partners who take active part in the conduct of day-to-day business of the firm are called active partners. These partners carry on business on behalf of the other partners. Sleeping partners are those who do not take active part in the management of the business. Such partners only contribute capital in the firm and are bound by the activities of other partners. However, they share in the profits and losses of the business.

2.2.2 Advantages: Some advantages of partnerships include as under:

A. Easy to Establish: Partnership requires minimal paperwork and legal documents to form. Partners just need to develop a partnership agreement.

B. Pooling of Financial Resources: A partnership commands more financial resources compared to sole proprietorship. This helps in expanding business and earning more profits. As and when a firm requires more money, more partners can be admitted.

C. Pooling of Expertise: With more than one like-minded individual, there are more opportunities to increase their collaborative skill set. Partners may have complementary skills. A partnership facilitates pooling of managerial skills of all its partners. This leads to greater efficiency in business operations.

D. Workload Distribution: People in partnerships commonly share responsibilities so that one person does not have to do all the work. Thus, in a big partnership firm, one partner can handle production department, another partner can look after all marketing activity, still another can attend to legal and personnel problems, and so on.

E. Risk Sharing: Unlike sole proprietary organization, the risks of partnership business are shared by partners on a pre-determined basis. This encourages partners to undertake risky but profitable business activities.

2.2.3 Disadvantages: These can be as follows:

A. Unlimited Liability: In a partnership, all members are personally liable for business-related debts and may be pursued in a lawsuit. The liability of partners is unlimited as in the case of sole proprietorship. In case some obligation arises then not only the partnership assets but also the private property of the partners can be attached for the payment of liabilities of the firm. Moreover, the liability of a partner may arise not only from his own acts but also from the acts and mistakes of co-partners over whom he has no control. This discourages many persons with money and ability, to join a partnership firm as partner.

B. Risk of Disagreements: By having more than one person involved in taking decisions, partners may disagree on some aspects of running the business operations. In partnership, since decisions are taken unanimously, it is essential that all partners reconcile their views for the common good of the organization. However, there may arise situations when some partners may adopt rigid attitudes and make it impossible to arrive at a commonly agreed decision. Lack of harmony may paralyze the business and cause conflict and mutual bickering. Business may come to a halt when partners disagree and choose to end their partnership.

C. Difficulty in Exiting: Investment in a partnership can be easily made but cannot be easily withdrawn. This is so because the withdrawal of a partner's share requires the consent of all other partners.

D. Lack of Public Confidence: A partnership business does not enjoy much confidence of banks, financial institutions and the general public. This is so because the nature of its activities is not disclosed to public. As a result large financial resources cannot be raised by partnership firms for business expansion.

E. Uncertainty of Existence: The existence of a partnership firm is very uncertain. The retirement, death, bankruptcy or lunacy of any partner can put an end to the partnership. Further, the partnership business can come to a close if any partner demands it.

Partnership form of business organization is good when the size of business is medium, i.e. neither too small not too large, and when the partners can work in full co-operation with one another.

2.2.4 Limited Liability Partnership: Unlike limited liability entities, where the liability of the shareholder is limited to the extent of the contribution made or due from him, in proprietorships or partnerships there is no separation of personal and business liability. When a business fails, not only do the assets of the business but the entrepreneur's personal assets also get attached to pay off business dues. Further, all guarantors which are drawn from the critical social safety net of the small entrepreneur, get personally involved and in the eventuality of failure they also get implicated and the whole safety net crumbles.

In many countries reforms have taken place that allows insolvency of businesses to be dealt with in a comprehensive manner that enables revival or rescue before liquidation and winding up. Insolvency is treated as a commercial phenomenon requiring to be dealt with in accordance with commercial principles in a framework of fairness and equity. There is an independent institutionalized process of providing a grace period for businesses to deal with distress. This is intended to enable a revival plan if the business is inherently viable, puts all creditors on hold pending revival, gets business out of holding period if it revives or takes action on winding up if the business is non-revivable. Both personal as well as business insolvency are dealt with on the basis of similar principles with ease of filing for bankruptcy and securing of certain protection from creditor action once this is done.

India's Limited Liability Partnership (LLP) Act, 2008 provides for a flexible governance structure to be determined by the partners themselves by mutual agreement, easy compliance requirements in comparison to companies, combined with limitation of liability to the extent of the partner's contribution.

2.3 Joint Stock Company
2.3.1 Meaning and Features: A joint stock company or simply a company may be defined as a voluntary association of persons having separate legal existence, perpetual succession and a common seal. There must be a group of persons who voluntarily agree to form a company. Once formed the company becomes a separate legal entity with a distinct name of its own. Its existence is not affected by change of members. It must have a seal to be imprinted on documents whenever required. The capital of a company consists of transferable shares, and members have limited liability. A large company may employ thousands of people.

A company is considered by law to be a unique entity, separate from those who own it. A company can be taxed, sued and enter into contractual agreements. A company has a life of its own and does not dissolve when ownership changes.

A company is taxed separately from its owners. It gives the owners limited liability, which can encourage more risk-taking and potential investment. In regards to transfer of ownership, shareholders can sell their shares. Capital is easier to raise through the sale of stock.

A company comes into existence only after its registration. For that purpose, necessary legal formalities have to be completed as prescribed under the law of the land. A company is regarded as a legal entity separate from its members. Thus a company can carry on business in its own name, enter into contracts, sue, and be sued.

A company is the creation of law and has a distinct entity. It is, therefore, regarded as an artificial person. The business is run in the name of the company. Since it is an artificial person, its functions are performed by the elected representatives of members, known as directors. In other words, a company has no physical existence. The activities of the company are carried through a group of natural persons elected by its members.

2.3.2 Advantages: Advantages of company form of business organization include the following:

A. Limited Liability: The liability of the members of a company is limited. It is limited to the extent of capital agreed to be contributed. Beyond that amount, the members cannot be personally held liable for payment of the company's debts. With the liability of members limited to the value of their shares, company is able to attract many people to invest in its shares. It is thus in a position to undertake business ventures involving risks.

B. Large Financial Resources: A company is able to collect large amounts of funds. This is so because a company can raise capital by issuing shares to a large number of persons. Shares of small value can be subscribed even by people with small savings. Besides, a company can also raise loans from the public as well as from different lending institutions. Availability of necessary funds makes it possible for a company to undertake business activities on a large scale.

C. Transferability of Shares: The capital of a company is divided into parts called shares. Normally the shares of a company are freely transferable by its members. A company permits its members to transfer their shares. Free transferability of shares ensures liquidity of investment made by the shareholder. Thus, if a member needs cash he can sell his shares.

D. Growth and Expansion: With large resources at its command, a company can organize business on a large-scale which gives it strength to grow and expand. Economies of large-scale production lead to lower costs which, in turn, are reflected in higher profits.

E. Managerial Efficiency: Since a company undertakes large-scale activities, it can afford the services of professional managers. Competent managers can be easily hired by a company because it commands large financial resources. Thus, efficient management is ensured in a company.

F. Widely-held Ownership: Since a large number of persons are associated with a company as members, its ownership is widely dispersed. Thus the benefits of the company's operations are distributed among a large section of people. It, thus, leads to curtailment of concentration of economic power in few hands.

G. Corporate Social Responsibility: Large companies often undertake and contribute to social welfare activities by making donations to schools and colleges, developing rural areas, running healthcare institutions, and so on. For example, Section 135 of the India Companies Act, 2013 provide that every company having a specified net worth shall constitute the corporate social responsibility committee of the board. This committee shall formulate the policy, *inter alia*, regarding eradicating extreme hunger and poverty, promotion of education and reducing child mortality and improving maternal health.

H. Durability, Stability and Continuity: A company is the only form of organization which enjoys continuous existence and stability. Any change in the company's membership does not affect its life. Death, insolvency, or change of members has no effect on the life of a company. As a result of this, a company can undertake projects of long duration and attract people to invest in the business of the company. The life of the company can come to an end only through the prescribed legal procedure.

2.3.3 Disadvantages: These are as under:

A. Lengthy and Expensive Legal Procedures: The registration of a company is a long-drawn process. A number of documents need to be filled and filed. For preparing documents, experts need to be hired who charge heavy fees. Besides, registration fees have also to be paid to the relevant public authorities.

B. Double Taxation: A company must pay income tax at its own level before profits are transferred to the shareholders, who must then pay tax at individual level.

C. Annual Record-keeping Requirements: The company business structure involves a substantial amount of paperwork. Companies have to disclose the results of their activities and financial position in the annual reports. A company is required by law to have annual meetings, notify stockholders about the meetings and keep minutes of meetings.

D. Excessive Government Regulations: A company is subject to government regulations at every stage of its working. A company has to file regular returns and statements of its activities with the relevant public authorities. Penalties can be imposed for non-compliance of the legal requirements. Filing returns and reports, involving considerable time and money, is the responsibility of a company. All this reduces flexibility in operations.

E. Lack of Incentive among Paid Officials: A company is not managed by shareholders but by directors and other paid officials. Officials do not have investment in the company and also do not bear the risks. As such, they may not be as much motivated to safeguard the interests of the company as the shareholders.

F. Delay in Decision-making and Action: In large companies, decision making and its implementation happen to be a time consuming process. This is so because individual managers are unable to take decisions on their own. They may have to consult others which may take a lot of time. Similarly, after decisions are taken, they have to be communicated to people working at various levels of the organization. It also delays the implementation of already delayed decisions.

G. Conflict of Interest: A company is generally characterised by a large organisation with many groups operating in it. So long as the interests of these groups do not clash with each other they work for the good of the organisation. However, at times individual and group interests become difficult to reconcile. In such a situation, the business suffers in course of time unless there is a reconciliation of the conflicting view points. The company management may seem to be fully democratic, but in actual practice, it may be controlled by a small group of persons. Such individuals often exploit the company for personal interests instead of working in the interest of shareholders. A company organisation provides scope for speculation in shares by the directors. Since directors have knowledge of all information about the functioning of company, they can use it to their personal advantage. As a result of this, innocent shareholders may suffer loss.

H. Growth of Monopolistic Tendencies: A company because of its large size has the tendency to grow into a monopoly so as to eliminate competition, control the market and charge unreasonable prices to maximise profits. Moreover, big companies are generally in a position to influence government officials to make decision in their favour. This is because such companies have large financial resources and are in a position to bribe even high officials.

From the preceding discussion it is clear that the company form of organisation is best suited to those lines of business activity which are to be organised on a large-scale.

2.4 Co-operative

2.4.1 Meaning and Features: A co-operative is an organization that a group of individuals owns and runs to meet a common goal. These owners work together to operate the business, and they share the profits and other benefits.

In a co-operative, the membership is voluntary. Anybody having a common interest is free to join a co-operative society. The member can also leave the society anytime after giving proper notice.

In a co-operative society, the principle of *one-man, one vote* is adopted. A member has only one vote irrespective of the number of shares held by him. Thus, a co-operative society is run on democratic principles.

A co-operative society is required to be registered with the relevant authority. Registration provides it a separate legal entity. Its existence is quite different from its members. The death, insolvency or lunacy of a member does not affect its existence. It can sue and be sued in its own name. It can make agreements as well as purchase and sell properly in its own name.

A co-operative society is based on the service motive of its members. Its main objective is to provide service to the members and not to maximize profits as is the case with other forms of business organization.

Out of the profits of the cooperative, members are paid dividend and bonus. The bonus is given according to the volume of business transacted by each member with the co-operative society.

2.4.2 Types of Co-operative: A co-operative is a voluntary association of persons for mutual benefit and its aims are accomplished through self-help and collective efforts. The main principle underlying a co-operative is mutual help. To be called a co-operative society, it must be registered with the relevant authority.

Co-operative societies may be classified into different categories according to the nature of activities performed by them. The main types of co-operative societies are as follows:

A. Credit Co-operatives: Such societies are formed to provide financial help in the form of loans to members. The funds of these societies consist of share capital contributed by the members and the deposits made by them and outsiders. The funds are used in giving loans to needy members on easy terms. Thus, the members are protected from the exploitation of moneylenders, who charge very high rates of interest.

B. Consumer Co-operatives: Consumer co-operatives are organized by consumers to eliminate middlemen and establish direct relation with the manufacturers or wholesalers. These societies are formed by consumers to ensure a steady supply of goods and services of high quality at reasonable prices. It purchases goods either from the manufacturers or wholesalers for sale at reasonable prices to its members. The profit, if any, is distributed among members as dividend in the ratio of capital contributed.

C. Producer Co-operatives: Producer co-operatives are formed to help the members in procuring inputs for production of goods or services. These societies generally provide raw material, tools and equipment and other common facilities to its members. This helps them to concentrate attention on production of goods.

D. Marketing Co-operatives: Co-operative marketing societies are voluntary associations of small producers, who find it difficult to individually sell their products in the market. The main purpose of such a society is to ensure a steady and favourable market for the output of its members. The output is pooled together and sold at the best available price.

E. Housing Co-operatives: These are formed to provide residential accommodation to the members. They undertake the purchase and development of land and/or construction of houses/flats on the land. Some housing co-operatives provide their members with necessary loans at low rates of interest to build houses.

F. Farming Co-operatives: In these co-operatives, small farmers join together and pool their resources for cultivating their land collectively. Their objective is to achieve economies of large-scale farming and maximising agricultural output. Co-operative farming makes it possible for members to use modem tools and implements, better quality seeds, fertilizer and irrigation facilities in order to achieve higher production.

2.4.3 Advantages: These are as under:

A. Easy to Form: A co-operative society is voluntary association and may be formed with a specified minimum of members. Its registration is very simple and can be done without much legal formalities.

B. Democratic Structure: Members of a co-operative follow the *one member, one vote* philosophy. It means that everyone has an equal say, regardless of his/her investment in the co-operative. Co-operatives allow members to join and leave the business without disrupting its structure or dissolving it.

C. Government Support: Co-operatives generally have access to government-sponsored grant/loan programmes depending on the type of co-operative. Relief in taxation is also provided.

D. Limited Liability: The liability of the members of a cooperative society is limited to the extent of capital contributed by them. They do not have to bear personal liability for the debts of the society.

E. Stability and Continuity: A co-operative society has a separate legal existence. It is not affected by the death, insolvency, lunacy or permanent incapacity of any of its members. It has a fairly stable life and continues to exist for a long period.

F. Economical Functioning: The functioning of a co-operative society is quite economical due to elimination of middlemen and the voluntary services provided by its members.

2.4.4 Disadvantages: Following can be the disadvantages of a co-operative:

A. Limited Capital: Co-operatives are usually at a disadvantage in raising capital because of the low rate of return on capital invested by members.

B. Inefficient Management: Co-operatives are more relaxed in terms of structure, so members who do not fully participate or contribute to the business leave others at a disadvantage and risk turning other members away. The management of a co-operative society is generally inefficient because the managing committee consists of part-time and inexperienced people. Qualified managers are not attracted towards a co-operative on account of its limited capacity to pay adequate remuneration.

C. Lack of Motivation: A co-operative society is formed for mutual benefit and the interest of individual members are not fully satisfied. There is no direct link between effort and reward. Hence members are not inclined to put in their best efforts in a co-operative society.

D. Rigid Rules and Regulations: Excessive government regulation and control over co-operatives adversely affects their functioning. Plethora of rules and regulations deprives a co-operative society to adopt flexibility of operations and efficiency of management.

2.5 Choice of Business Organization

Choice of a suitable form of organisation is important because the success and growth of a business depends a great deal on it. The form of organisation determines availability of finance, risk associated with business, division of profit, control of ownership, stability and durability of business etc.

Which is the most suitable form of business structure? No cut and dried answer can be given to this question. Since entrepreneurial objectives vary, no single form of organisation can be considered as the best for all kind of businesses. The selection of a suitable form of organisation is generally made after careful consideration of the following factors:

1. Scale of business operations (small, medium or large).
2. Nature of business (manufacturing, trading or service).
3. Scope of market (local, national or international).
4. Degree of direct control desired by owners.
5. Degree of risk and liability.
6. Division of profit.
7. Flexibility of operations.
8. Legal requirements and procedures to establish the business.

Evidently, sole proprietorship, partnership and co-operative organisations are not capable of undertaking large-scale activity due to lack of adequate capital and limited managerial abilities. The company form of organisation is considered to be most suitable for organising business activities on a large-scale as it does not suffer from the limitations of capital and management. It has the advantage of attracting huge capital from the public due to the limited liability of members. With adequate capital it can also employ trained and experienced managers to run the business activities efficiently.

2.6 Start-ups

Start-ups are the platform for entrepreneurs who have the ability to think out of the box and innovate to conceive products that can create a niche for themselves in a dynamically changing world.

2.6.1 What is a Start-up? A start-up company (or simply a start-up) is an entrepreneurial venture which is typically a newly emerged, fast-growing business that aims to meet a marketplace need by developing a viable business model around an innovative product, service, process or a platform. A start-up is usually a company designed to effectively develop and validate a scalable business model. Start-ups have high rates of failure, but the minority of successes includes companies that have become large and influential.

Although there are start-ups created in all types of businesses, and all over the world, some locations and business sectors are particularly associated with start-up companies. The internet bubble of the late 1990s was associated with huge numbers of internet start-up companies, some selling the technology to provide internet access, others using the internet to provide services. Most of this start-up activity was located in the most well-known start-up ecosystem—Silicon Valley, an area of northern California renowned for the high level of start-up company activity.

2.6.2 Start-up Ecosystem: The size and maturity of the start-up ecosystem where the start-up is launched and where it grows have an effect on the volume and success of the start-ups. The start-up ecosystem consists of the following:

1. Individuals, i.e. entrepreneurs, venture capitalists, angel investors, mentors.
2. Institutions and organizations, i.e. top research universities and institutes, business schools and entrepreneurship programmes operated by universities and colleges.
3. Non-profit entrepreneurship support organizations.
4. Government entrepreneurship programmes and services.
5. Chambers of commerce.
6. Business incubators and business accelerators.

A region with all of these elements is considered to be a *strong* start-up ecosystem. Some of the most famous start-up ecosystems are Silicon Valley in California, where major computer and internet firms and top universities such as Stanford University create a stimulating start-up environment. Boston [where Massachusetts Institute of Technology (MIT) is located] and Berlin, home of WISTA (a top research area) are other examples of start-up ecosystem.

Large or well-established companies often try to promote innovation by setting up internal start-ups, i.e. new business divisions that operate at arm's length from the rest of the company.

Then, there are re-starters, i.e. failed entrepreneurs who after some time restart in the same sector with more or less the same activities.

2.6.3 Characteristics of a Start-up: Start-ups can come in all forms and sizes. Some of the critical tasks are to build a co-founder team to secure key skills, know-how, financial resources, and other elements to conduct research on the target market. Co-founders are people involved in the initial launch of start-up companies.

1. Anyone can be a co-founder, and an existing company can also be a co-founder, but frequently co-founders are entrepreneurs, engineers, hackers, web developers, web designers and others involved in the ground level of a new, often high-tech, venture.

2. Typically, a start-up will begin by building a first minimum viable product (MVP), a prototype, to validate, assess and develop the new ideas or business concepts. In addition, start-ups founders do research to deepen their understanding of the ideas, technologies or business concepts and their commercial potential.

3. A shareholders' agreement (SHA) is often agreed early on to confirm the commitment, ownership and contributions of the founders and investors and to deal with the intellectual properties and assets that may be generated by the start-up.

4. Beyond founders' own contributions, some start-ups raise additional investment at some or several stages of their growth (called investing rounds). The first round is called *seed round*. The seed round generally is when the start-up is still in the very early phase of execution when their product is still in the prototype phase. At this level angel investors will be the ones participating. The next round is called Series A. At this point the company already has traction and may be making revenue. In Series A rounds venture capital firms will be participating alongside angels or super angel investors. The next rounds are Series B, C, and D. These three rounds are the ones leading towards the IPO. Venture capital firms and private equity firms will be participating. Not all start-ups trying to raise investments are successful in their fundraising.

5. Business models for start-ups are generally found via a *bottom-up* or *top-down* approach. A company may cease to be a start-up as it passes various milestones, such as becoming publicly traded on the stock market in an initial public offer (IPO), or ceasing to exist as an independent entity via a merger or acquisition.

6. Companies may also fail and cease to operate altogether, an outcome that is very likely for start-ups, given that they are developing disruptive innovations which may not function as expected and for which there may not be market demand, even when the product or service is finally developed. Given that start-ups operate in high-risk sectors, it can also be hard to attract investors to support the product/service development or attract buyers.

7. Investors are attracted to start-ups because of the latter's strong co-founding team, a balanced *risk/reward* profile—in which high risk due to the untested, disruptive

innovations is balanced out by high potential returns—and *scalability*, i.e. the likelihood that a start-up can expand its operations by serving more markets or more customers.

8. Attractive start-ups generally have lower *bootstrapping* (self-funding of start-ups by the founders) costs, higher risk, and higher potential return on investment.

9. Successful start-ups are typically more scalable than an established business, in the sense that the start-up has the potential to grow rapidly with a limited investment of capital, labour or land.

10. Start-ups have several options for funding. Venture capital firms and angel investors may help start-up companies begin operations, exchanging seed money for an equity stake in the firm. Venture capitalists and angel investors provide financing to a range of start-ups, with the expectation that a very small number of the start-ups will become viable and make money. In practice though, many start-ups are initially funded by the founders themselves using *bootstrapping*, in which loans or monetary gifts from friends and family are combined with savings and credit card debt to finance the venture.

11. Start-ups usually need to form partnerships with other firms to enable their business model to operate. To become attractive to other businesses, start-ups need to align their internal features, such as management style and products with the market situation.

12. Start-up founders often have a more casual or offbeat attitude in their dress, office space and marketing, as compared to traditional corporations. Thus, instead of *tie culture*, start-up founders may wear bermudas, hoodies, sneakers and other casual clothes to business meetings. Their offices may have recreational facilities in them, such as pool tables, ping pong tables and pinball machines, which are used to create a fun work environment, stimulate team development and team spirit, and encourage creativity. Some start-ups do not use a strict command and control hierarchical structure, with executives, managers, supervisors and employees.

Successful business owners build a business around what they love doing the most. People who have a passion for making specialty items or a desire to change the world by offering a unique service may choose to form a start-up that allows for flexibility and creativity. Once you have a solid understanding of your goals, it is easier to move on to the next stage of planning.

3

Location of Industry: Determinants and Theories

Location of industry refers to establishment of an industry or cluster of industries in a particular location or region due to availability of cheap factors of production, transport and infrastructural facilities, demand incentives, raw materials etc. These are some of the factors which attract entrepreneurs to set up their plants in a particular area. Once the process starts, it has a tendency to accelerate.

A series of location factors influence the location patterns of various individual industries during their respective periods of evolution. No single location factor on its own absolutely determines or clearly indicates the right location of a given industry. Among the principal factors enumerated by the theorists, transportation costs in general, and those of finished products in particular, seem decisive in the choice of the location of most industrial plants.

Importance of each locational factor varies for different geographic areas and for different types of industries. In general, following are the factors which affect the location of industry.

3.1 Land and its Attributes

The issue of land and its attributes is of initial concern to an industrialist. Although land cost may be a major cost item in the initial setting up of a firm, it becomes much less important when considered over a long period and may be relatively insignificant in determining choice between comparable sites. Nonetheless it may rule out certain very expensive locations. It is also important that the land be physically suitable for its intended purpose or at least adaptable to development. Climatic, geological and other physical attributes may affect the location of some Industries while others remain indifferent.

Of considerable advantage is land which is already serviced prior to development. Industries will be attracted to sites where infrastructure, public utilities and amenities are easily accessible. Other industries will be drawn to the occurrence of large quantities of water while others will be concerned with the deposit of industrial effluence. Also significant to location is the size of land parcels and their related costs. Sites that are otherwise desirable may have to be eliminated either because they are not of adequate proportions or due to the prohibitively high cost of the land. This is generally true of city or town-centre locations where plots are small or a manufacturer is not able to outbid commercial users.

Climate of the area selected for the industry is important. Very harsh climate is a discouraging factor in the location of industry.

3.2 Accessibility of Capital

The accessibility of a proposed industrialist to finance capital is another factor of industrial location. Finance capital is necessary before land or other inputs like machinery, equipment, buildings and so forth, are acquired. For small firms and those just getting established, capital may be obtainable more easily in some places than in others. Frequently too, industrialists would prefer to locate within easy reach of financiers.

3.3 Availability of Raw Materials

This is one of the important factors in an industrial location. The mere location of industries itself may be determined by the availability or location of the raw materials.

The essence of industrial process is the conversion of one thing into another of greater value, hence all manufacturing activities require raw materials. Industrial raw materials can be grouped into organic and inorganic. The leading organic raw materials are those derived from agriculture, i.e. agro-industrial raw materials. Inorganic materials include minerals and water-power resources for hydroelectric generation. The effects of raw materials on industrial location arise from the issue of transportation costs. Materials vary enormously in terms of bulk, weight, and perishability, while others need special treatment in transport, handling or storage.

The outlay incurred in acquiring raw materials involves the costs of both production and transportation to the factory. The cost of extracting a mineral or manufacturing a component will affect locational choice only if there are significant variations in the price from different places. Owing to a dependence on transport charges, the cost of raw materials varies with distance from the source in a fairly regular manner. However, where a uniform delivered price is adopted, the cost of the particular raw materials would be the same anywhere and its effects on plant location insignificant.

3.4 Transportation

Transport always influences the location of the industry. So the junction points of waterways, roadways and railways become humming centres of industrial activity. Transport is often considered to be the most important determinant of plant location. Few firms can overlook the transport factor when making their location decision, and for many the total freight charge will be the largest difference between costs at alternative sites. Important innovations undertaken in the recent past have had considerable impact on the factor of transportation and its related costs with regard to raw materials and finished goods. The use of pipelines for moving tricky commodities like petroleum and oil, and the development of container systems have greatly facilitated the transfer of goods by road, rail, air and water. The more efficient transportation becomes in terms of decreasing costs of overcoming distance, the more flexible the manufacturer's choice of location.

The nature of material or product to be transported affects the means of transport to be adopted. Bulky goods of relatively low value such as iron ore and coal are cheaply shipped on water. A commodity of high value in relation to its weight and volume, on the other hand, may justify air transport. If it is crucial that goods are moved quickly, then road is preferable to rail which is preferable to water. Other goods require special facilities such as refrigeration or careful handling and the selected mode of transport should cater to these needs. The distance over which the goods are to be moved is also important. For a majority of items trucking is the cheapest mode of transport over relatively short distances, railway suitable for medium distances and waterway best for long hauls. All in all, a good transport system with direct access to primary distributor roads is a prerequisite for industrial areas.

3.5 Access to Market

The finished goods should reach the market at the end of the process of manufacturing. Thus, nearness to the market is an important factor in the process of selecting a location for industry.

For many industries the significance of the market is growing in relation to such considerations as the cost of labour and materials. Freed from the original necessity of being close to sources of raw materials, many firms now show a distinct preference for a location close to major urban centres. The market is not the only attraction of a metropolitan location. The large concentration and relatively affluent body of final consumers found in the city, together with its large industrial market, is certainly one of the main reasons for relatively rapid industrial growth in and around major urban areas. The market can also influence plant location through its effects on costs. Finished products have to be transported to the consumer and for many industries the outgoing freight bill can be a substantial addition to the cost incurred in acquiring the inputs and conducting the process of manufacture. Proximity to the market if it is spatially concentrated, or a central location if consumers are dispersed, can thus be an advantage.

3.6 Sources of Power and Water

Power is a necessity condition for any industrial establishment. Electricity is one of the key inputs for the overall economic development of the country. The basic responsibility of the power supply industry is to provide adequate electricity at economic cost, while ensuring reliability and quality of the supply. The demand for power in both rural and urban areas is increasing rapidly.

Electricity is the main source of power for most industries today. It is more mobile geographically than the earlier forms of industrial energy (water and steam power) since it can be transmitted from one place to another at little cost. This means that over fairly large areas the cost of electricity may not vary much if there are no significant differences in local production costs, and in those circumstances its influence on industrial location will be negligible. However, there can be instances where large supplies of cheap power are necessary and this will have an important effect on industrial location. Certain metallurgical and chemical industries such as aluminium and copper processing and the production of fertilizers are especially sensitive to the cost of power. Areas that can produce electricity cheaply have been able to attract important manufacturing industries of this type.

Some industries like iron and steel, textiles and chemical require large quantities of water for their proper functioning. Such industries are established near rivers, canals, and lakes.

3.7 Skilled Workforce and Managerial Skills

The amount and type of labour necessary for operation varies from one industry to another and one firm to another. Some industries require thousands of employees while others can run with a few operatives. Some industries need a highly skilled labour force, some a large clerical and managerial staff, and others need numerous unskilled manual workers. The distinctive labour requirements of some concerns make certain locations more suitable them others. A firm needing a large labour force supplying a diverse range of skills would find it easier to obtain in a metropolitan area than in a small town. However, labour is likely to be more costly to the industry in large cities or national core regions than in the periphery where the cost of living is lower. However, if the right labour is not available at an otherwise attractive location, it is possible to obtain it from elsewhere since labour is mobile both geographically and in terms of occupation.

Skilled labour is important because of its contribution to enhancing productivity at the individual, industry and also national levels. Complementarities exist between physical capital and human capital on the one hand and between technology and human capital on the other. Fast changing knowledge economies call for new core competencies among all learners in the society.

Managerial skill is a category of labour and has a vital bearing on the success or failure of a business. Other than the policy-making function and organization structuring, management has the important decision-making task beginning with the initial choice on location, the balancing of various considerations and the assessment of *local business climate*. The need for skilled managerial employees may bestow locational advantages to areas best able to supply them. A firm requiring a range of managerial personnel with specific skills is more likely to locate where it can find it which would probably be in major urban area rather than in a small town.

3.8 Agglomeration

The area concentration of industrial activity often provides firms with collective benefits that they would not enjoy in an isolated location. These collective benefits take the form of external economies or agglomeration.

The advantages of a new firm locating among other firms engaged in the same activity include a pool of labour with particular skills and special educational institutions geared to the needs of the particular industry, both of which reduce the cost of training workers. Firms may also join together to develop a research institute, a marketing organization, and other collective facilities that individual manufacturers would be unable to provide for themselves. In addition, a region specializing in one industry will often have machine-makers, repair-works, suppliers of components etc., and other activities ancillary to the main one and providing goods and services for it. All these benefits of agglomeration when added together offer considerable cost advantages over alternative locations.

There are also benefits that arise in any large urban industrial area and which are potentially available to any firm irrespective of the industry to which it belongs. The main advantages of a large city or industrial region arise from the existence of a relatively well-developed infrastructure, i.e. highways, railways, airports, utilities, commercial facilities, educational institutions, research organizations and many other services that might not exist or would be less developed in a smaller place. However, a city location is not always to the advantage of the firm which may instead experience diseconomies of urbanization or deglomeration. In addition to the high price for land, taxes, labour etc., a firm may also have to contend with traffic congestion, lack of space, pollution and so forth. Nevertheless the balance of advantages still appears to favour the city.

3.9 Backward and Forward Linkages

It is important to make a clear distinction between industrial linkage and agglomeration. Linkages, both within and between firms, may encourage the geographical concentration, i.e. agglomeration of interdependent activities. More often than not such activities are separated by considerable distances. This suggests that linkages only reflect other factors and conditions that are the explanatory variables in industrial location. One of the key determinants of an industry's actual and potential importance for industrial development is the range of its backward and forward linkages.

Backward linkages occur when finished goods of a firm are used in the manufacturing process of another firm. Backward linkage is extremely common because so much of the activity in any region is producing for and oriented to the regional market.

Forward linkages occur when a firm produces raw materials or intermediate products that are used in the manufacture of finished goods by another firm. This means that an impact of change is transmitted to an activity further along in the sequence of operations. Large food processing industry can develop linkages with agricultural producers, transporters and packaging suppliers. The agro-related industry has probably the most significant linkages. For instance the textile industry is mainly cotton-based and is linked to primary cotton production via cotton-growing enterprises, to suppliers of dyes, printing and finishing chemicals and producers of synthetic fibres for blended textiles. The main forward linkages are to tailors and to final consumers through retail outlets. Significant potential exists for other linkages of the textile industry to engineering workshops for machines parts, to specialised tailors, hotels and service for curtain and upholstery materials, and for exports to regional and world markets. The motor vehicle assemblers and coach builders can establish some linkages with smaller workshops for a few components.

3.10 Public Policy

Many countries now seek to actively direct industry to particular problem regions or when they believe that certain economic, social or strategic objectives can be achieved more readily by planning than by leaving manufacturers to locate where they please. National or local government bodies can influence industrial location in two ways:
1. Freedom of choice of site may be restricted through land use zoning or by some tax penalty in an area where new industrial development is to be discouraged.
2. Encouraging firms to locate in certain areas which need new development by

offering financial inducements in the form of loans, subsidies or tax incentives. Aid at the local level is more often organizational than financial. Local help with regard to matters such as housing requirements and planning permission can be a real factor in the choice between alternative locations. In addition, many local authorities band together to sponsor regional scale industrial development associations, each seeking to lure the limited supply of mobile industry to its own constituent authority through a combination of publicity campaigns, industrial promotion and political pressure.

In countries where industry is state-owned or where the positive direction of industry to selected areas is possible, public action can modify existing location patterns speedily and effectively. In a free-enterprise economy, however, the adjustment is likely to be less rapid and predictable since whatever the national government may think is best for the nation, and whatever inducements are offered, location decisions are still subject to the capriciousness of the individual entrepreneur.

3.11 Personal Considerations

Almost any industry reveals cases of plant location that cannot be explained by obvious economic factors. The choice of one site over possible alternatives might seem to be entirely a matter of chance, with historical accident or the personal whim of the entrepreneur as the only possible explanation. The random factor in the diffusion of industrial innovation can also have a bearing on the spatial pattern of the adoption of new techniques, with some places and some entrepreneurs being more receptive to change than others. Once a plant has been built, personal factors as well as immobility of fixed capital may prevent relocation, even if it seems desirable on other economic grounds. In addition to leaving familiar surroundings, a move involves an increase in managerial effort while it is planned and undertaken, with some degree of risk and uncertainty as to the outcome. Some manufacturers may simply prefer to stay put, no matter how attractive an economic proposition an alternative location may be. Such attitudes make an important contribution to industrial inertia and existing industrial location patterns a degree of stability and permanence that economics alone may not justify.

To sum up, there are various economic and social criteria to determine location of industries. Economic criteria include availability of raw materials, nearness to market and infrastructural facilities. These may be available in already developed areas. Social criteria include employment opportunities and laying of social and economic overheads in backward areas. Zoning and land use regulations as well as environmental legislations in different countries also regulate industrial locations.

3.12 Theories of Industrial Location

A discussion of theories of industrial location seeks an answer to the question of what is the most rational location or pattern of land use for industries, describing why and how industries choose their actual sites or situations. Basically, location theory attempts to idealise the rational factors which ought to be considered before any use can be given a specific location. Concern would be to find that pattern of locational decisions which give the maximum amount of real goods and services from the sources available.

Industrial location analysis is structured around three approaches:

1. Least-cost approach which attempts to explain location in terms of the minimisation of factor costs.
2. Market area analysis where there is more emphasis on the demand or market factors.
3. Profit maximisation approach which is the logical outcome of the two.

Least-cost location theory rests upon the work of Alfred Weber (see section 3.14 on the next page) who began on the premise that the best location was the one at which costs are minimized. Considerable emphasis was placed upon the transport costs involved in assembling materials at the manufacturing site and in delivering the finished product to the market, although Weber also recognised the influence of labour costs and the possibility that economies may be achieved as a result of the agglomeration of several plants in close proximity to one another.

One of the fundamental weaknesses of the least cost approach is the over-emphasis of the input side (cost minimisation) and the under-emphasis of the output or demand side, simply assuming that the firm can sell all it produces wherever it locates. However, the market is a variable: buyers are scattered over a wide area and the intensity of demand varies from place to place. Firms will seek to gain access to the market and serve the greatest demand. Both these approaches are nonetheless one-sided, holding either the input supply or market demand constant.

In practice, both costs and revenue vary with location and the optimum location is the one which yields the greatest profit as upheld by the profit maximisation approach.

3.13 William Launhardt's Location Triangle Model

The analysis of William Launhardt provided the basis for the theory of industrial location. It was his contention that the decision to locate in a particular place would be based on transport costs of raw materials, inputs, finished goods etc. Using a simple model called the *location triangle* and the concept of ton-mileage, Launhardt suggested that as bulky products incur high transportation costs, the profits of finished goods should make these costs worthwhile; If not, a rational manufacturer would opt to relocate, always seeking the point of least transportation costs.

In his contribution, Alfred Weber considered transportation costs, labour costs and agglomeration forces as the major factors of industrial location given the location of raw material and market, assuming that raw material locations are sporadic. On the basis of the *location triangle*, Weber concluded that transportation costs were the primary determinants of industrial location. A new aspect in Weber's refashioned *triangle* was the use of isodapanes. He described these as hypothetical lines joining places of equal additional transportation costs from the least cost location of the industry that would be located somewhere within the *triangle*. An industry would face increasing costs the further away it was located from the least cost location.

Weber extended his analysis using isodapanes to include the effect of labour costs on industrial location, showing how cheap labour productivity would influence the decision of entrepreneurs in selecting the location of their industry. Through the same model Weber introduced the concept of raw material and market orientation where an industry would be attracted to the factor input product that is most costly to transport. If the finished product demanded in a particular market were bulky and thus costly to transport, the industry would be drawn to locate near the market, i.e. market orientation. Conversely, the Industry would be raw material or resource-oriented if its finished product were *weight-losing* through the process of manufacture. Thus, furniture-making and saw-milling would be market and raw material oriented respectively.

3.14 Alfred Weber's Theory of Industrial Location

Alfred Weber, a German economist, enunciated a systematic theory of industrial location in 1909. Weber's theory of location is purely deductive in its approach. He formulated a theory of industrial location in which an industry is located where the transportation costs of raw materials and final product is a minimum. He singled out two special cases. In one the weight of the final product is less than the weight of the raw material going into making the product.

He analyzed the factors that determine the location of industry and classified these factors into two divisions. These are as under:

1. Primary causes of regional distribution of industry (regional factors).
2. Secondary causes (agglomerative and deglomerative factors) that are responsible for redistribution of industry.

3.14.1 Primary Causes: According to Weber, transport costs and labour costs are the two regional factors on which his pure theory is based. Assuming that there are no other factors that influence the distribution of industry, except transportation costs, then it is clear that the location of industry will be pulled to those locations which have the lowest transportation costs. The key factors that determine transportation costs are as follows:

1. The weight to be transported.
2. The distance to be covered.

Weber lists some more factors which influence the transportation costs such as: (a) the type of transportation system and the extent of its use, (b) the nature of the region and kinds of roads, (c) the nature of goods themselves, i.e. the qualities which, besides weight, determine the facility of transportation.

However, the location of the place of production must be determined in relation to the place of consumption and to the most advantageously located material deposits. Thus, *locational figures* are created. These locational figures depend upon: (a) the type of material deposits and (b) the nature of transformation into products.

3.14.2 Secondary Causes: We have so far been discussing primary causes of industrial location. Weber has also discussed secondary causes responsible for industrial location. He has taken into account agglomerative and deglomerative factors. An agglomerative factor, according to him is a factor which provides an advantage in production or marketing a commodity simply because industry is located at one place. On the other hand deglomerative factor is one which gives such advantage because of decentralization of production.

Agglomerative factors include gas, water etc. and are conducive for concentration of industry and deglomerative factors include land values and taxes and lead to decentralisation. Pulls of agglomerative factors are index of manufacture and locational weight. According to Weber, ratio of manufacturing cost of locational weight is co-efficient of manufacture.

According to Weber, agglomeration is encouraged with high co-efficient and deglomeration with low. According to him, we shall do well to bear in mind that labour orientation is one form of deviation from the minimum point; agglomeration to another.

When agglomerative forces appear in an industry oriented towards labour, there takes place a competition between the agglomerative deviation and the labour deviation, a struggle to create, locations for agglomeration, as compared with labour locations, both bearing upon the foundations of the transport ground work.

The contribution of Alfred Weber was monumental and subsequent location theorists have upheld his analysis, emphasising transport costs as the basic factor of location.

3.15 Sargent Florence's Theory of Industrial Location

Sargent Florence started with the idea that some of Weber's assumptions are not realistic. According to him geographical location of an industry is not as important as the distribution of occupied population. His main consideration is that occupational distribution of population should be the main and primary factor for taking into consideration the location of an industry.

His theory is mainly based on inductive analysis and while explaining location factor of an industry he has taken into consideration location factor and co-efficient of localisation. According to him, location factor is an index of the degree of concentration of an industry in a particular region. This index is calculated by taking into consideration two ratios, namely the percentage of workers of the industry in question found in the region under consideration and the percentage of all industrial workers in the country. In calculating index to find out the location factor the first one is divided by the second and if the quotient is one, the location factor is said to be unity and it can be said that the industry is evenly distributed over the whole country. If quotient is above unity, then it means the region under reference has higher share of industry.

3.15.1 Co-Efficient of Localisation: By this he meant prosperity of an industry for concentration. It indicates an industry's tendency for localisation anywhere in the country. It is primarily concerned with a particular industry and not a particular region. It will thus be a single figure for the industry and also for the country as a whole. On the basis of coefficients it becomes possible to divide the industries into three categories namely high, medium and low. Thus coefficient helps in classifying industries according to their dispersion or concentration.

However, his theory is not in a position to explain the causes responsible for the choice of location of an industry. It can only help in finding out the existing state of industrial distribution in a country. It can be said that the theory is only the investigation of status quo and nothing beyond that.

According to his theory, the number of workers is the only factor as the indicator of concentration of an industry. Choosing this one factor alone for finding out concentration of an industry is unrealistic assumption.

Still, his theory is of considerable use for studying location dynamics and guiding the trends of industrial development in a country.

4

Market Structure (or Types of Market)

Market structure means the type of market in which a firm operates. The number of buyers and sellers, and the nature of the product traded are important characteristics of market structure. Perfect competition and monopoly are the two extreme market situations. In between these two extremes lie a number of other market structures such as monopolistic competition, oligopoly and duopoly. All these in-between market structures are collectively called imperfect competition.

4.1 Perfect Competition

Perfect competition is a market situation with the following features:

1. A perfectly competitive market has a large number of buyers and sellers so that no individual buyer or seller can influence the market price. A firm is a price-taker, i.e. it must accept the price ruling in the market. Since price is given, neither marginal revenue nor average revenue varies with output, and both are equal to price. Technically speaking, the marginal and average revenue curves are the same and parallel to the horizontal axis.
2. All the firms in a competitive market sell homogeneous product. Thus, if a firm tries to charge more than the prevailing market price, it will lose all buyers. There is apparently no reason for the firm to charge less when it can sell any quantity at the going price.
3. Firms enjoy freedom of entry into and freedom of exit from the industry. In other words, existing firms cannot bar the entry of new firms and there are no legal restrictions on entry or exit.
4. Buyers and sellers are well informed about market conditions. For example, a buyer knows when one firm is asking a higher price than other firms.

4.2 Monopoly

Monopoly is a market situation characterised by one seller and many buyers. It is the opposite extreme of perfect competition. Being the sole seller, a monopolist has the power to influence the market price. Unlike a competitive firm, a monopolist firm is a price-setter, not a price-taker. Since a monopolist is the only producer of his product, the distinction between a firm and the industry vanishes.

Monopoly may arise due to any of the following reasons:

1. A firm may control the entire supply of raw materials needed to produce the commodity.
2. A firm may own a patent which prohibits other firms from producing the same commodity.
3. A monopoly may be established by government order.
4. Increasing returns to scale in a firm may operate over a sufficiently large range of

output so that only one firm is left in the industry.

4.2.1 Single-price Monopoly and Price Discriminating Monopoly: The study of monopoly behaviour is attempted under two categories: (a) monopoly which charges a single price for the commodity it sells (single-price monopoly) and (b) a monopoly which sells its commodity at different prices either to different classes of customers or in different geographical markets (price discriminating monopoly).

4.2.2 Price Discriminating Monopoly: Price discrimination occurs when a monopolist sells different units of his output at different prices. There are two types of this discrimination: (a) discrimination among units sold to the same buyer as, for example, offering the first shirt at full price and the second for only half price, (b) discrimination among buyers as, for example, a doctor charging more fees from a rich patient and fewer fees from a poor patient for the same services.

4.2.3 Why is Price Discrimination Beneficial for the Monopolist? If a monopolist can discriminate among units sold, he can always earn a higher total revenue than by charging a single price. In other words, price discrimination is always advantageous to the monopolist. This is so because price discrimination allows the monopolist to capture some of the consumer surplus which would otherwise go to the buyers.

4.2.4 Conditions for Price Discrimination: Price discrimination is always profitable for the monopolist. However, there is a basic condition if price discrimination is to succeed. Successful price discrimination requires that goods cannot be resold by the buyer who faces lower price to the buyer who faces higher price. The ability to prevent resale depends on the following factors.

1. It is associated with the character or the nature of the product traded. It is fairly easy to resell movable commodities like sugar, butter and milk. However, it is pretty difficult to resell those goods which are installed like sanitary and electrical fittings. The resale of direct services like a haircut is impossible. That is why price discrimination is more successful in case of direct services.

2. Resale may not take place owing to consumers' peculiarities. For example, buyer A may be unaware that buyer B is paying a lower price for the same commodity. Similarly, if price differences are very small, buyers may just ignore them.

3. Resale will be difficult when consumers are separated by distance. Clearly, so long as the transportation cost is more than the price differential, resale will not be profitable. Apart from geographical barriers, resale may be prevented by artificial barriers like tariffs and import quotas. Duties on imports into a country would allow a monopolist producing in that country to charge a higher price in his home market.

4.2.5 Is Price Discrimination Desirable? There is no straight answer to this question. Whether price discrimination is good or bad depends on the merit of the case. It is also a matter of value judgement.

It is wrong to suggest that price discrimination is always undesirable because situation may arise justifying discrimination. In a college, students belonging to rich families are charged full fee, others pay half-fee and poor students are exempted from paying fee. Certainly, discrimination is preferable to non-discrimination in this case.

There is nothing in economic theory to suggest that price discrimination is undesirable.

4.3 Monopolistic Competition

Perfect competition and monopoly are two extreme market situations. In the real world, most firms operate under intermediate market structures like oligopoly, duopoly and monopolistic competition. These intermediate market structures are collectively called *imperfect competition*. Monopolistic competition is the most representative example of *imperfect competition*.

In perfect competition, firms sell a homogenous product and face a market price which they cannot influence. In monopolistic competition, firms sell differentiated products as, for example, different brands of soap, toothpaste and soft drinks. Though a firm is not a monopolist of a product as such yet it is the only producer of a particular brand of that product. Various brands of a product produced by different firms are close substitutes but not exactly alike. A producer in such a market has close rivals. Therefore, the market is competitive as well as monopolistic. It is competitive because there are rivals; it is monopolistic because each firm has monopoly over its own brand of the product. Since a firm is the only producer of its own brand of the product, it can exercise some control over its price. In other words, a firm is not a price-taker (as in perfect competition) but a price-setter.

4.4 Oligopoly

It is a market structure characterised by few sellers and many buyers. An oligopoly is an industry comprising only a few competing firms. These firms are strong rivals constantly watching jealously each other's decisions and reacting accordingly. This type of market structure is frequently observed in real life as, for example, car manufacturers.

An oligopolistic market may emerge because of falling costs due to the economies of large-scale production. In some cases, an industry may be dominated by a few large firms because they are successful in preventing the entry of new firms.

This type of market situation has a strange phenomenon called *price stickiness* or *price rigidity*. It means firms in oligopoly prefer to keep prices unchanged unless there are violent fluctuations in demand or cost conditions. The explanation for sticky prices lies in the possible reactions of competitor firms.

4.5 Duopoly

Duopoly is a market situation characterised by two sellers and many buyers as, for example, two firms selling identical spring water. Duopoly is the simplest and special case of oligopoly. Since in duopoly there are only two producers, any price or output change by one is bound to affect the other significantly. Among the various models for the behaviour of a duopolist firm, the one given by the French economist A.A. Cournot (1801-1877) is the most widely accepted.

Cournot's equilibrium assumes that there are two firms selling identical product (e.g. spring water) under conditions of zero cost of production. Therefore, the profit-maximising level of sales of each firm occurs at the mid-point of its negatively sloped straight line demand curve, where elasticity of demand is one, marginal revenue is zero and total revenue is maximum.

Basic assumption of the Cournot model is that each firm assumes that the other firm will hold its output constant.

If Cournot's equilibrium is achieved, neither firm will wish to depart from it. In the Cournot's equilibrium, the two firms make profits which exceed those earned under perfect competition but are less than those that would be earned by a monopoly.

4.6 Monopsony

It is a market situation where there is only one buyer but the number of sellers is very large. For example, owner of a sugar mill in a remote area is the only buyer of the labour services of the inhabitants of that area.

4.7 Bilateral Monopoly

It is a market structure where there is one buyer and one seller. If the inhabitants in the above example form a trade union and deal with the owner of the sugar mill collectively, it will be a case of bilateral monopoly.

5

Production Function, Cost Function and
Revenue Function of a Firm

5.1 Objective Function of a Firm

A firm is a unit which takes decisions regarding production and sale of commodities. A firm seeks profit by producing and selling commodities. More precisely, profit maximisation is the objective function of every firm. Profit (P) is the difference between revenue (R) received from the sale of output (Q) and the cost (C) of producing the output. $P = R - C$.

For determining the profit maximising output of a firm, it is necessary to understand the relationship between cost and output as well as revenue and output. The theories of cost and revenue are then combined to determine the most profitable output for a firm. However, before relating cost to output, it is necessary to know the relationship between output and input. Thus, the sequence of analysis becomes as follows:

1. How is output related to inputs (production function)?
2. How is cost related to output (cost function)?
3. How is revenue related to output (revenue function)?
4. Combination of cost and revenue functions to determine equilibrium of the firm, i.e. profit-maximising output.

It may be noted that cost conditions are common to all firms irrespective of the type of market in which they operate. However, revenue conditions differ depending upon the market structure in which a firm operates. Perfect competition, monopoly, oligopoly and monopolistic competition are the important types of market in which firms generally operate.

5.2 Production Function

A production function explains the technological relationship between inputs and output.
$P = f(F_1, F_2, ...F_n)$

In the above, P is the quantity of production and F_1, F_2, ...F_n are the quantities of different factors of production. Modern economists emphasise the importance of labour (L) and capital (K) in the production process. Land as a factor of production is considered unimportant or as a part of capital and thus ignored. Therefore, the simplified production function becomes:
$P = f(L, K)$

The relationship between inputs and output can be studied in two ways:

1. What happens to output as more of the variable factor is applied to a given quantity of the fixed factor. This is the study of the *law of diminishing returns*. It is also called the *law of variable proportions*.

2. What happens to output when all inputs are increased in a given proportion. This is the study of the *laws of returns to scale*.

5.2.1 Law of Diminishing Returns: Historically, the law of diminishing returns is associated with agricultural operations, with land being the fixed factor and labour the variable factor. However, this law holds good for all those productive activities where increasing quantities of a variable factor are applied to a given quantity of a fixed factor. Modern economists regard labour (L) and capital (K) to be the most significant factors of production, considering land as either unimportant or a part of capital.

The law of diminishing returns states that if increasing quantities of a variable factor (labour) are applied to a given quantity of fixed factor (land), the marginal product of the variable factor will eventually decline. The law is based on the following assumptions.

1. If one factor is kept fixed and increasing quantities of the other factor are applied, variations in the proportions of the two factors are implicitly assumed. This law will apply only to those cases where possibilities of variable proportions exist.
2. Since it is assumed that some factors are fixed therefore this law pertains to short-run.
3. Production technology is assumed to be given. A change in technology may postpone the operation of the law for sometime.
4. Different units of the variable factor are assumed to be homogenous.

Let us consider a fixed amount of land (say 1 hectare) on which increasing units of labour are employed. Table 5.1 records the variations in output as the quantity of the variable factor (labour) is increased. Before we analyse these variations, certain terms used in the table may be explained.

A. Total Product (TP): It is simply the total amount produced by all the factors of production employed.

B. Average Product (AP): Total product divided by the units of the variable factor gives the per unit or the average product of the variable factor. Symbolically,

AP = TP/L

C. Marginal Product (MP): It means the change in total product resulting from the use of one more unit of the variable factor. Thus,

MP = $\triangle$TP/$\triangle$L

According to Table 5.1, both average and marginal product move upward as more and more quantities of labour are applied to 1 hectare of land. In other words, the marginal as well as average product of labour increases in the initial stages. After that the marginal product of labour reaches the maximum point and then starts declining. The law of diminishing returns starts operating when the marginal product begins to decline. The declining marginal product may become zero or even negative if too much labour is used to work on 1 hectare of land.

Why does the law of diminishing returns hold good? There are valid explanations for the operation of this law. The marginal product increases in the first instance because increasing quantities of labour lead to division of labour and its advantages. In the beginning, the amount of labour is inadequate to utilise the fixed factor optimally and therefore there are increasing rather than decreasing returns. However, the scope for increasing returns must disappear eventually, i.e. marginal product of additional workers must decline. This is so because too many workers on the fixed factor will spoil the optimum ratio between land (fixed factor) and labour (variable factor). If the process of increasing the number of workers continues, they will start getting in each other's way and the marginal product may become zero or even negative. Were it not for the law of diminishing returns, the world food production could be raised on 1 hectare of land by simply increasing the quantity of labour on it.

Table 5.1: Total, Average and Marginal Product of Labour

Land (hectare)	Quantity of labour	Production of wheat (in quintals)		
		Total product	Average product	Marginal product
1	0	0	0	0
1	1	10	10	10
1	2	22	11	12
1	3	39	13	17
1	4	48	12	9
1	5	55	11	7
1	6	60	10	5
1	7	64	9.1	4
1	8	64	8	0
1	9	63	7	- 1

5.2.2 Law of Returns to Scale: This law pertains to production situation under which all factors of production can be increased in a given proportion. By assuming that all factors are variable, the law deals with long-run variations in output. Only two factors of production, viz. labour and capital are taken into account.

If there is an increase or decrease in labour and capital in a given proportion, the scale of production is changed. What is the relationship between increase in factors of production and the consequent increase in output? There are three dimensions of returns to scale. They are the following:

A. Increasing Returns to Scale: This is a situation where if factors are increased in a given proportion, output increases in a greater proportion. For example, if labour and capital are doubled, output is more than doubled.

What is the explanation for increasing returns to scale? The main reason for increasing returns to scale lies in the advantages of division of labour and specialisation. Higher scale of production facilitates greater division of labour and specialisation and as a result labour productivity increases. Large scale of production generates various types of *economies of scale* or *internal economies* for the firm. These include technological economies, managerial economies, financial economies and marketing economies. The firm also overcomes the problem of indivisibility of specialised and costly machines.

B. Constant Returns to Scale: This case refers to that situation where if factors are increased in a given proportion, the output also increases in the same proportion. For example, if capital and labour are doubled, the output is also doubled. We may come across such a production situation in real life. If one worker working on a machine produces 5 units of a commodity, it can be expected that two workers working on two identical machines will produce 10 units of the commodity.

C. Decreasing Returns to Scale: If factors of production are increased in a given proportion and output increases in a smaller proportion, it will be a situation of decreasing returns.

Under this production situation if inputs are increased by say 50 percent, the output will increase by less than 50 percent.

There are various reasons for the operation of decreasing returns. As the firm goes on expanding its size, it becomes increasingly difficult to co-ordinate and properly manage the activities of various departments of the firm. The firm may find it difficult to procure more and more raw material or finance for its production process. Marketing of the finished product may also become difficult. Excessive use of machines may result in more wear and tear. All these disadvantages put together are termed as *diseconomies of scale* or *internal diseconomies* which are related to the expanding size of the firm.

It is noteworthy that whereas all other factors of production can be purchased from the market and therefore increased but the services of the entrepreneur himself are fixed. There are limits on the supervisory and decision-making capabilities of the entrepreneur. If we assume the services of an entrepreneur as fixed while other factors are progressively increased, the law of decreasing returns to scale turns out to be a special case of the *law of variable proportions*.

In short, a firm normally experiences increasing returns to scale in the initial stages of its production, constant returns to scale at medium level and decreasing returns at very high levels of production.

5.3 Cost Function

Profit maximisation is the objective of all firms. Profit is the difference between revenue and cost. It is, therefore, necessary to know how cost and revenue vary with output. The study of cost behaviour of a firm is more important because a producer can influence his cost by varying the proportions of factors of production, or by economising on the use of factors, or through better and more efficient co-ordination of factors. Under perfect competition, the price of the product is determined by market forces and a firm has to sell at that price. In other words, a firm has no control over its revenue (price) and it can earn more profit only by reducing its cost of production. Any firm that is trying to maximise its profits must also try to produce a given output at lowest possible cost.

5.3.1 Various Concepts of Cost: The term cost has various meanings in economics.

A. Real Cost and Money Cost: Production process involves exertion on the part of labour, abstinence on the part of saver, and risk-taking on the part of entrepreneur. In other words, production process involves pain, discomfort and disutility for factors of production.

These exertions of labour and abstinences of savers constitute, according to British economist Alfred Marshall (1842-1924), the real cost of production. Obviously, the notion of real cost is subjective and defies measurement and hence has little practical utility.

In the real world, it is the money cost of production which is more important for the producer and the economist. Money cost refers to monetary payments by a firm to different factors of production which help the firm to produce a commodity. Thus, wages paid to labour and payment made for capital borrowed, raw material, equipment, transportation etc. all form part of money costs of a firm.

B. Explicit Cost and Implicit Cost: A producer hires factors of production for use in the production process. Apart from the hired factors, he also uses factors owned by him. He makes payments to factors which do not belong to him. Such payments relate to wages of labour hired, interest on borrowed funds, rent of hired lands and buildings etc. These are all explicit costs of production. However, the producer does not make payments for the factors which belong to him and are used in the production process. Thus, he has not to pay: (a) any rent for the buildings owned by him, (b) any interest for his own funds invested in the business or (c) any salary to himself for his own services rendered in running the business. Yet, one cannot ignore the services of a firm's own factors in calculating the cost of production. This is so because a firm could have earned a return by supplying its factors to other parties. Thus, a firm which uses its own resources incurs implicit costs equal to the amount it could have earned by offering these resources to other users. In other words, implicit costs are the costs of using a firm's own factors of production. Both explicit and implicit costs are taken into account while studying the cost structure of a firm.

C. Opportunity Cost: It is well known that resources of an economy are limited and can be put to alternative uses. A hectare of land may be used to produce say 100 quintals of wheat or 75 quintals of rice but it cannot produce both the items simultaneously. If a farmer decides to cultivate the hectare of land for wheat production, he will have to forego the amount of rice which he could have produced instead of wheat. Thus, 75 quintals of rice is the opportunity cost of producing 100 quintals of wheat. Hence, opportunity cost (also called user cost) denotes the output sacrificed or foregone when a society uses resources for one product rather than another. It is called so because one forgoes the opportunity of producing a commodity when another commodity is produced instead.

D. Private Cost and Social Cost: Private cost is simply the money cost of producing a commodity by a private producer. It includes all explicit and implicit costs of production. The concept of social cost is broader. Apart from private cost, the production process may generate socially undesirable effects like pollution of air and water by private factories. Pollution, in turn, may adversely affect health of the people. Thus, social cost consists of private costs plus other costs (pollution etc.) imposed on society at large.

E. Fixed Cost and Variable Cost: Total cost is divided into two parts: total fixed cost (TFC) and total variable cost (TVC). In the short-run, some factors (machinery, equipment etc.) are fixed in quantity. Total fixed costs are those which are incurred by a firm for all fixed inputs. Apparently, these costs do not vary with output, i.e. they remain the same whether output is more or less or even zero. Total variable costs are those which are incurred by a firm for all variable inputs (labour etc.). These costs vary positively with output, i.e. they rise as more is produced and fall as less is produced. Fixed costs are also called *overhead costs* or *unavoidable costs*. Likewise, variable costs are also called *direct costs* or *avoidable costs*. Thus, TC = TFC + TVC.

F. Total Cost, Average Cost and Marginal Cost:

(a) Total Cost (TC): Total cost is self-explanatory. It is simply the total cost of producing a given level of output.

(b) Average Cost (AC): Average cost or per unit cost is the total cost of producing a given level of output divided by the number of units produced. As in the case of total cost, average cost (AC) is divided into average fixed cost (AFC) and average variable cost (AVC). AFC equals total fixed cost divided by output while AVC equals total variable cost divided by output. Thus,

AC = TC/X =(TFC + TVC)/X = AFC + AVC.

C. Marginal Cost (MC): Marginal cost is the increase in total cost resulting from increasing the output by one unit. Marginal cost of producing the 10th unit (or the nth unit) of a commodity is the change in total cost when production increases from 9 units (n-1 units) to 10 units (n units). Symbolically, $MC = TC_n - TC_{n-1}$.

A hypothetical numerical example showing relationship between output and various type of costs is given in the Table 5.2.

Table 5.2: Total, Average and Marginal Costs at Various Production Levels

Units of output	TFC	TVC	TC	AFC	AVC	AC	MC
1	60	30	90	60	30	90	-
2	60	40	100	30	20	50	10
3	60	45	105	20	15	35	5
4	60	56	116	15	14	29	11
5	60	75	135	12	15	27	19
6	60	120	180	10	20	30	45
7	60	185	245	8.5	26.4	35	65
8	60	276	336	7.5	34.5	42	91

5.4 Revenue Function

Profit of a firm is the difference between total revenue derived from selling its product and the cost of producing it.

5.4.1 Total Revenue, Average Revenue and Marginal Revenue: Total revenue means the total amount of money which a firm receives from the sale of its output. Total revenue (TR) is equal to the quantity sold (q) multiplied by the price per unit (p) of the commodity. Thus, TR = pq. Average revenue (AR) is total revenue divided by the quantity sold. Thus, AR = TR/q. Marginal revenue (MR) is the change in total revenue resulting from an increase of 1 unit in the sale of a commodity. The marginal revenue resulting from the sale of the nth unit of a commodity is the change in total revenue when sales increase from n-1 units to n units. Symbolically,

$MR = TR_n - TR_{n-1}$

Cost-output relationship is applicable to all firms irrespective of the market structure in which they operate. However, this is not so in case of revenue. In other words, there is no single theory of revenue which applies to all firms. Revenue-output relationship of a firm is governed by the market situation in which a firm operates. Thus, a firm working under perfect competition is faced with different revenue conditions than a monopoly firm.

5.5 Macroeconomics and Microeconomics

Economic analysis has two phases: macroeconomics and microeconomics. Macroeconomics or aggregative economics is the study of the economy as a whole. It examines factors which govern the aggregate size of the economy. Thus, it deals with such aggregates as national income, total consumption, savings and investments in the economy, general price level and total exports and imports of a country.

Microeconomics is a branch of economics that studies the behaviour of individuals and firms in making decisions regarding the allocation of scarce resources and the interactions among these individuals and firms. Microeconomics is that part of economic analysis which examines particular components of the national economy. It studies adjustments of the various parts of the economy in detail. Thus, it includes the study of consumer behaviour, equilibrium of a firm, pricing of a product, pricing of a factor of production, location of an industry, choice of technology, exports and imports of individual items, and family income, consumption and saving.

Whether an economic phenomenon is macro or micro depends upon the definition of the whole. In the context of the formulation of world economic model, the study of the Indian economy would be micro in nature. Both macro and micro economic concepts are complementary to understand the working of an economy.

5.6 Economic Models

An economic model is a statement of relationship among economic variables. It is used to explain the cause and effect relationship among variables. Economic models are helpful in explaining and predicting economic phenomena like cost behaviour of firms. Aggregate models deal with the economy as a whole. Sectoral models examine particular sectors of the economy like industry or agriculture. Inter-industry models explain relationship among various sectors of the economy, using the popular technique of input-output matrices.

A demand model expressed relationship between the demand for a commodity and factors influencing it (like the price of the commodity, income of the consumer etc.).

5.7 Economic Laws and Their Assumptions

As a social science, economics deals with human behaviour i.e., behaviour of human beings as consumers and producers. An economic law is a statement that has been successfully tested again and again. Since human behaviour is not accurately predictable, the laws of economics are not as exact as those of physical sciences. Alfred Marshall compared economic laws with the law of tides rather than the law of gravitation which states exactly the force with which a thing falls to the ground.

Most economic laws hold good under several assumptions. Although techniques have been developed (multiple regression) to study the influence of several independent variables on a dependent variable simultaneously yet it is desirable, for the sake of simplicity, to ignore the influence of relatively unimportant factors on the dependent variable. Therefore, it is usual to make the ceteris paribus (other things being equal) assumption.

Economics deals with the behaviour of rational human beings. The assumption of rationality is at the core of economic analysis.

Rationality demands maximisation or optimisation behaviour. A consumer must try to maximise his satisfaction while a producer must try to maximise his profits.

6

Profit Maximization by a Firm: The Marginal Rule

A firm is a unit which takes decisions regarding production and sale of commodities. A firm seeks profit by producing and selling commodities.

6.1 Profit Maximization Objective of a Firm

Profit maximization is the objective function of every firm. Profit (P) is the difference between revenue (R) received from the sale of output (Q) and the cost (C) of producing the output. P = R - C.

For determining the profit maximising output of a firm, it is necessary to understand the relationship between cost and output as well as revenue and output. The theories of cost and revenue are then combined to determine the most profitable output for a firm. However, before relating cost to output, it is necessary to know the relationship between output and input. Thus, the sequence of analysis becomes as follows:

1. How is output related to inputs (production function)?
2. How is cost related to output (cost function)?
3. How is revenue related to output (revenue function)?
4. Combination of cost and revenue functions to determine equilibrium of the firm, i.e. profit-maximising output.

Production function, cost function and revenue function have already been discussed in chapter 5 of this book.

It may be noted that cost conditions are common to all firms irrespective of the type of market in which they operate. However, revenue conditions differ depending upon the market structure in which a firm operates. Perfect competition, monopoly, oligopoly and monopolistic competition (imperfect competition) are the important types of market in which firms generally operate.

6.2 Equilibrium (Profit Maximization) of a Firm under Perfect Competition

Equilibrium refers to the condition where a firm earns maximum profit. In this condition, there is no tendency to change the level of output. A firm does not want to increase or decrease the level of output under this condition.

Perfectly competitive market is a situation characterised by a large number of buyers and sellers so that no individual buyer or seller can influence the market price. All the firms in a competitive market sell homogeneous product. Firms enjoy freedom of entry into and freedom of exit from the industry. The buyers and sellers are well informed about market conditions.

Under perfect competition, each firm faces a perfectly elastic demand curve for its product. It follows that the demand curve facing the firm is identical with both the average revenue (AR) and marginal revenue (MR) curves so that all the three coincide in the same straight line showing price = AR= MR.

In a perfect competition market, MR curve is parallel to x-axis. In this market a firm can achieve equilibrium position when two conditions are fulfilled:

MC = MR and MC curve cuts MR curve from below.

6.3 The Marginal Rule

Profit maximisation is the objective function of a firm. What should be the level of a firm's output so that profit is maximised? This question is answered with the help of marginal rule. If at the present level of output a firm finds the cost of making another unit (marginal cost) less than the revenue gained by selling that unit (marginal revenue), total profit can be increased by producing the additional unit. Therefore, whenever a firm finds that marginal revenue exceeds marginal cost, it must expand output to increase profit.

Conversely, if the firm finds that the cost of producing the last unit of its current output exceeds the revenue gained by selling it, total profit can be increased by not producing the last unit. Thus, whenever marginal cost (MC) exceeds marginal revenue (MR), a firm can increase profit by contracting output.

In short, a firm should change its output whenever marginal cost is not equal to marginal revenue. According to marginal rule, a firm should raise output if MR exceeds MC and lower it if MC exceeds MR. It follows that at the profit-maximising output MR=MC. This is shown by point E in Figure 6.1.

Figure 6.1: Equilibrium of the Firm under Perfect Competition

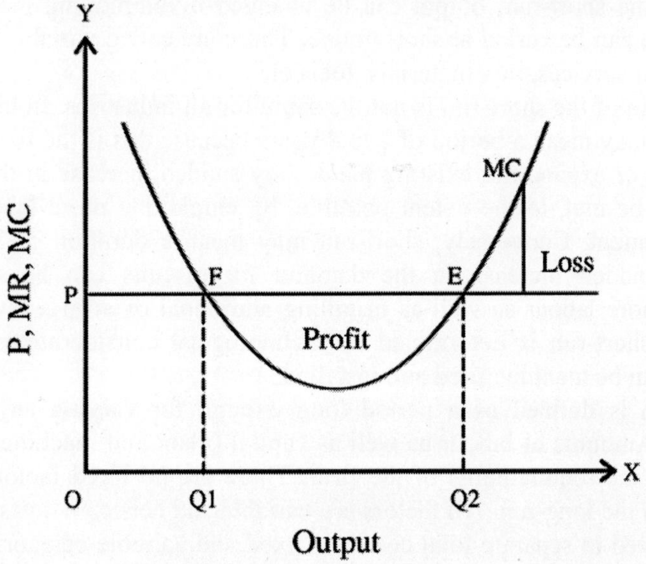

In Figure 6.1, output is measured on x-axis whereas price, marginal revenue and marginal cost are measured on y-axis. At point F, MR and MC are equal and MC cuts MR from above so that point F is not the equilibrium point because if the producer produces more than Q_1 then profit amount is increased. So, he wants to produce more which is against equilibrium position.

However, point E is equilibrium position because if he produces more than Q_2 there is no chance of profit. So, producer wants to remain at point E by producing Q_2 output which gives maximum revenue and MC = MR and MC curve cuts MR curve from below.

The equality of marginal cost and marginal revenue is necessary but not sufficient for profit maximisation. In Figure 6.1, there are two output levels where MC=MR (points F and E). These two points represent entirely different situations: point E showing maximum profit while point F' depicting minimum profit. Since we are interested in maximum profit situation, we add another condition to the marginal rule. Geometrically, this condition states that at the profit maximising output, the marginal cost curve should intersect the marginal revenue curve from below (as is the case at point E in Figure 6.1).

When the firm has chosen its profit-maximising output (or optimum output), it achieves equilibrium. It has no incentive to increase or decrease output from this equilibrium level. The marginal rule of profit-maximisation is applicable not only to perfect competition but to all types of market situations.

6.4 Short-run and Long-run

In economics, short-run is defined as a period of time over which certain factors of production cannot be changed. These factors are called fixed factors and usually pertain to plant, machinery, rent for buildings, insurance charges and other payments fixed by contract. In the short-run, output can be changed by employing more or less of those factors which can be varied at short notice. These are called variable factors and usually refer to labour services, raw materials, fuels etc.

The length of the short-run is not the same for all industries. In the case of a modern steel plant it may mean a period of 3 to 4 years because this is the likely time required to set up a new or expand the existing plant. Any sudden increase in the demand for steel will have to be met, to the extent possible, by employing more labour on the existing capital equipment. Conversely, short-run may mean a duration of 3 to 4 weeks for a bakery. A sudden increase in the demand for biscuits can be met adequately by employing more labour as well as installing additional oven in a few weeks. Thus, the duration of short-run is determined by technological considerations, i.e. how quickly equipment can be manufactured and installed.

Long-run is defined as a period long enough for varying any of the factors of production. Amounts of labour as well as capital (plant and machinery) can be changed according to the requirements of the firm. There are no fixed factors and therefore no fixed costs in the long-run. All factors are variable and hence all costs are variable. Thus, there is no need to separate total cost into fixed and variable categories as is the case in short-run. The absence of fixed costs is the essential characteristic of long-run which distinguishes it from short-run. In the long-run, we deal with the total cost and average cost without further classification. However, the concept of marginal cost is applicable to both short-run and long-run analysis. Marginal cost refers to the change in total cost when output is increased by one unit from its present level.

In the long-run, new firms can enter and existing firms exit the industry without any difficulty. In the short-run, existing firms cannot leave in view of constraints imposed by fixed costs, and similarly new firms cannot join the industry because it takes time to set up new plants.

In the short-run, firms may earn supernormal profits or suffer losses (i.e. subnormal profits). In case they are earning supernormal profits, new firms will enter the industry to share these profits. This means, at a given price more will be supplied because there are more suppliers. Supply will increase and if market demand remains unchanged, the equilibrium price will fall.

As the equilibrium price decreases, both new and old firms will have to adjust their output to this new price. Entry of new firms will continue and so also the decrease in price. This process will go on till all firms in the industry are just earning normal profit.

Conversely, if firms are suffering losses in the short run, some of them will leave the industry in the long-run. Supply will decrease and if market demand remains unchanged, the equilibrium price will increase. Firms continue to exit and price continues to rise until the remaining firms can cover their total costs and earn normal profit.

In the context of exit from the industry, it is sometimes important to distinguish between marginal and intra-marginal firms. A marginal firm is one which is just covering its full costs and would exit if price fell by even a small amount. An intra-marginal firm is that which is earning profits and would require a larger fall in price to decide to exit.

Since long-run equilibrium is normal profit equilibrium, there is no incentive for new firms to enter the industry or for the existing firms to leave the industry. It is pertinent to note that long-run equilibrium depicts the most efficient manner of production.

6.4.1 Shut-down Point: It is possible that a firm suffers losses in the short-run. In spite of incurring losses, it may prefer to remain in business. This is so because short-run is characterised by certain fixed costs which the firm must bear whether it remains in business or not. These fixed costs pertain to plant, machinery, rent for buildings, insurance charges and other payments fixed by contracts. Contrarily, there are variable costs which can be dispensed with in the short-run as, for example, labour on daily wages, raw materials, fuels etc.

It is clear that if a firm ceases operation in the short-run, its loss will be equal to fixed costs. It follows that a firm should stay in production even if it cannot cover its full fixed cost. However, there is no doubt that the firm must cover all its variable costs. As soon as the price becomes less than average variable cost, the firm must shut-down. In other words, a firm should produce only if total revenue is not less than total variable cost.

7

Industrial Productivity and Efficiency

Production system converts various resources and raw materials to produce goods and services. Industrial productivity deals with the relationship between output and input in a firm.

7.1 Factors of Production and Their Rewards

Production is creation of utility. Whosoever creates utility is a producer. One may create utility by transferring a commodity from one place to another. The utility of sand is increased when it is transferred from the river bank to the construction site of a building. Similarly, utility of a commodity may increase if preserved over a period of time. It is generally believed that older the wine the more utility it has. In most cases, utility is created by changing the shape of a commodity. A log of wood has less utility than a table made out of it. Thus, a carpenter who makes the table is a producer.

Basically, there are four factors of production: land, labour, capital and enterprise. Production becomes possible with the help of these factors of production.

7.1.1 Land: Land means all free gifts of nature including land as such, fertility of soil, sea, sunshine and rainfall. Land as a factor of production possesses the following characteristics: (a) it is fixed in supply, (b) it is immobile, (c) it is a passive factor of production and (d) it is heterogeneous.

The reward for the services of land is called rent.

7.1.2 Labour: Labour refers to various types of physical and mental exertions of man. According to British classical economist Adam Smith (1723-1790), labour is the source of all wealth. It has the following characteristics: (a) labour is an active factor of production, (b) labour is mobile, (c) labour is perishable, (d) labour cannot be separated from the labourer, (e) efficiency of labour varies and (f) labour needs incentives to work.

Reward for the services of labour is called wages.

7.1.3 Capital: Capital refers to man-made machines, equipment, tools and implements which are used for further production of wealth.

The reward for the services of capital is called interest.

7.1.4 Enterprise: Enterprise means bearing risks and uncertainties associated with business. He who bears these risks and uncertainties is called entrepreneur. He combines and organises other factors of production.

Reward for the services of an entrepreneur is called profit. Profit is a residual income after other factors of production have been paid. Unlike the rewards of other factors, profit cannot be determined in advance and it can be negative (loss) also.

7.2 What is Industrial Productivity?

It is a measurement of the efficiency of production. Basically, it is the relationship between the amount of output and the amount of inputs used to produce goods. In other words, it is the ratio of output to input.

Productivity = output ÷ input

With the help of modern technology, output per person can be increased, resulting into greater gross domestic product (GDP). More a man creates per unit time the higher the productivity.

Productivity can be improved in any situation by increasing the ratio of output to input. This ratio can be increased in the following manner:

1. Increasing output by using the same amount of input.
2. Producing the same level of output by using reduced input.

Productivity is a crucial factor in production performance of firms and nations. Increasing national productivity can raise living standards because more real income improves people's ability to purchase goods and services and enjoy leisure. Productivity growth can also help businesses to be more profitable.

7.3 Partial Productivity and Multi-factor Productivity

Productivity measures that use one class of inputs or factors, but not multiple factors, are called partial productivities. In practice, measurement in production means measures of partial productivity. Interpreted correctly, these components are indicative of productivity development, and approximate the efficiency with which inputs are used in an economy to produce goods and services. However, productivity is only measured partially or approximately. In a way, the measurements are defective because they do not measure everything, but it is possible to interpret correctly the results of partial productivity and to benefit from them in practical situations. At the company level, typical partial productivity measures are such things as worker hours, materials or energy used per unit of production.

In macroeconomics, a common partial productivity measure is labour productivity. Labour productivity is a revealing indicator of several economic indicators as it offers a dynamic measure of economic growth, competitiveness, and living standards within an economy. It is the measure of labour productivity which helps explain the principal economic foundations that are necessary for both economic growth and social development.

When multiple inputs are considered, the measure is called multi-factor productivity (MFP). MFP is typically estimated using growth accounting. If the inputs specifically are labour and capital, and the outputs are value added intermediate outputs, the measure is called total factor productivity (TFP). TFP measures the residual growth that cannot be explained by the rate of change in the services of labour and capital.

When all outputs and inputs are included in the productivity measure it is called total productivity. A valid measurement of total productivity necessitates considering all production inputs. If we omit an input in productivity this means that the omitted input can be used unlimitedly in production without any impact on accounting results. Because total productivity includes all production inputs it is used as an integrated variable when we want to explain income formation of production process.

MFP replaced the term TFP used in the earlier literature, and both terms continue in use (usually interchangeably).

7.4 Individual and Team Productivity

A team is a group of people working towards common goal or objective and with complementary skills. Usually the teams executing the projects in information technology (IT) organizations are known as project teams. In IT organizations, existence of software development teams, software maintenance teams, testing teams, quality teams, and support teams is very common. Each team has its own objective and purpose. It is led by a team leader or project manager. Team consists of team members and team leader or project manager.

Teams are supposed to be better suitable for executing complex tasks because team members share workload, observe behaviour of other team members and contribute to the sub tasks of the complex task. Technological advancements have catalyzed the usage of teams in modern software organizations.

Large scale software development is a collaborative activity which requires human resources and coordination among them. Essential characteristics of teams include enough team size, complementary skills, meaningful purpose, mutually accountable, specific goals, and clear working approach.

Productivity is influenced by effective supervision and job satisfaction. An effective or knowledgeable supervisor has an easier time motivating his subordinates to produce more in quantity and quality. An employee who has an effective supervisor, motivating him to be more productive is likely to experience a new level of job satisfaction thereby becoming a driver of productivity itself.

Technology—computers, spreadsheets, e-mails, and other advances—has enabled massive personal productivity gains. It has made it possible for a knowledge worker to seemingly produce more in a day than was previously possible in a year.

7.5 Business Productivity

Productivity is one of the main concerns of business management. Many companies have formal programmes for continuously improving productivity, such as a production assurance programme. Whether they have a formal programme or not, companies are constantly looking for ways to improve quality, reduce downtime and inputs of labour, materials, energy and purchased services. Often simple changes to operating methods or processes increase productivity, but the biggest gains are normally from adopting new technologies, which may require capital expenditures for new equipment, computers or software.

Modern productivity science owes much to formal investigations that are associated with scientific management. Although from an individual management perspective, employees may be doing their jobs well and with high levels of individual productivity, from an organizational perspective their productivity may in fact be zero or effectively negative if they are dedicated to redundant or value destroying activities. In office buildings and service-centred companies, productivity is largely influenced and affected by operational upgradation. The past few years have seen a positive uptick in the number of software solutions focused on improving office productivity. In truth, proper planning and procedures are more likely to help than anything else.

7.6 National Productivity

In order to measure productivity of a nation or an industry, it is necessary to operationalize the same concept of productivity as in a production unit or a company, yet, the object of modelling is substantially wider and the information more aggregate. The calculations of productivity of a nation are based on the time series of the System of National Accounts (SNA). National accounting is a system based on SNA recommended by United Nations Organization (UNO) to measure total production and total income of a nation and how they are used.

National productivity growth stems from a complex interaction of factors. Some of the most important immediate factors include technological change, organizational change, industry restructuring and resource reallocation, as well as economies of scale and scope. A nation's average productivity level can also be affected by the movement of resources from low-productivity to high-productivity industries and activities. Over time, other factors such as research and development and innovative effort, the development of human capital through education, and incentives from stronger competition, promote the search for productivity improvements and the ability to achieve them. Ultimately, many policy, institutional and cultural factors determine success in improving productivity of a country.

At the national level, productivity growth raises living standards because more real income improves people's ability to purchase goods and services (whether they are necessities or luxuries), enjoy leisure, improve housing and education and contribute to social and environmental programmes. Nothing contributes more than increase in productivity to reduction of poverty, increases in leisure, and the country's ability to finance education, public health, and better environment.

Productivity is considered basic statistical information for many international comparisons and country performance assessments and there is strong interest in comparing them internationally. Organization for Economic Co-operation and Development (OECD) publishes an annual Compendium of Productivity Indicators that includes both labour and multi-factor measures of productivity.

7.7 Benefits of Productivity Growth

Productivity growth is a crucial source of growth in living standards. Productivity growth means more value is added in production and this means more income is available to be distributed.

At a firm (or industry) level, the benefits of productivity growth can be distributed in a number of different ways:

1. To the workforce through better wages and conditions.
2. To shareholders and superannuation funds through increased profits and dividend distributions.
3. To customers through lower prices.
4. To the environment through more stringent environmental protection.
5. To governments through increase in tax payments.

Productivity growth is important to the firm because it means that it can meet its obligations to workers, shareholders, and government (taxes), and still remain competitive or even improve its competitiveness in the market place.

7.8 Determinants of Productivity

In the most immediate sense, productivity is determined by the available technology or know-how for converting resources into outputs, and the way in which resources are organized to produce goods and services. Historically, productivity has improved through evolution as processes with poor productivity performance are abandoned and newer forms are exploited. Process improvements may include organizational structures, management systems, work arrangements, manufacturing techniques, and changing market structure. Famous examples include assembly line, process of mass production and electrification.

There is a general understanding of the main determinants of productivity growth. Following factors are critical for determining productivity growth.

7.8.1 Technological Development and Innovations: Technological development plays an important part to influence the industrial productivity. The application of mechanical improvements to the process of production has accelerated the peace of industrialisation to an unprecedented degree, and has given us the vision of the vast and unexplored frontiers that still lie ahead of us in the realm of applied science and technology. The technological factors include degree of mechanisation, technical know-how, product design etc. Improvement in any of the technological factors will contribute towards the increase in industrial productivity.

Successful exploitation of new ideas is of crucial importance. New ideas can take the form of new technologies, new products or new corporate structures and ways of working. Speeding up the diffusion of innovations can boost productivity.

7.8.2 Quality of Human Resources and Skills: Manpower plays a significant role in raising industrial productivity in most of the industries. If the labour force is not adequately qualified and/or is not properly motivated, all the steps taken to increase the industrial productivity will have no result. Employees' performance and attitudes have an immense effect on the productivity of any industrial unit. Three important factors which influence the productivity of labour area: (a) ability of the worker, (b) willingness of the worker, and (c) the environment under which he has to work.

Labour enters the production process from the supply side as well as from the demand side. The focal point for both aspects is higher productivity because it is through higher productivity that higher real wages can be ensured, cost of production can be brought down and higher demand for products can be generated, which would lead to further growth. The role of labour has to be perceived in this broad perspective.

The success of labour policy has to be adjudged on the basis of the productivity standard that it helps the economy to achieve. While technical factors and the state of technology are crucial in determining productivity levels, there is no denying the fact that discipline and motivation of workers, their skill, the state of industrial relations, the extent and effectiveness of participation of workers, the working climate and safety practices are also of great importance. While maximising employment generation, requisite attention has to be directed to the improvement of labour productivity through the adoption of up-to-date technology in productive processes in major sectors and corrective measures for industrial sickness.

Skills are defined as the quantity and quality of labour of different types available in an economy. Skills complement physical capital, and are needed to take advantage of investment in new technologies and organisational structures.

7.8.3 Availability of Finance: The ambitious plans of an industrial unit to increase the productivity will remain mere dreams if adequate financial resources are not available to introduce technical improvements and give appropriate training to the workers. The greater the degree of mechanisation to be introduced, the greater is the need for capital. Capital will also be required for investment in research and development activities, advertisement campaign, better working conditions to the workers, up-keep of plant and machinery etc.

The more capital (machinery, equipment and buildings) workers have at their disposal, generally the better they are able to do their jobs, producing more and better quality output.

7.8.4 Managerial Talent: The significance of managerial talent has increased with the advancement in technology. Professional managers are required to make better use of the new technological development. Since the modern enterprises are run on a large-scale, the managers must possess imagination, judgment and willingness to take imitative.

The managers should be devoted towards their profession and they should understand their social responsibilities towards the owners of the business, workers, customers, suppliers, government, and the society. This is essential if the managers want to manage their organisations effectively. The managers should have conceptual, human relations and technical skills in order to increases the productivity of the enterprise.

7.8.5 Enterprise and Competition: It is defined as the seizing of new business opportunities by both start-ups and existing firms. New enterprises compete with existing firms by new ideas and technologies, increasing competition in the industry. Entrepreneurs are able to combine factors of production and new technologies forcing existing firms to adapt or exit the market.

Competition improves productivity by creating incentives to innovate and ensures that resources are allocated to the most efficient firms. It also forces existing firms to organise work more effectively through imitations of organisational structures and technology.

7.8.6 Government Policy: The industrial policies of the government have an important impact on the industrial productivity. Government should frame and implement such policies which create favourable conditions for saving, investment, flow of capital from one industrial sector to another and conservation of national resources. Certain industries may be granted protection, and incentives may be given to the others for the development in view of the national interest.

Government should follow taxation policy which does not discourage the further expansion of business. It is also the duty of the government to check the growth of monopolistic enterprises so that the interest of the consumers and the workers are not jeopardized.

7.8.7 Natural Factors: The natural factors (such as physical, geographical and climatic) exercise considerable impact on the industrial productivity. The relative importance of these factors depends upon the nature of the industry, goods and services produced and the extent to which physical conditions are controlled.

The geological and physical factors play a very dominant role in determining the productivity of extractive industries likes coal-mining in which the physical output per head is greatly influenced by the depth of the coal-mines, the thickness of the coal seams, the topography of the region and the quality of coal available. In other industries like tailoring, grain-milling, hosiery, soap-making, confectionary, medium and coarse cotton manufacturing.

7.9 Factors Harming Productivity

Workplace bullying results in a loss of productivity. Over time, victims of bullying will spend more time protecting themselves against harassment by bullies and less time fulfilling their duties. Workplace incivility has also been associated with diminished productivity in terms of quality and quantity of work.

A toxic workplace is marked by significant drama and infighting, where personal battles often harm productivity. While employees are distracted by this, they cannot devote time and attention to the achievement of business goals. When toxic employees leave the workplace, it can improve the culture overall because the remaining staff becomes more engaged and productive.[The presence of a workplace psychopath may have a serious detrimental impact on productivity in an organization.

In companies where the traditional hierarchy has been removed in favour of an egalitarian, team-based set-up, the employees are often happier, and individual productivity is improved. Companies that have this hierarchy removed and have their employees work more in teams are called liberated companies.

The factors affecting industrial productivity are inter-related and inter-dependent and it is a difficult task to evaluate the influence of each individual factor on the overall productivity of industrial units.

8

Trademarks, Patents, Industrial Designs and Geographical Indications

8.1 Intellectual Property Rights (IPRs)

IPRs refer to the legal ownership by a person or business of an invention/discovery attached to particular product or process which protects the owner against unauthorized copying or imitation.

The Agreement establishing the World Trade Organization (WTO) contains, *inter alia*, an Agreement on Trade-related Aspects of Intellectual Property Rights (TRIPS).

TRIPS Agreement, which came into effect on January 1, 1995, is to date the most comprehensive multilateral agreement on intellectual property.

TRIPS provides, among others, for norms and standards in respect of following areas of intellectual property:

1. Trademarks.
2. Patents.
3. Industrial designs.
4. Geographical indications.

8.2 Trademarks

A trademark means a mark capable of being represented graphically and which is capable of distinguishing the goods or services of one undertaking from those of other undertakings. A trade mark can be a device, brand, heading, label ticket name, packaging, sign, word, letter, number, drawing, picture, emblem, colour or combination of colours, shape of goods, signature or a combination thereof.

A trademark is used or proposed to be used to distinguish the goods or services of one person from those of others in the course of trade. Though the registration of trademark is not compulsory, it is a prima facie proof of the title and it gives the registered proprietor an exclusive right to use the trademark and take legal action in case of infringement. If a trademark is not registered and if someone not having the right in the trademark uses that trademark, the proprietor of the trademark can take the common law action of passing off.

In the TRIPS Agreement, the basic rule is that any sign, or any combination of signs, capable of distinguishing the goods and services of one undertaking from those of other undertakings, must be eligible for registration as a trademark, provided that it is visually perceptible. Such signs, in particular words including personal names, letters, numerals, figurative elements and combinations of colours as well as any combination of such signs, must be eligible for registration as trademarks.

Where signs are not inherently capable of distinguishing the relevant goods or services, member countries of WTO are allowed to require, as an additional condition for eligibility for registration as a trademark, that distinctiveness has been acquired through use. Members are free to determine whether to allow the registration of signs that are not visually perceptible (e.g. sound or smell marks).

Members may make registrability depend on use. However, actual use of a trademark shall not be permitted as a condition for filing an application for registration, and at least 3 years must have passed after that filing date before failure to realize an intent to use is allowed as the ground for refusing the application.

The owner of a registered trademark must be granted the exclusive right to prevent all third parties not having the owner's consent from using in the course of trade identical or similar signs for goods or services which are identical or similar to those in respect of which the trademark is registered where such use would result in a likelihood of confusion. In case of the use of an identical sign for identical goods or services, a likelihood of confusion must be presumed.

Cancellation of a mark on the grounds of non-use cannot take place before 3 years of uninterrupted non-use has elapsed unless valid reasons based on the existence of obstacles to such use are shown by the trademark owner. Circumstances arising independently of the will of the owner of the trademark, such as import restrictions or other government restrictions, shall be recognized as valid reasons of non-use. Use of a trademark by another person, when subject to the control of its owner, must be recognized as use of the trademark for the purpose of maintaining the registration.

It is further required that use of the trademark in the course of trade shall not be unjustifiably encumbered by special requirements, such as use with another trademark, use in a special form, or use in a manner detrimental to its capability to distinguish the goods or services.

8.3 Patents

A patent is granted for an invention which is a new product or process, that meets conditions of novelty, non-obviousness and industrial use. Inventive step is the feature(s) of the invention that involves technical advance as compared to existing knowledge and that makes the invention not obvious to a person skilled in the art. Industrial use means that the invention is capable of being made or used in an industry.

The TRIPS Agreement requires member countries to make patents available for any inventions, whether products or processes, in all fields of technology without discrimination, subject to the normal tests of novelty, inventiveness and industrial applicability. It is also required that patents be available and patent rights enjoyable without discrimination as to the place of invention and whether products are imported or locally produced.

There are three permissible exceptions to the basic rule on patentability. One is for inventions contrary to *ordre public* or morality; this explicitly includes inventions dangerous to human, animal or plant life or health or seriously prejudicial to the environment. The use of this exception is subject to the condition that the commercial exploitation of the invention must also be prevented and this prevention must be necessary for the protection of *ordre public* or morality.

The second exception is that member countries may exclude from patentability diagnostic, therapeutic and surgical methods for the treatment of humans or animals.

The third is that member countries may exclude plants and animals other than micro-organisms and essentially biological processes for the production of plants or animals other than non-biological and microbiological processes. However, any country excluding plant varieties from patent protection must provide an effective *sui generis* system of protection. Moreover, the whole provision is subject to review 4 years after entry into force of the Agreement.

The exclusive rights that must be conferred by a product patent are the ones of making, using, offering for sale, selling, and importing for these purposes. Process patent protection must give rights not only over use of the process but also over products obtained directly by the process. Patent owners shall also have the right to assign, or transfer by succession, the patent and to conclude licensing contracts.

Countries may provide limited exceptions to the exclusive rights conferred by a patent, provided that such exceptions do not unreasonably conflict with a normal exploitation of the patent and do not unreasonably prejudice the legitimate interests of the patent owner, taking account of the legitimate interests of third parties.

Member countries shall require that an applicant for a patent shall disclose the invention in a manner sufficiently clear and complete for the invention to be carried out by a person skilled in the art and may require the applicant to indicate the best mode for carrying out the invention known to the inventor at the filing date or, where priority is claimed, at the priority date of the application.

If the subject-matter of a patent is a process for obtaining a product, the judicial authorities shall have the authority to order the defendant to prove that the process to obtain an identical product is different from the patented process, where certain conditions indicating a likelihood that the protected process was used are met

Compulsory licensing and government use without the authorization of the right holder are allowed, but are made subject to conditions aimed at protecting the legitimate interests of the right holder.

8.4 Industrial Designs

A design refers only to the features of shape, configuration, pattern, ornamentations, composition of colour or line or a combination thereof, applied to any article, whether two or three dimensional or in both forms by any industrial process or means which in the finished article, appeal to and are judged solely by the eye.

Every design, to be registrable must pass the universal test of novelty. A registered design is valid for 10 years and can be further extended by another 5 years. A design cannot be registered if it is not new or original or has been disclosed to the public in India or anywhere in the world by publication.

TRIPS Agreement obliges member countries of WTO to provide for the protection of independently created industrial designs that are new or original. They may provide that designs are not new or original if they do not significantly differ from known designs or combinations of known design features. It may also be provided that such protection shall not extend to designs dictated essentially by technical or functional considerations.

There is a special provision aimed at taking into account the short life cycle and sheer number of new designs in the textile sector: requirements for securing protection of such designs, in particular in regard to any cost, examination or publication, must not unreasonably impair the opportunity to seek and obtain such protection. Member countries are free to meet this obligation through industrial design law or through copyright law.

Owner of a protected industrial design may be granted the right to prevent third parties not having the owner's consent from making, selling or importing articles bearing or embodying a design which is a copy, or substantially a copy, of the protected design, when such acts are undertaken for commercial purposes.

Limited exceptions to the protection of industrial designs may be given, provided that such exceptions do not unreasonably conflict with the normal exploitation of protected industrial designs and do not unreasonably prejudice the legitimate interests of the owner of the protected design, taking account of the legitimate interests of third parties.

The duration of protection available shall amount to at least 10 years.

8.5 Geographical Indications

A geographical indication identifies agricultural or natural or manufactured goods as originating or manufactured in the territory of a country or region or locality in that territory, where a given quality, reputation or other characteristic of such goods is essentially attributable towards geographical origin and in case where such goods are manufactured goods one of the activities of either the production or a processing of preparation of the goods concerned takes place in such territory, region, or locality as the case may be.

In the TRIPS Agreement, geographical indications are defined as indications which identify a good as originating in the territory of a region or locality in that territory, where a given quality, reputation or other characteristic of the good is essentially attributable to its geographical origin. Thus, this definition specifies that the quality, reputation or other characteristics of a good can each be a sufficient basis for eligibility as a geographical indication, where they are essentially attributable to the geographical origin of the good.

In respect of all geographical indications, interested parties must have legal means to prevent use of indications which mislead the public as to the geographical origin of the good, and use which constitutes an act of unfair competition.

The registration of a trademark which uses a geographical indication in a way that misleads the public as to the true place of origin must be refused or invalidated *ex-officio* if the legislation so permits or at the request of an interested party.

Interested parties must have the legal means to prevent the use of a geographical indication identifying wines for wines not originating in the place indicated by the geographical indication. This applies even where the public is not being misled, there is no unfair competition and the true origin of the good is indicated or the geographical indication is accompanied be expressions such as "kind", "type", "style", "imitation" or the like. Similar protection must be given to geographical indications identifying spirits when used on spirits. Protection against registration of a trademark must be provided accordingly.

There are certain exceptions to the protection of geographical indications. These exceptions are of particular relevance in respect of the additional protection for geographical indications for wines and spirits. For example, countries are not obliged to bring a geographical indication under protection, where it has become a generic term for describing the product in question. Measures to implement these provisions shall not prejudice prior trademark rights that have been acquired in good faith. Under certain circumstances, continued use of a geographical indication for wines or spirits may be allowed on a scale and nature as before. Countries availing themselves of the use of these exceptions must be willing to enter into negotiations about their continued application to individual geographical indications. The exceptions cannot be used to diminish the protection of geographical indications that existed prior to the entry into force of the TRIPS Agreement.

8.6 Intellectual Property Rights (IPRs) in India

IPRs are private rights recognized within the territory of a country and given to (or conferred upon) an individual(s) or a legal entity in order to protect their creativity or innovation. India has a well-established legislative, administrative and judicial framework to safeguard IPRs which meet the country's international obligations while utilizing the flexibilities provided in the international regime to address its developmental concerns.

The Indian government has taken several initiatives to create conducive environment for the protection of intellectual property rights of innovators and creators by bringing about changes at legislative and policy level. In addition, specific focus has been placed on improved service delivery by upgrading infrastructure building capacity and using state-of-the-art technology in the functioning of intellectual property offices in the country. This measure has resulted in sweeping changes in intellectual property administration within the country. Aims of the Indian intellectual property administration are as under:

1. Establishing a vibrant intellectual property regime in the country.
2. Efficient processing of intellectual property applications by inducting additional manpower, judgment IT facilities and automation in intellectual property offices.
3. Adopt best practice in intellectual property processing.
4. Strengthening public delivery of intellectual services.
5. Highest levels of transparency and user-friendliness.

The IPR framework in India is stable and well-established from a legal, judicial and administrative point of view and is fully complaint with the WTO Agreement on Trade-related aspects of Intellectual Property Rights (TRIPS).

India is committed in a wide range of international treaties and conventions relating to intellectual property rights. Wide range of awareness programmes are being conducted by the Government.

During the last few years, Indian intellectual property offices have undergone major improvement in terms of upgradation of IP legislation including infrastructure facilities, human resources, processing of intellectual property applications, computerization, database, quality services to stakeholders, transparency in functioning and free access to intellectual property data through a dynamic website.

India is a member of World Trade Organization and committed to the Agreement on Trade Related Aspects of Intellectual Property. India is also a member of World Intellectual Property Organization (WIPO), a body responsible for the promotion of protection of intellectual property rights throughout the world.

The Department of Industrial Policy and Promotion (DIPP) under the Ministry of Commerce and Industry, Government of India is responsible for administration of trademarks, patents, industrial designs and geographical indications.

9

Mergers and Acquisitions (M&A)

9.1 Meaning of M&A

Mergers and acquisitions (M&A) is a general term used to describe the consolidation of companies or assets through various types of financial transactions, including mergers, acquisitions, consolidations, purchase of assets, and management acquisitions.

Collectively, M&A are transactions in which the ownership of companies or other business organizations is transferred or consolidated with other entities. As an aspect of strategic management, M&A can allow enterprises to grow and change the nature of their business or competitive position.

The terms *mergers* and *acquisitions* are often used interchangeably, although, in fact, they hold slightly different meanings.

9.1.1 Merger: A merger is the combination of two firms, which subsequently form a new legal entity under the banner of one corporate name. A merger describes two firms, of approximately the same size, that join forces to move forward as a single new entity, rather than remain separately owned and operated. This action is known as a merger of equals. In a merger, the boards of directors for two companies approve the combination and seek shareholders' approval.

A. Demerger: The term *demerger* is sometimes used to indicate a situation where one company splits into two, generating a second company which may or may not become separately listed on a stock exchange.

9.1.2 Acquisition: An acquisition (or takeover) is the purchase of one business or company by another company or other business entity. In an acquisition, one company purchases the other outright. In a simple acquisition, the acquiring company obtains the majority stake in the acquired firm, which does not change its name or alter its organizational structure.

When one company takes over another and establishes itself as the new owner, the purchase is called an acquisition.

Acquisition usually refers to a purchase of a smaller firm by a larger one. Sometimes, however, a smaller firm will acquire management control of a larger and/or longer-established company and retain the name of the latter for the post-acquisition combined entity. This is known as a *reverse takeover*. It occurs when a privately held company—often one that has strong prospects and is eager to raise financing—buys a publicly listed shell company, usually one with no business and limited assets. It enables a private company to be publicly listed in a relatively short time frame. The private company merges into the public company, and together they become an entirely new public company with tradable shares.

Acquisitions are divided into *private* and *public* acquisitions, depending on whether the merging company (also called *target company)*) is listed or not on a stock market.

9.1.3 Difference between Mergers and Acquisitions (M&A): A merger is a legal consolidation of two entities into one, whereas an acquisition occurs when one entity takes ownership of another entity's stock, equity interests or assets.

A deal may be called a *merger of equals* if both entities agree that joining together is in the best interest of both of their companies, while when the deal is unfriendly—i.e. when the management of the target company opposes the deal—it may be regarded as an acquisition.

In general, the term *merger* is used when the purchasing and target companies mutually combine to form a completely new entity. *Acquisition* describes a transaction, where one firm absorbs another firm via a takeover.

Because each combination is a unique case with its own peculiarities and reasons for undertaking the transaction, use of these terms tends to overlap. From a commercial and economic point of view, both types of transactions generally result in the consolidation of assets and liabilities under one entity, and the distinction between a *merger* and an *acquisition* becomes nebulous.

9.1.4 Consolidation (or Amalgamation): It occurs when two companies combine to form a new enterprise altogether, and neither of the previous company remains independent. Consolidation creates a new company by combining core businesses and abandoning the old corporate structures. Stockholders of both companies must approve the consolidation, and subsequent to the approval, receive common equity shares in the new firm.

9.2 Brief History of M&A

History of M&A began in the late 19th century USA. However, mergers coincide historically with the existence of companies. In 1708, for example, the East India Company merged with an erstwhile competitor to restore its monopoly over the Indian trade. In 1784, the Italian Monte dei Paschi and Monte Pio banks were united as the Monti Reuniti. In 1821, the Hudson's Bay Company merged with the rival North West Company.

9.2.1 Great Merger Movement: 1895-1905: The Great Merger Movement was a predominantly USA business phenomenon that happened from 1895 to 1905. During this time, small firms with little market share consolidated with similar firms to form large, powerful institutions that dominated their markets, such as the Standard Oil Company, which at its height controlled nearly 90 percent of the global oil refinery industry.

Companies such as DuPont, U.S. Steel, and General Electric that merged during the Great Merger Movement were able to keep their dominance in their respective sectors due to growing technological advances of their products, patents, and brand recognition by their customers. One of the major factors that sparked the Great Merger Movement was the desire to keep prices high. However, high prices attracted the entry of new firms into the industry.

A major catalyst behind the Great Merger Movement was the Panic of 1893, which led to a major decline in demand for many homogeneous goods. For producers of homogeneous goods, when demand falls, these producers have more of an incentive to maintain output and cut prices, in order to spread out the high fixed costs these producers faced (i.e. lowering cost per unit) and the desire to exploit efficiencies of maximum volume production. However, during the Panic of 1893, the fall in demand led to a steep fall in prices.

In recent years, *corporate marriages* have involved more diverse companies. Acquirers more frequently buy different industries. Sometimes this is done to smooth out cyclical bumps, to diversify, the hope being that it would hedge an investment portfolio.

Similarly, cross-sector convergence has become more common. For example, retail companies are buying tech or e-commerce firms to acquire new markets and revenue streams. Many companies are being bought for their patents, licenses, market share, name brand, research staff, methods, customer base, or culture.

9.3 Categorization of M&A

M&A process is multifaceted which depends upon the type of merging companies.

9.3.1 Horizontal and Vertical M&A: Horizontal integration and vertical integration are competitive strategies that companies use to consolidate their position among competitors. Horizontal integration is the acquisition of a related business. A company that opts for horizontal integration will take over another company that operates at the same level of the value chain in an industry.

A horizontal merger is usually between two companies in the same business sector. An example of horizontal merger would be if a publisher purchases the business of another publisher. This means that synergy can be obtained through many forms such as increased market share, cost savings and exploring new market opportunities.

Vertical integration refers to the process of acquiring business operations within the same production vertical. A company that opts for vertical integration takes complete control over one or more stages in the production or distribution of a product.

A vertical merger represents the buying of supplier of a business as, for example, a publisher acquiring the business of a paper merchant. The vertical buying is aimed at reducing overhead cost of operations and economy of scale.

A. Conglomerate M&A: It is a form of M&A process which deals the merger between two irrelevant companies. The relevant example of conglomerate M&A would be if a publisher acquires a hotel. The objective is often diversification of goods and services and capital investment.

9.3.2 Statutory and Consolidated M&A: A statutory merger is a merger in which the acquiring company survives and the target company dissolves. The purpose of this merger is to transfer the assets and capital of the target company into the acquiring company without having to maintain the target company as a subsidiary.

A consolidated merger is a merger in which an entirely new legal company is formed through combining the acquiring and target company. The purpose of this merger is to create a new legal entity with the capital and assets of the merged acquirer and target company. Both the acquiring and target company are dissolved in the process.

9.3.3 Friendly and Unfriendly M&A: A deal can be classified as a merger or an acquisition, based on whether the acquisition is friendly or hostile and how it is announced. In other words, the difference lies in how the deal is communicated to and perceived by the board of directors of the target company, its employees and shareholders.

Friendly acquisitions are most common, and occur when the target firm agrees to be acquired. Its board of directors and shareholders approve of the acquisition and these combinations often work toward the mutual benefit of the acquiring and target companies.

Unfriendly acquisitions (commonly known as *hostile takeovers*) occur when the target company does not consent to the acquisition. Hostile acquisitions do not have the same agreement from the target firm, and so the acquiring firm must actively purchase large stakes of the target company to gain a controlling interest, which forces the acquisition. Unfriendly takeover deals are always regarded as acquisitions.

It is normal for M&A deal communications to take place in a so-called *confidentiality bubble* wherein the flow of information is restricted pursuant to confidentiality agreements. In the case of a friendly transaction, the companies co-operate in negotiations; in the case of a hostile deal, the management of the target company is unwilling to be bought or has no prior knowledge of the offer. Hostile acquisitions can, and often do, ultimately become *friendly*, as the acquiror secures endorsement of the transaction from the board of the acquiree company. This usually requires an improvement in the terms of the offer and/or through negotiations.

9.3.4 Asset Purchases and Equity Purchases: Corporate acquisitions can be characterized for legal purposes as either *asset purchases* in which the seller sells business assets to the buyer, or *equity purchases* in which the buyer purchases equity interests in a target company from one or more selling shareholders. Asset purchases are common in technology transactions where the buyer is most interested in particular intellectual property rights but does not want to acquire liabilities or other contractual relationships. An asset purchase structure may also be used when the buyer wishes to buy a particular division or unit of a company which is not a separate legal entity.

9.4 Documentation of a M&A Transaction

The documentation of an M&A transaction often begins with a letter of intent. The letter of intent generally does not bind the parties to commit to a transaction, but may bind the parties to confidentiality and exclusivity obligations so that the transaction can be considered through a due diligence process involving lawyers, accountants, tax advisors, and other professionals, as well as business people from both sides.

After due diligence is complete, the parties may proceed to draw up a definitive agreement, known as a *merger agreement*, *share purchase agreement* or *asset purchase agreement* depending on the structure of the transaction. Such contracts typically focus on following key types of terms:

1. Conditions which must be satisfied before there is an obligation to complete the transaction. Conditions typically include matters such as regulatory approvals and the lack of any material adverse change in the target's business.

2. Representations and warranties by the seller with regard to the company, which are claimed to be true at both the time of signing and the time of closing.
3. Covenants which govern the conduct of the parties, both before the closing (such as covenants that restrict the operations of the business between signing and closing) and after the closing (such as covenants regarding future income tax filings and tax liability or post-closing restrictions agreed to by the buyer and seller parties).
4. Termination rights which may be triggered by a breach of contract, a failure to satisfy certain conditions or the passage of a certain period of time without consummating the transaction, and fees and damages payable in case of a termination for certain events.
5. An indemnification provision, which provides that an indemnitor will indemnify, defend, and hold harmless the indemnitee(s) for losses incurred by the indemnitees as a result of the indemnitor's breach of its contractual obligations in the purchase agreement
6. Provisions relating to obtaining required shareholder approvals under the law.

9.5 Business Valuation and Financing

The assets of a business are pledged to two categories of stakeholders: equity owners and owners of the outstanding debts of the business. The core value of a business, which accrues to both categories of stakeholders, is called the enterprise value (EV), whereas the value which accrues just to shareholders is the equity value (also called market capitalization for publicly listed companies). Enterprise value reflects a capital structure neutral valuation and is frequently a preferred way to compare value as it is not affected by a company's strategic decision to fund the business either through debt, equity, or a portion of both.

Both companies involved on either side of an M&A deal will value the target company differently. The seller will obviously value the company at the highest price possible, while the buyer will attempt to buy it for the lowest possible price. Fortunately, a company can be objectively valued by studying comparable companies in an industry, and by relying on the following metrics:
1. **Price-earnings Ratio (P/E Ratio):** With the use of P/E ratio, an acquiring company makes an offer that is a multiple of the earnings of the target company. Examining the P/E for all the stocks within the same industry group will give the acquiring company good guidance for what the target's P/E multiple should be.
2. **Enterprise-value-to-sales Ratio (EV/sales):** With EV/sales, the acquiring company makes an offer as a multiple of the revenues, while being aware of the price-to-sales ratio of other companies in the industry.
3. **Discounted Cash Flow (DCF):** A key valuation tool in M&A, DCF analysis determines a company's current value, according to its estimated future cash flows. Forecasted free cash flows (net income + depreciation/amortization − capital expenditures − change in working capital) are discounted to a present value using the company's weighted average costs of capital (WACC). Admittedly, DCF is tricky to get right.

Professionals who value businesses generally do not use just one method, but a combination. M&A advice is provided by full-service investment banks who often advise and handle the biggest deals in the world and specialist M&A firms, who provide M&A only advisory, generally to mid-market, select industries. Highly focused and specialized M&A advice investment banks are called boutique investment banks.

9.5.1 Financing: Mergers are generally differentiated from acquisitions partly by the way in which they are financed and partly by the relative size of the companies. Various methods of financing an M&A deal exist:

A. Cash: A company can buy another company with cash, stock, assumption of debt, or a combination of some or all of the three. Such transactions are usually termed acquisitions rather than mergers because the shareholders of the target company are removed from the picture and the target comes under the (indirect) control of the bidder's shareholders.

B. Stock: Payment in the form of the acquiring company's stock, issued to the shareholders of the acquired company at a given ratio proportional to the valuation of the latter. They receive stock in the company that is purchasing the smaller subsidiary.

In smaller deals, it is also common for one company to acquire all of another company's assets. Company A buys all of company B's assets for cash, which means that company B will have only cash (and debt, if any). Of course, company B becomes merely a shell and will eventually liquidate or enter other areas of business.

9.6 Motives for M&A

Why do companies keep acquiring other companies through M&A? Two of the key drivers of capitalism are competition and growth. When a company faces competition, it must both cut costs and innovate at the same time. One solution is to acquire competitors so that they are no longer a threat. Companies also complete M&A to grow, by acquiring new product lines, intellectual property, human capital, and customer bases. Companies may also look for synergies. By combining business activities, overall performance efficiency tends to increase and across-the-board costs tend to drop, as each company leverages off of the other company's strengths.

The following motives are generally considered for M&A:

1. **Economies of Scale:** This refers to the fact that the combined company can often reduce its fixed costs by removing duplicate departments or operations, lowering the costs of the company relative to the same revenue stream, thus increasing profit margins. It also includes managerial economies such as the increased opportunity of managerial specialization.

2. **Economy of Scope:** This refers to the efficiencies primarily associated with demand-side changes, such as increasing the scope of marketing and distribution, of different types of products.

3. **Increased Market Share:** This assumes that the buyer will be absorbing a major competitor and thus increase his market power to set prices. Due to increased order size, the firm can get bulk-buying discounts.

4. **Taxation Liability Reduction:** A profitable company can buy a loss making company to use the latter's loss to reduce its tax liability.
5. **Geographical Diversification:** This is designed to smooth the earnings results of a company, which over the long-term smoothens the stock price of a company, giving conservative investors more confidence in investing in the company.
6. **Innovative Intellectual Property:** Nowadays, intellectual property has become one of the core competences for companies. Studies have shown that successful knowledge transfer and integration after a merger or acquisition has a positive impact to the firm's innovative capability and performance.

10

Industrial Imbalances and the Need for Balanced Regional Development

In any comprehensive plan of development, it is axiomatic that the special needs of the less developed areas should receive due attention. The pattern of industrialization must be so devised as to lead to balanced regional development. The problem is particularly difficult in the early stages when the total resources available are inadequate in relation to needs. However, as the development proceeds and large resources become available for investment, the stress of developmental programmes should be on relatively underdeveloped regions. Only thus can a truly diversified economy be built up.

Apart from inter-regional imbalances, there can be intra-regional imbalances. Even in highly developed regions, there can be districts/blocks whose indicators are comparable to those of the poorest districts in the most backward regions. While some level of intra-region and inter-region disparity is bound to exist even in the best possible situation, economic policy must enable backward regions to substantially overcome the disadvantages and provide at least a certain minimum standard of services for their citizens. Disparities in regional performance are a matter of concern not just in terms of income indicators, but also human development indicators.

Livelihood options in industrially backward areas are limited as agriculture does not give adequate returns.

10.1 Causes of Industrial Imbalances

Industrial imbalances may be natural due to unequal distribution of natural resources and/or man-made in the sense of neglect of some regions and preference for others for investment and infrastructural facilities. Since different provinces are not equally endowed with resources, they have dissimilar industrial bases. As a result, the well-endowed provinces have a higher per capita income and hence a sound revenue base for their governments than the less-endowed provinces.

In India, apart from uneven distribution of geographical advantages, historical factors have also contributed to regional imbalances. The British rulers developed only those regions which possessed facilities for manufacturing and trading activities. Thus, in the pre-1947 period almost all industrial and commercial activities remained confined to major cities, viz. Bombay (in Maharashtra), Calcutta (in West Bengal), and Madras (in Tamil Nadu).

Industrial disparities are also attributed to inequities in access to social and physical infrastructure. Private sector investment tends to move to places where the enabling environment, i.e. investment climate is better (infrastructure availability and good governance). Another factor which explains industrial disparity is the quality of human capital which, in turn, depends on the level of education and health of the population.

Private sector activity depends on the extent of entrepreneurship within a region and the resources commanded by it and on the infrastructure and other developments within the region conducive to development of such activity. Attracting entrepreneurs from outside the region is also dependent mainly on the services and facilities available within the region. To a limited extent this can be stimulated by special concessions.

Development experience has shown that funds are not the only bottleneck in the industrialization process. Reforms in the administrative and fiscal structure, in policies related to the day-to-day life of the ordinary people and the manner of delegation of financial and administrative powers do have a multiplier effect on the economies of the concerned regions. More often, it pertains to the way in which existing rules and regulations are used/interpreted in the delivery of services and the working of the local economy.

Finally, regions with better law and order situation and governance benefit in the form of higher and sustained growth. In India, industrially better-off states have generally had better governance and followed growth-enhancing policies more effectively than others.

10.2 Need for Balanced Regional Development

Balanced regional development is needed to ensure the unity and integrity of the nation. Since not all parts of the country are equally well endowed to take advantage of growth opportunities, and since historical inequalities have not been eliminated, planned intervention is required to ensure that large regional imbalances do not occur. With greater freedom and choice of location that is now available to industry, it is more than likely that some regions would be able to attract more private investment than others. In such a situation it will be necessary to deliberately bias public investment in infrastructure in favour of the less well-off regions. However, it should be ensured that the regions which benefit from this reorientation do not dilute their own efforts at generating investible resources or divert their resources to other uses.

In the context of India, neglect of balanced regional development including the development of tribal areas, can lead to serious consequences such as the growth of left wing extremism which is evident in many districts in the country. Successful development in these areas is the only viable solution to the underlying discontent which leads to extremism. This calls for innovative approach, especially efforts to improve governance and participation of people.

There can be regions or pockets of poverty which are unable to benefit adequately from the over-all growth process. There is a strong probability that even in the future, market-based growth may elude these regions unless active intervention is made by the government. The role of the government in promoting equity among regions, therefore, has assumed added importance in the post-liberalization era. Redressing regional disparities is not only a goal in itself but is essential for maintaining the integrated social and economic fabric of a country without which it may be faced with a situation of discontent, anarchy and breakdown of law and order.

10.3 Constraints and Challenges

Balanced development of different parts of a country, extension of the benefits of economic progress to the less developed regions and widespread diffusion of industry should be the major aims of economic development. Expansion of the economy and more rapid growth has increased progressively the capacity of the economy to achieve a better balance between national and regional development. In striving for such a balance, certain inherent difficulties have to be met. As resources are limited, advantage lies in concentrating them at those points within the economy at which the returns are likely to be favourable. As development proceeds, investments are undertaken over a wider area and resources can be applied at a large number of points, thereby resulting in greater spread of benefits. In the interest of development itself, the maximum increase in national income should be achieved and resources obtained for further investment. The process is a cumulative one, each stage determining the shape of the next. In some fields, as in industry, intensive and localised development may be inevitable.

Along with this, in other areas, the aim should be to provide for more dispersed advance in sectors like agriculture, small industries, power, communications and social services. Equally with industry, investment in economic and social overheads helps to create numerous promising centres for growth. Once a minimum in terms of national income and growth in different sectors is reached, without affecting the progress of the economy as a whole, it becomes possible to provide for a larger scale of development in the less developed regions. A large country with extensive natural resources has the means not only to realise a high and sustained rate of growth but also to enable its less developed regions to come up to the level of the rest.

The two aims—increase in national income and more balanced development of different parts of the country—are thus related to one another and, step by step, it becomes possible to create conditions in which resources in terms of natural endowment, skill and capital in each region are fully utilised. Sometimes the sense of lagging behind in development may be due not so much to a slower rate of overall growth in the region as to inadequate or tardy development in specific fields, such as agriculture, irrigation, power or industry or employment. In each region the nature of the problem and the impediments to rapid development in particular fields should be carefully studied, and appropriate measures devised for accelerated development. The essential objective should be to secure the fullest possible utilisation of the resources of each region, so that it can contribute its best to the national pool and take its due share from the benefits accruing from national development.

Balanced regional development has been an important objective of economic policy in India and various instruments including fiscal incentives, industrial policies and directly targeted programmes have been deployed in the past to achieve it. Some policies, such as industrial licensing, are no longer relevant in today's economic environment since investment cannot be directed to particular locations. In a competitive world, investment must be allowed to flow to locations perceived to have an attractive investment climate and better infrastructural facilities. While this has definitely generated efficiency, there is, at the same time, evidence of increasing regional divides. Growth performances across states have been varied; the performance of poorer states with poorer infrastructure has been lagging.

It is recognized that the planning and development of an area within the state is primarily the responsibility of the concerned state governments. Within an overall state-oriented approach, certain regions across and within states have, for historical and special reasons, called for a focused area development approach. Developmental problems are faced by certain areas arising out of their distinct geo-physical structure and location and concomitant socio-economic development. To deal with the specific problems of these areas, region-specific plan strategies are formulated keeping in view the basic needs of the people and priorities of the state government concerned.

To sum up, an important objective of the development strategy must be to bring about a progressive reduction in regional inequalities. It should be generally accepted that the fulfilment of the objective requires upgrading the development process in the backward regions which have acquired a certain momentum.

The fact that there are vast areas of the country which have remained backward over the years is both a challenge and an opportunity. Diffusion of skills and technology to these areas should bring forth a proportionately greater improvement in productivity. Their resource base is low and many of them face one or the other of the adverse natural factors which inhibit the prospects of growth—scanty rainfall, frequency of floods, difficult terrain, desert areas and so on.

Backwardness does not recognise state boundaries and it may be necessary, over time, to take account of this in the policies concerning resource transfers. Relatively richer states need to pay adequate attention to the backward areas within their territories and the claims of the backward states must also be sustained on the basis of proven programmes for the benefit of the backward regions.

11

Infrastructure and Logistics for Industry

Supply chains in the modern world are complex and their performance is largely dependent on infrastructure and logistics.

11.1 Infrastructure: Meaning, Importance and Financing

Availability of adequate, efficient and affordable infrastructural facilities constitutes the core of development strategy and efforts. By their very nature, infrastructure projects (power, railways, ports, civil aviation, roads and telecommunications) involve huge initial investments, long gestation periods and high risk. The demand for infrastructural services has increased rapidly after industrial liberalisation of the Indian economy. Unfortunately, infrastructural bottlenecks remain the biggest stumbling block of industrial progress in the country.

11.1.1 What is Infrastructure? Infrastructure is generally defined as the physical framework of facilities through which goods and services are provided to the public. Its linkages to the economy are multiple and complex, because it affects production and consumption directly, creates positive and negative spill over effects (externalities), and involves large flows of expenditure.

In economic literature, infrastructure is popular by the name *overhead capital* which represents basic services without which primary, secondary and tertiary productive activities cannot function. The very success of social and economic transformation of an economy lies in providing inclusive and sustainable infrastructure amenities to the people and the pace of economic growth depends on how competently and judiciously an economy is able to address its infrastructure bottlenecks.

Generically, infrastructure has the following distinct components:

1. Energy (electricity, coal, petroleum and natural gas, renewable energy sources and atomic power for civil use).
2. Transport (railways, roads and road transport, shipping and ports and civil aviation).
3. Telecommunications and information technology.
4. Special economic zones (SEZs).
5. Harnessing water resources (irrigation)
6. Rural infrastructure (housing, transport, telephony, water supply and sanitation.
7. Urban infrastructure (housing, transport, slum clearance/development, water supply, sanitation and sewerage and solid waste management).

11.1.2 Why is Infrastructure Important? The availability of adequate infrastructure facilities is imperative for the overall economic development of a country. Infrastructure adequacy helps determine success in diversifying production, expanding trade, coping with population growth, reducing poverty and improving environmental conditions. Infrastructure contributes to economic development both by increasing productivity and by providing amenities which enhance the quality of life. The services provided lead to growth in production in several ways.

1. Infrastructure services are intermediate inputs to privatisation and any reduction in these input costs raises the profitability of production, thus permitting higher levels of output, income, and/or employment.
2. They raise the productivity of other factors, including labour and other capital. Infrastructure is thereby often described as an 'unpaid' factor of production, since its availability leads to higher returns obtainable from other capital and labour.

The infrastructure sector covers a wide spectrum of services. Some of these services have a direct impact on the working of a business enterprise, while others are more important from a societal point of view. Each sub-sector of an infrastructural service is inherently unique in terms of its administration and operational structure, the regulatory framework governing its operations, the level of technology and the degree of commercialisation. In addition, while some services such as telecommunications can be provided on a strictly commercial basis, others like roads are expected to be fully provided by the State or at least part-subsidised.

Typically, as incomes rise, the composition of infrastructure changes significantly. For low-income countries, basic infrastructure is more important—water, irrigation, and transport. As economies mature, most of the basic consumption demands for water are met, the share of agriculture in the economy shrinks, and more transport infrastructure is provided. The share of power and telecommunications is greater in high-income countries.

Most directly, productive activities in industry, agriculture and services use electricity, telecommunications, water and transport as intermediate inputs. Even in the informal sector, infrastructure can be a major share of business expenses. A measurable benefit of investment in infrastructure is the reduced cost to users of each service unit consumed. This benefit is greater, the more the service is characterised by economies of scale.

If enterprises are unable to realise the benefit of efficient generation of infrastructure services, they are forced to seek higher-cost alternatives that may have unfavourable impacts on profits and production levels. Unreliability (erratic water pressure, call interruptions etc.) and lack of access to infrastructure services lead to under-utilisation of existing productive capacity and constrains short run productive efficiency and output growth. Users are forced to invest in alternative sources such as captive power plants and tube wells, thereby raising capital costs. This has ripple effects, creating bottlenecks and slack capacity utilisation in other sections of the economy. Problems like under-maintenance of facilities and poor service quality shifts the burden of infrastructure provision and increase overall costs to produce outcomes which are not the most economically efficient.

Infrastructure is central to the basic patterns of demand and supply, and to the economy's ability to respond to changes in prices or endowments of other resources. The expansion of service, high-technology and financial sectors relative to manufacturing industries increases the demand for telecommunications, but decreases the relative requirements for industrial waste disposal and transportation of manufacturing inputs and outputs.

The ultimate goal of infrastructure policy is to effectively deliver infrastructure services of high quality and at low prices, to households and firms in the country. The success of policies in infrastructure must be judged by the quality, quantity and prices that end-users are charged for these services, and comparisons with global standards on each of these three fronts.

Provision of quality infrastructure services at reasonable cost is a necessary condition for achieving sustained economic growth. In fact, one of the major challenges being faced by the Indian economy is to enhance infrastructure investment and to improve the delivery system and quality of services. Investment in infrastructure involves high risk, low return, lumpiness of huge investment, high incremental capital/output ratio, long payback periods and superior technology. These prerequisites pose a constraint on the Government's efficient delivery of quality infrastructure services. Government is moving away from its traditional role as a *provider* of services to one of *facilitator* and *regulator* by ensuring that infrastructure services are actually delivered in a desirable manner.

11.1.3 Nature of Infrastructure Services: Infrastructure projects are characterised by large financial outlay requirements and long generation periods. Investment involves high upfront costs and long-term financing since the payback period is long.

Infrastructure services are often monopolistic in nature, they usually involve high upfront costs and long payback periods, and investments are typically bulky and lumpy. They are also characterised by the existence of externalities which make it difficult for infrastructure entities to recoup investment costs and operational expenses through the levy of user charges. Consequently, infrastructure services have been predominantly provided by the public sector in almost all countries for most of the 20th century.

Historically, initiatives to implement infrastructure projects in India have generally been vested in the public sector. With infrastructure services being perceived as natural monopolies, it was argued that only the government should be entrusted with its provision. There was also the view that the financial outlays involved were beyond the resources available with the private sector. Both these views have since undergone a change. In the current fiscal situation, the government will be very constrained to raise resources from the market for providing budgetary support to departments or public sector enterprises engaged in infrastructure development. Technological improvements and organizational innovations have enabled unbundling of services and this, in turn, has debunked the view about economies of scale and the purely monopolistic nature of infrastructure activities.

A solution to the problems associated with the traditional approach to infrastructure can be found in commercialising these projects. The recovery of investments should be through a system of user charges which bears a direct relation to the specific benefits that the facility provides to the user.

11.1.4 Financing of Infrastructure: The importance of infrastructure financing towards economic growth can hardly be overemphasized. It has remained a principal area of government intervention in India and many other countries, given the sector's fundamental contribution to economic growth and social welfare. Developing countries have to make massive investments of financial, human and managerial resources in infrastructure.

Future investment needs are expected to be much higher, because of demand created by economic growth, rising population, rapid urbanisation as well as the need to reconstruct some economies and make up for lack of adequate investment in others in the recent past. This is particularly true for the East Asia Region, whose increasing investment needs are driven by its very high economic growth rate. The need for investment in infrastructure rises exponentially with economic growth rate.

Till recently, as the government implemented and financed the bulk of infrastructure outlays, all the attendant project risks were also borne by the government. Resource mobilisation, mainly domestic, was through pre-emption of funds from banks and insurance companies backed by issue of dated securities. Foreign funds, mainly in the form of project-specific aid from bilateral and multilateral sources, supplemented domestic resources. Hence, infrastructure financing was relatively simple and straightforward, but undoubtedly inefficient and lacking accountability.

The pattern of financing witnessed in the past will undergo a change as the transition from predominant state investment in infrastructure to increasing private/foreign participation occurs. While the reliance on domestic sources would continue as in the past, these would need to be augmented by foreign funds in the form of equity as well as debt.

A. Role of Financial Institutions: The nature of infrastructure projects and their inherent complexities make them different from traditional industrial projects with which the financial institutions (FIs) have been familiar. In addition to traditional financial, technical and economic appraisal capabilities of project financing, infrastructure projects require deep understanding of the legal, regulatory and institutional arrangements under which the project promoters would operate. Most infrastructure projects are limited-resource financing and hence bear higher risk compared to traditional industrial lending where the risk is covered by the balance sheet of the sponsor, with tangible assets as security.

Privately financed infrastructure projects need well developed domestic capital markets and provide an opportunity to develop them. Since most of these investments generate revenues in local currency, it may not be sustainable in the long run to finance these investments out of foreign savings. There is both the scope and the need to develop financial instruments and the market systems to tap domestic capital markets to finance infrastructure investments.

Private investment and financing while offering the benefit of additional funds, will also importantly encourage better risk sharing, accountability, monitoring and management. Empirical evidence suggests that infrastructure projects, irrespective of their sectoral characteristics, have high leverage ratios. Since the level of retained earnings over and above the depreciation provisions is low, infrastructure firms typically fund projects through debt finance. They also tend to diverge from the conventional pecking order of corporate finance, i.e. using retained earnings in preference to debt and debt in preference to public issues of equity capital to fund asset acquisition. Not only is the initial recourse to debt funding very high for infrastructure investments, but subsequent expansion, renovation, and modernisation are also funded substantially through debt finance.

The central financial issue in infrastructure investment is not adequacy of funds, but more importantly the institutional framework and other related mechanisms which facilitate convergence of investment horizons of ultimate savers and borrowers in the economy.

In developed countries, infrastructure projects raise financing from institutional investors (insurance companies, pension funds, endowments, and the like) either through the bond markets, or through direct private placements. In India also, the contractual savings institutions [like Life Insurance Corporation of India (LIC), and General Insurance Corporation of India (GIC)] that have long-term liabilities, make natural investors in private infrastructure projects.

Apart from these institutions, other institutional investors such as charitable and religious trusts can also be a source of substantial funds. With the development of an active and liquid market for securitised corporate debt, mutual funds, commercial banks and financial institutions, they could also emerge as potentially large investors. However, all this calls for substantial reform in the debt market.

At present all the contractual savings institutions are under the control of the government which largely pre-empts their funds. If infrastructure has to be financed through the capital markets, it is necessary to initiate major reforms in the area of contractual savings institutions, allowing for the entry of private companies and institutions in each of these areas. The government's programme to reduce its fiscal deficit would also bring down its pre-emption of funds in existing institutions. The more widespread availability of contractual savings instruments which provide good returns can be expected to lead to increasing financial savings rates of the households.

In order to leverage their core competence of project appraisal, the FIs would need to adopt a number of strategies, such as taking of loans onto their books and then syndicating them, or lending to projects during the construction and start-up stages, and securitising the loans or selling down the bonds, once operations have begun and the project is investment graded. FIs would thus bear their risk-assessment capabilities during the riskier pre-operative phase, with securitisation made easier in the post completion phase. Such turnover of portfolio would have a salutary effect on the quantum of funds mobilised. However, securitisation as a financing mechanism would require a fair amount of reforms in the legal framework.

B. Debt Market: If the trend towards private investment in infrastructure is to continue, financial markets will have to respond by providing the necessary long term resources. Parallel to the innovations in the structuring of contractual agreements, which are critical to making a project finance worthy, delivering long-term finance through alternative institutions and instruments would be critical success factors. Overall balance of payments constraints and the sheer size of infrastructure investments imply that a sustained infrastructure programme will have to be accompanied by a strategy for mobilising domestic funds. In turn, an increasing share of domestic savings will need to come from private sources as the government reduces its involvement in infrastructure.

Synergistic links can develop between private infrastructure projects and domestic financial intermediation through capital markets. Infrastructure developments and private (especially contractual) savers share a long term horizon. Bringing compatible savers and investors together is the task of the capital markets. At the same time, the financing of infrastructure projects improves appraisal capabilities and expands risk-diversification possibilities for local commercial banks, equity and bond markets, and institutional investors such as insurance companies and pension funds.

Successful implementation of the envisaged investment would call for reforms in all segments of the financial system. The major areas, where comprehensive polity and procedural changes would be necessary would largely be in the institutional segment of contractual savings—insurance, pension and provident funds and the debt market. The policies relating to the equity and forex markets, ECB and fiscal concessions to infrastructure projects also need to be reviewed. Deepening and widening of the market in debt instruments through financial innovations are expected to go a long way in stepping up the overall domestic savings rate. This of course, also crucially hinges on the speed with which the policy framework is made conducive.

International experience suggests that the traditional approaches to financing that involve term loans from FIs and banks and equity offerings in the domestic capital markets, are inadequate to match the risk returns profile and payback periods of infrastructure projects. FIs and banks are constrained by the time profile of their own liabilities and hence cannot prudently lend large volumes of debt. Hence, an intermediary would be needed to provide credit enhancements to extend the maturity of the funding raised for infrastructure projects.

Even after the various reforms proposed for developing a debt market are put in place there may be difficulty in actually issuing long-term debt instruments since few borrowing agencies at present have a credit quality that is high enough to go to the market. Even the all-India financial institutions are currently finding it difficult to raise long term funds in the capital market.

However, while raising these funds, these institutions have had to offer basically similar interest rates for different term maturities that have been provided for in these instruments. Long-term real interest rates of over 10 percent will not be suitable for infrastructure investment. Innovative institutional interventions would be required to help kick-start the debt market, particularly for medium and long term bonds.

India is lucky to already have a reasonably well-developed framework of financial institutions. The liberalization of the financial sector and the capital markets that has taken place in the last few years has also seen the entry of newer institutions such as Infrastructure Leasing and Financial Services Ltd. (ILFS). It is, however, likely that even these established Institutions may need additional enhancement of their credit quality in order to borrow in both domestic and international markets.

In most countries, special arrangements have been made to make possible the issuance of different kinds of bonds meant mainly for raising resources from the capital market at the lowest possible cost and with the longest possible debt maturities. For example, in the US, much of urban infrastructure is financed through the sale of municipal bonds which have been given tax-free status by the Federal Government. A complex market structure exists to make these bonds marketable. The availability of credible ratings, financial guarantees, bond insurance and the like helps in this respect.

Similarly, the development of the widespread housing mortgage system in the US was helped by government intervention through the creation of government sponsored agencies such as Fannie Mae. In Germany, much of infrastructure finance is done through the sale of mortgage bonds which are backed either by state guarantees or mortgages that can be conveyed. In Japan, the widespread postal savings system provides funds to different infrastructure financing institutions such as the Japan Development Bank and the Long Term Credit Bank.

Given the complexity of risks inherent in infrastructure projects, lenders and investors may often perceive the project cash flows and the collateral as insufficient inducement to take up the financing risks. In such a situation, to gain the confidence of lenders and investors, credit enhancement mechanisms may be needed to improve the overall credit quality of the project. In simple terms, credit enhancement mechanisms enable the issuers of debt to secure a higher credit quality assessment than would have been possible on a standalone basis. Credit enhancement benefits the issuer in terms of possibly lower interest costs and easier marketability due to the high safety of the instrument. Credit enhancements thus essentially provide a risk-mitigating mechanism to investors and lenders.

The principal credit enhancement measures used so far in India have been government guarantee and special reserve accounts (SRAs). While guarantees increase the comfort levels of the lenders in the initial phases, extensive use of these measures can lead to a strain on government finances and ultimately impact the overall sovereign range. In the SRA arrangement, the inflows from the concerned project are pooled into a separate bank account, managed by the trustees, and all debt servicing obligations are fulfilled before releasing them for further utilisation.

C. External Sources: In addition to the standard sources of foreign funds like the multilateral financial institutions, much greater effort will have to be made to tap commercial sources. This will be increasingly necessary since the future outlook for official debt flows is not optimistic. Syndicated loans and direct borrowing will have to be resorted to in foreign markets, along with an increased openness to foreign investment. The process of granting approvals for external commercial borrowing (ECB) would have to be made more transparent and systematic. Borrowing in foreign markets would also be helped by sovereign benchmark issues of government debt instruments.

A new important source of equity finance for infrastructure is the set of infrastructure funds that are increasingly being set up for investment in developing countries, particularly in Asia. At present, each equity investment sought to be made from these funds has to be routed through the foreign direct investment approval route of the Foreign Investment Promotion Board (FIPB). Equity investment from such funds could be put on a special footing, allowing them ease of investment in eligible infrastructure projects.

D. Value Guarantees: Governments are increasingly providing guarantees to private lenders rather than directly financing infrastructure projects. Though government guarantees targeted at specific sovereign risks are relatively new, loan guarantees that cover some or all of the repayment risk have been frequently used by governments to pursue policy objectives. It has been observed that such loan guarantees are of significant value, particularly when the underlying risk is high and the term of the loan exceeds 10 years. As such, when governments give guarantees, they are providing substantial comfort to lenders.

However, government guarantees for infrastructure projects involve risks which are often unexpectedly high for both the government, and the private investor. The government faces the risk of such unforeseen liabilities that may occur when the guarantee is called and when it may possibly lack the necessary budgetary resources to honour the commitment.

Similarly, because of this possibility of unforeseen future risk, the private investor also funds such guarantees to be less than credible, particularly at lower levels of government. Often, the market may not also attach much value to them and hence the credit enhancement provided by government guarantees is negligible. It is, therefore, suggested that government at both central and state levels should consider setting up Contingent Valuation Funds for providing additional back-up to any infrastructure project guarantees that are given. It is possible to value guarantees and thereby set aside specific funds from the budget on an annual basis so that the Contingent Valuation Fund has adequate resources to fund the guarantees in case they are called. Such a mechanism would provide both safety to the government as well as additional comfort to creditors.

11.1.5 Commercialisation of Infrastructure Services: With greater demand, changing technology, increasing complexity for financing the infrastructure projects and the budgetary constraints, the public sector is no longer able to discharge efficiently its role as a provider of infrastructure services. The Government has recognised that private sector participation including foreign investment is required to supplement the public sector efforts. Various reforms have been made in infrastructure sectors, and rules and procedures for investment have been liberalised in order to provide an enabling environment conducive for private participation.

A wave of privatisation and deregulation has been sweeping infrastructure sectors around the globe over the last decade or so. These bold new approaches promote improvement in efficiency and service quality. Whereas the specific motivations and circumstances vary by countries, and in countries by sectors, there are five factors that are leading economies all over the world to consider enhanced commercialization of infrastructure provision.

1. The massive investment requirement arising from sharply rising economic growth

rates are pushing countries to look for additional sources of financing against the backdrop of fiscal stringency in most countries.

2. The rising awareness of the importance of efficiency in investment and delivery in the context of tight fiscal conditions, is leading to rethinking on the ability of government owned entities to supply infrastructure services in a business like manner.

3. Changes in technology now make it easier to charge for marginal use of infrastructure services. Such technological changes are making possible the introduction of competition horizontally and unbundling of services vertically.

4. The increasing need for countries to compete in the global marketplace is putting additional pressure on countries to provide efficient infrastructure services to their businesses in a cost-effective and competitive manner. Higher infrastructure costs in terms of both price and time delays can make the difference between firms being globally competitive or otherwise.

5. The new dynamism and integration of world capital markets have vastly increased the possibility of raising large funds for infrastructure investment on a commercial basis whereas earlier, it was governments which had better access to resources. In many cases, it is now the private sector which has the capability of sourcing large funds internationally.

While these forces are pushing most countries towards the commercialisation of infrastructure investment services, there is also increasing understanding of the social dimension of infrastructure in poor countries in particular. The state bears a responsibility to provide the impoverished, access to basic services such as health, education, water supply, sanitation and sewerage.

Moreover, despite the new possibilities of competition mentioned above, most infrastructure services retain very strong monopolistic elements. As such, the State continues to be responsible for providing appropriate regulatory frameworks which assist investors and infrastructure entities on the one hand and protect consumers from monopolistic exploitation on the other. The commercialisation of infrastructure and unbundling also lead to a considerable increase in transaction costs which have to be mitigated through transparent and appropriate regulation.

The general condition is that whereas the possibility of commercialisation of infrastructure investment and services has increased tremendously over the last decades, the role of the public sector in investment delivery of services and in regulation will continue to be vital. The future therefore, suggests the introduction of a new framework for public-private-partnership (PPP) in different forms so that appropriate infrastructure investment can fructify.

A. Involvement of Private Sector in Infrastructure Projects: A major problem in the commercialisation of infrastructure projects is the appropriate allocation of risk. When infrastructure is provided by the public sector, all the risks are internalised within the government and hence the issue of risk allocation does not arise. Successful design of an infrastructure project involves the appropriate demarcation and allocation of risks to the different stakeholders in the project. Clarity in this allocation is essential to avoid confusion in the financing and implementation of commercialised infrastructure projects as the tendency of each stakeholder is to shift the risk to others. In other words, the question is what recourse the lenders have if investments fail to produce the expected returns. The financing is usually non-recourse, with lenders being repaid only from the cash flow generated by the project.

Of late, different countries have adopted various methods for attracting private sector funds for infrastructure development. The most prominent, and possibly the most widely used, is the build-operate-transfer (BOT) arrangement. As the term suggests, the private investor (concessionaire) builds, operates and transfers the facility back to the government at the end of a specified period, called the concession period. A transparent regulatory framework is needed to make BOT type projects easier to negotiate and implement.

Recent years have witnessed substantial progress from the old paradigm of public monopoly provision of infrastructure services to the new paradigm which also encourages private investment and provision of infrastructure services within a stable, predictable and commercially viable regulatory framework.

11.2 Logistics: Meaning, Importance and Improvement Strategies

11.2.1 Logistics Defined: Logistics refers to a series of services and activities, such as transportation, warehousing, and brokerage, that help to move goods and establish supply chains across and within borders. Although these services and activities are carried out by private firms for the benefit of private firms, service delivery and the efficiency of supply chains depend on public sector provisions and interventions in a number of domains. Logistics uses publicly funded or regulated infrastructure. International trade is processed by border agencies. Services and logistics activities are regulated with fiscal, environmental, safety, land use, and competition objectives.

Logistics organizes the movement of goods through a network of activities and services operating at global, regional, and local scale. Logistics encompasses more than freight transportation. Traders delegate increasingly sophisticated tasks to networks of specialized service providers. Efficient logistics connects people and firms to markets and opportunities and helps achieve higher levels of productivity and welfare. Crucially, logistics is not only a private endeavour, but also a public policy concern. The performance and reliability of supply chains depend on an array of interventions, ranging from trade facilitation at the border to infrastructure and regulations and to urban planning and skills. Empirical evidence confirms that logistics and connectivity-related interventions have the highest potential to reduce the cost of trade and to boost integration in global value chains. Policy makers know that logistics matters and that they can improve the efficiency of the supply chains connecting their countries internally and externally.

11.2.2 Importance of Logistics: Logistics performance both in international trade and domestically is central to the economic growth and competitiveness of countries, and the logistics sector is now recognized as one of the core pillars of economic development. Policy makers not only in the best performing countries, but also in emerging economies, increasingly see the need to implement coherent and consistent policies to foster seamless and sustainable supply chain operations as an engine of growth. Efficient logistics connects firms to domestic and international markets through reliable supply chain networks. Conversely, countries characterized by low logistics performance face high costs, not merely because of transportation costs but also because of unreliable supply chains, a major handicap in integrating and competing in global value chains.

Logistics firms have a strong incentive to provide predictable deliveries in both the developed and the developing world. Supply chain reliability continues to be a major concern among traders and logistics providers. In a global environment, consignees require a high degree of certainty on when and how deliveries will take place. This is much more important than the speed of the delivery. Predictability also carries a premium, which many shippers are willing to pay. In other words, supply chain predictability is a matter not merely of time and cost, but also of shipment quality.

Efficient clearance procedures at the border are critical to eliminating avoidable delays and to improving supply chain predictability. To achieve this, governments need to facilitate trade, while safeguarding the public against harmful activities ranging from health hazards to crime and terrorism. Realizing these two objectives—facilitating trade and safeguarding the public interest—is a challenge for policy makers and authorities, especially in countries with a low performance record, where delays and unexpected costs are more common.

Trade facilitation tools and principles have taken hold in many countries thanks to growing awareness and international initiatives to support trade facilitation reforms in developing countries. Co-ordination among government-controlled agencies continues to require attention, including the need to introduce best practices in automation and risk management in non-customs control agencies.

Implementation of trade and transport reform is lagging in the logistically constrained countries that are most in need of attention from the international community. Many landlocked developing countries and small island states also fall into this category because their connectivity with global markets is severely challenged by their economic size or geography.

In logistics-friendly countries, manufacturers and traders already outsource much of their basic transport and logistics operations to third-party providers and focus on their core business, while managing more complex supply chains. The more such advanced services are available at a reasonable price-cost ratio, the more shippers will outsource their logistics.

The demand for environmentally friendly logistics solutions, or green logistics, is gradually becoming a common feature in most advanced logistics environments

11.2.3 Strategies to Improve Logistics: Comprehensive strategies increasingly focus not merely on looking at the sources of costs, but on steering a sector with a large footprint in the economy and with links to concerns about the environment, jobs, land use, urban planning, and other issues.

Logistics performance depends on the availability to traders of reliable supply chains and predictable service delivery. Global supply chains are becoming more complex, and the safety, social, environmental, and other regulations affecting traders and operators are becoming more demanding. Efficient management and information technology (IT) solutions in both the private and public sectors are vital tools of the trade in high-quality logistics. The ability to manage logistics processes in today's global business environment is a crucial factor in national competitiveness. More than ever, comprehensive reform and long-term commitments from policy makers and private stakeholders are needed.

The two main objectives of current logistics strategies in all types of economies are as under:

First, logistics is an input to much of the economy, i.e. industry, commerce, and so on. The performance of logistics impacts productivity in other sectors. This is most often presented in negative language in terms of average costs of logistics. Secondly, logistics can be a sector of development in and of itself, where countries with high global or regional connectivity expect to play the role of a logistics and trade hub, such as the Netherlands in Europe and Dubai or Singapore in Asia.

11.2.4 Recent Global Initiatives: Recently, at least two initiatives of global scale have emerged that are likely to have positive impacts on the logistics performance of the participating countries.

A. One Belt, One Road: One Belt, One Road Initiative is likely to have significant implications for logistics operators. Led by China, this initiative targets 60+ countries. This ambitious programme seeks to improve trade connectivity among Silk Road economies and also countries on the main sea routes from China. Though in its early stages, the initiative has an ambitious scope. It will target physical infrastructure in a variety of locations, catalyzing finance and investment resources. However, hard infrastructure is not enough. There also needs to be a soft component, involving regulatory reform in service markets such as transport, logistics, and telecommunications. The initiative can help develop a broad, business-focused programme that can work on multiple fronts to bring improvements in trade facilitation and logistics to participating countries.

B. Trans-Pacific Partnership: The 12-country Trans-Pacific Partnership agreement was signed in February 2016, after seven years of negotiations. Member countries include Australia, Brunei, Canada, Chile, Japan, Malaysia, Mexico, New Zealand, Peru, Singapore, the United States, and Vietnam.

From a logistics standpoint, there are a number of relevant aspects of the agreement. First, logistics is a service, so the agreement provisions on trade in services could facilitate international exchange involving logistics providers. The agreement also includes provisions on trade facilitation, in line with existing international agreements. One innovative aspect of the agreement that is important to the logistics community is the annex on express delivery services, which is designed to level the playing field among private sector delivery services and traditional postal operators. If implemented, there is potential for these provisions to facilitate the expansion of delivery services in countries where accessibility to such services is low.

12

Special Economic Zones (SEZs) and Technology Parks

SEZs are seen as vehicles for inducing industrial growth in the backward regions, backward areas within a state or rural areas within a district. SEZs are linked to the idea of urban dispersal and are seen mainly as a provision of land in locations which are usually distant from the major urban centres. Usually the goal is an increase in foreign investment. World's first SEZ was set up at Shannon in Ireland in 1958. Seven years after, India set up its first export processing zone (EPZ) at Kandla (Gujarat) in 1965, which was also the first in Asia.

12.1 Meaning of SEZs

SEZs are geographical regions in a country subject to economic laws which are liberal than typical economic laws of that country. The word *special* mainly means special economic system and policies. A SEZ can be deemed as a *foreign territory* for the purposes of trade operations, duties and tariffs. Units in SEZs enjoy lot of fiscal pampering.

SEZs are self-contained islands providing high-quality infrastructural facilities. SEZs offer industrial, residential and commercial areas with developed plots/pre-built factories, power, telecommunications, water supply, sewerage and drainage, and educational and medical facilities.

SEZs have been established in several countries, including China, India, Iran, Jordan, Poland, Kazakhstan, Philippines and Russia. SEZs are known by different names in different countries. Some close variants of SEZs are growth centres, industrial estates, export zones, industrial parks etc. In the United States, SEZ are referred to as urban enterprise zones.

12.2 Types of SEZs

SEZs can be developed either as general SEZs, catering to all types of industries or specialised SEZs, focusing on a specific industry, such as chemicals, automobiles or software. A specialised SEZ offers an opportunity for the industries in the zone to synergise their operations with the local industries in the region, and position themselves close to the local raw material sources. The zone can offer specific facilities such as a common effluent treatment plant, integrated design centre etc. to cater to the needs of the target industries. However, development of such a zone involves high risk and requires a longer time to sell the developed plots or pre-built factories. Therefore, a specialised SEZ is viable only in industries like information technology, plasters and textiles which are fast growing and have a large market. SEZs are of varying sizes in terms of land occupied. A SEZ may be as small in size as 10 hectares. It can be as large as a self-contained township across thousands of hectares having airports, roads, hospitals, schools, movie theatres, shopping malls, homes and manicured parks.

12.3 Configuration of a SEZ

Normally a SEZ is divided into three zones.

1. The industrial zone encompasses industrial units catering to both domestic and export markets. It offers two options for entrepreneurs: (a) developed land and (b) pre-built factory space.
2. The residential zone houses the employees of the units. Additionally, in order to commercially exploit certain locational advantages, a portion may be developed for sale to outsiders.
3. The commercial zone provides facilities such as offices, banks, post and telecom services, shopping centres, restaurants, clubs and recreation facilities.

12.4 Advantages of SEZs

In the context of the huge demand-supply gap in infrastructure, SEZs are ideal vehicles for providing integrated infrastructural facilities. SEZs are essential for industrialisation in developing countries which, unlike the developed world, do not have uniformly good infrastructural facilities across regions. They can serve as an intermediate solution to the lack of well-developed and uniformly good infrastructural services.

SEZs have been used as engines of growth by many Asian countries such as China, Thailand, Indonesia, Malaysia and Singapore.

Following are the advantages of setting up SEZs:

1. Developed plots and pre-built factories mean that the entrepreneur can immediately set up an industrial unit without spending scarce resources in developing the necessary infrastructure and land by himself. He also saves on costs because the cost of development is spread over a large number of users.
2. SEZs can serve as catalysts for the development of surrounding region by providing opportunities for employment and creation of ancillary industries.
3. They can help develop social infrastructure like healthcare centres, educational and training facilities. They provide an opportunity to cross-subsidise development and maintenance costs of social infrastructure with surpluses from other components through a common implementing agency.
4. SEZs can be tailored to capitalise on the strengths and needs of a region such as traditional skills and industries, availability of raw materials and locational advantages. Industrial units in the SEZs can take advantage of the synergies arising from forward and backward integration with others in the same sector.
5. SEZs can also act as incubators of small and medium industries until the time these are ready to stand on their own feet.

12.5 Pre-conditions for the Success of SEZs: These can be listed as follows:

1. The location of a SEZ is key factor determining its success. Location should be decided based on an analysis of the competitive advantage and inherent strengths of the region.
2. As foreign direct investment is very important for the success of SEZs, the foreign investment policy with reference to the SEZs should be clarified. Establishment of

holding companies for investment in the SEZs should be encouraged.

3. Land acquisition by the private sector should be in tune with the policy of commercialisation of SEZs through private sector participation. In this case, terms of negotiated land purchase should be primarily determined by the market forces. The government may acquire land in exceptional cases where private sector acquisition of land is difficult and where there is a clear case for public good in the acquisition of the land.

4. Since compensation for the land acquired is often a major cause for dissatisfaction, an independent valuer should be asked to fix the price which should be related to the average of the market prices in the recent past. The government should also encourage the provision of alternative locations for displaced owners. It should be recognised that the government should assist in the land acquisition process and not fix any price.

5. The government should announce a comprehensive legal policy for SEZs based on transparency and enforceability. It is essential to recognise SEZs as infrastructure projects and provide the same incentives including tax/tariff reliefs and special dispensations that are available to an infrastructure project in the power, telecommunications or transport sector.

6. A promotional authority may be set up in each state, on the lines of bodies such as the Industrial Estates Authority of Thailand, as a one-stop agency involved in development of SEZs either by itself or through joint ventures with the private sector. The authority should focus on monitoring and adjudicating.

7. Uninterrupted and quality power supply is a key success factor for any SEZ. State governments should encourage the supply of adequate power to the SEZs either through small captive power plants or through the support of the State Electricity Boards (SEBs) which must announce a clear policy for cogeneration so that captive power plants set up to serve SEZs can be of economic size.

8. Adequate financing through long-term debt is of critical importance for the projects. SEZs should be eligible to receive financing.

9. In order to encourage private sector financing of SEZs, financial institutions providing loans to SEZs may also be granted exemption from income tax on the profits from loans to SEZs. To encourage further investments in SEZs and also to discourage repatriation by foreign investors, tax rebate may be allowed on profits reinvested in the SEZs or in any other infrastructure project.

10. SEZs must develop connection with technological research institutions, universities, colleges and technical training institutes. Also, appropriate linkages are necessary with transportation facilities such as airports, ports, and railway terminals.

12.6 Role of the Government

International experience indicates that SEZs need active support from the government by way of a clear industrial policy and incentives for private sector development of SEZs.

State governments must formulate an integrated development plan for the region. In the short term, existing industrial parks should be upgraded while in the long-run, a suitable policy should be identified for their commercialisation. While private sector participation in the development of SEZs would increase with time, in the medium term, the State Industrial Development Corporation (SIDCs) which hold larger pieces of land can strike an alliance with the private sector for development of SEZs.

Commercialisation requires a collaborative approach and participation from various parties including private sector financial institutions, and the state and local government. Even if the government does not opt for equity participation, it should play the role of facilitator in the project. MoU which includes a mutually agreed-upon time-table with penalties for time and cost overruns should be signed. As a partner, the government should provide an exit policy which facilitates the pullout of the private sector from a venture which turns out to be unviable. A suitable dispute redressal system would need to be designed and put in place right at the beginning of the project to facilitate smooth operation of the park after construction.

In order to facilitate speedy statutory clearances and provision of other civic facilities, the government should encourage the setting up of business support centres (BSCs) in SEZs. The BSCs should be delegated the authority to grant clearances/approvals subject to specified norms. A system of public audit should be introduced to ensure that accountability and discipline work, in respect of both the partners and that the public purpose remains secure.

12.7 Role of the Private Sector

Participation of the private sector in partnership with the government in ownership and operation of SEZs helps in the emergence of a more commercial approach. Private sector participation generally leads to the following favourable effects:

1. Competition resulting in better services and an increase in efficiency in design and focus of the SEZ, its implementation and operation.
2. Greater accountability and responsibility.
3. Professional management.
4. Use of appropriate technologies.
5. Innovation and dynamism in the design and management of the SEZ.
6. Fund mobilisation from private sector to bridge the gap due to lack of government funds.

The commitment of the project sponsors through their financial and managerial inputs, the immense opportunities for generating profits and surpluses and the competition due to an increase in the number of players would lead to proper choice of the location, design and development of infrastructural facilities.

12.8 SEZs and Small Enterprises

Very large industries are capable to acquire large tracts of land and create all necessary infrastructure facilities on their own. Small and medium scale units need quality infrastructure but may not have the means to pay for such facilities. For the SEZs to be viable, the user industries must be able to pay for the cost of the services provided.

Only industries with a high value addition may be able to afford such high costs of developing infrastructural facilities.

SEZs should be targeted at small and medium scale industries with a focus on high value-added output. Pre-built factories provide readymade factory space which can cater to the needs of small and medium scale industries, serving as incubators before they grow in size and shift to a larger industrial space.

12.9 Global Experiences

SEZs have been established in many countries as testing grounds for implementation of liberal market economy principles. They are viewed as instruments to enhance the acceptability and credibility of transformation policies, to attract domestic and foreign investment, and generally for the opening up of the economy.

EPZs and SEZs were employed with considerable success by China and other ASEAN countries in the 1970s and 1980s to create regional islands, where export-oriented manufacturing could be undertaken. While EPZs in some of these countries had their share of early difficulties, they provided scope for cultivating manufacturing competitiveness when licensing, labour rigidities and high import duties and taxes acted as a disincentive for investment in the rest of the areas.

12.9.1 China: SEZs are called economic development areas (EDAs) in China. China set up four SEZs in the late 1970s on experimental basis to attract foreign capital, technology and managerial expertise. This was part of Chinese model of export-led growth. The astounding success of the SEZs in China has inspired other countries, including India to follow suit. Many in India believe that SEZs will create thousands of skilled and semi-skilled jobs in export-oriented industries and services and ensure double-digit growth rate in the future.

In China, the central government gives SEZs special policies and flexible measures, allowing SEZs to utilize a special economic management system.

1. Special tax incentives.
2. Greater independence on international trade activities.
3. Economic characteristics are represented as "4 principles":
- Construction primarily relies on attracting and utilising foreign capital.
- Primary economic forms are Sino-foreign joint ventures and partnerships as well as wholly foreign-owned enterprises.
- Products are primarily export-oriented.
- Economic activities are primarily driven by market.

SEZs are listed separately in the national planning (including financial planning) and have province-level authority on economic administration. Following is the list of SEZs in China.

1. Guangdong Province: Shenzhen, Zhuhai and Shantou.
2. Fujian Province: Xiamen.
3. Hainan Province (whole province).

12.9.2 North Korea: The Rajin-Sonbong Economic Special Zone was established under a UN economic development programme in 1994. Located on the bank of the Tumen River, the zone borders on the Yanbian Korean Autonomous Prefecture (or Yeonbyeon in Korean) of China, as well as Russia. In 2000 the name of the area was shortened to Rason and became separate from the North Hamgyeong Province.

12.9.3 Philippines: Philippine economic zones (eco-zones) are collections of industries, brought together geographically for the purpose of promoting economic development. Although designed to operate separately from the political and economic milieu of surrounding communities, Philippine economic zones do in fact interact with their neighbours. There are 41 private-owned economic zones and 4 government-owned economic zones in the Philippines. Of the 41 private economic zones, the biggest exporter is Gateway Business Park in General Trias, Cavite and the second biggest private eco-zone is Laguna Techno-park Inc. The four government-owned are Cavite Economic Zone, Bataan Economic Zone, Mactan Economic Zone and Baguio City Economic Zone.

12.9.4 India: India was one of the first in Asia to recognize the effectiveness of the Export Processing Zone (EPZ) model in promoting exports, with Asia's first EPZ set up in Kandla (Gujarat) in 1965. However, the EPZs were not able to emerge as effective instruments for export promotion on account of multiplicity of controls and clearances, absence of world-class infrastructure and an unstable fiscal regime.

Considering the need to enhance foreign investment and promote exports from the country and realising the need that level playing field must be made available to the domestic enterprises and manufacturers to be competitive globally, the Special Economic Zones (SEZs) Policy was announced in April 2000. This policy intended to make SEZs an engine for economic growth supported by quality infrastructure complemented by an attractive fiscal package, both at the Centre and the State level, with the minimum possible regulations. SEZs in India functioned from November 1, 2000 to February 9, 2006 under the provisions of the Foreign Trade Policy and fiscal incentives were made effective through the provisions of relevant statutes.

To instil confidence in investors and signal the Government's commitment to a stable SEZ policy regime and with a view to impart stability to the SEZ regime thereby generating greater economic activity and employment through the establishment of SEZs, a comprehensive draft SEZ Bill was prepared after extensive discussions with the stakeholders. The Special Economic Zones Act, 2005, was passed by Parliament in May 2005 which received Presidential assent on June 23, 2005. After extensive consultations, the SEZ Act, 2005, supported by SEZ Rules, came into effect on February 10, 2006, providing for drastic simplification of procedures and for single window clearance on matters relating to Central as well as State Governments. The main objectives of the SEZ Act are the following:

1. Generation of additional economic activity.
2. Promotion of exports of goods and services.
3. Promotion of investment from domestic and foreign sources.
4. Creation of employment opportunities.

5. Development of infrastructure facilities.

The SEZ Act, 2005 envisages key role for the State Governments in export promotion and creation of related infrastructure. A single window SEZ approval mechanism has been provided through a 19 member inter-ministerial SEZ Board of Approval (BoA). The applications duly recommended by the respective State Governments/UT Administrations are considered by BoA periodically. All decisions of the BoA are with consensus.

The SEZ Rules provide for differentiated minimum land requirements for different classes of SEZs. Every SEZ is divided into a processing area where alone the SEZ units would come up and the non-processing area where supporting infrastructure is to be created. The SEZ Rules also provide for simplified procedures for development, operation and maintenance of the SEZ, setting up units in SEZs, single window clearance both relating to Central as well as State Governments for setting up of an SEZ and units in a SEZ, and simplified compliance procedures/documentation with emphasis on self-certification. A Board of Approval has been constituted by Government in exercise of the powers conferred under the SEZ Act.

SEZs in India seek to promote value addition component in exports, generate employment and mobilize foreign exchange. SEZs when operational are expected to offer high quality infrastructure facilities and support services, besides allowing for the duty free import of capital goods and raw materials. Additionally, attractive fiscal incentives and simpler customs, banking and other procedures are offered in such zones. Setting up of SEZs is also treated as an infrastructure development activity and offered same incentives. SEZs in India closely follow the Chinese model.

SEZs are intended as engine for economic growth supported by quality infrastructure, with minimum possible regulations, and an attractive fiscal package, both at the level of Central and State Governments.

Various incentives and facilities are offered to both SEZ developers and units in SEZs for attracting investments, including foreign investment, into SEZs. These incentives and facilities are expected to trigger a large flow of foreign and domestic investment in SEZs, in infrastructure and productive capacity, leading to generation of additional economic activity and creation of employment opportunities.

12.10 Technology Parks

The foundations of industrial and agricultural advance lie ultimately in the availability and effective use of human skills. Human skills are a formidable asset since they last not merely during one working life but because they are transmitted for generations. If these assets are used effectively, they may well turn out to be one of the most fruitful results of planning.

12.10.1 Importance of Science and Technology: The per capita income and quality of life that a nation enjoys is, in the final analysis, dependent largely on the technology it adopts, and which in turn has to be appropriate to its endowments, resources and skills.

The pace of economic development depends on a variety of factors which constitute the psychological and sociological setting within which the economy operates. A major element in this setting is the community's will to progress and its readiness to develop and adopt new and more efficient methods and processes of production. Basically, development involves securing higher productivity all round and this is a function of the degree of technological advance the community is able to make. The problem is not one merely of adopting and applying the processes and techniques developed elsewhere, but of developing new techniques specially suited to local conditions.

Modern technology is changing rapidly and no country can hope to maintain a steady pace of advance unless it keeps abreast of current developments. Techniques in turn affect and are affected by economic and social organisation. Certain forms of economic and social organisation are unsuited to or incapable of absorbing new techniques and utilising them to the best advantage. To some extent techniques must of course be adapted to economic and social organisation, but the latter has also to change in order to accommodate new techniques which need to be applied not merely in one or two isolated lines but in several lines of economic activity.

The vital role of science in modern life is now generally recognised. Apart from the vast changes it has brought about, the development of a scientific temper in the people is considered important. Improvements in techniques evolved as a result of scientific research bring about great increases in production in the different sectors of the economy. National resources are augmented by the substitution of cheap and abundant materials for those in scarce supply and by finding uses for materials which have remained unutilised. A balanced programme of research covering every sector of the economy is essential therefore for the development of a country.

High standards of living in the more advanced countries are the direct result of progress in science and technology and the rapid pace of development associated with it. The flow of new scientific knowledge is continuous and ever expanding and covers both pure and applied research. Pure research leads to new knowledge and understanding of nature and its laws, and creates the scientific capital from which practical applications of knowledge are drawn. New products and processes are based on new principles and concepts. The advance of technology presents new problems to science and also provides new tools with which to resolve them.

12.10.2 Technology Park Defined: The ultimate objective of a technology park is to provide an environment that will enable the localization of various tech-related companies. It is a development that brings together office spaces, residential areas, and retail developments in order to enhance the operations of tech corporations, thereby providing various benefits and economies of scale to each individual business entity.

Technology parks are able to perfectly integrate row houses, residential complexes, villas, as well as low-rise and high-rise apartments with commercial and convenience establishments, clubs and resorts, and various facilities that make living and working as comfortable as possible. All of these amenities are ideally supposed to help in attracting investors and to promote the setting up of various businesses, ensuring that they get all they need to thrive and reach their operating objectives.

Usually, technology parks take some land space, and there is usually a lot of consideration given to them in order to thrive and wok towards their full potential.

12.10.3 Objectives of Technology Parks: However, the major purposes of technology parks are usually any of the following:

A. Advancement of Technology: The primary aim for the establishment of a technology park is usually the advancement of scientific and technological endeavours. Millions are usually poured into the creation of technology parks, and a large chunk of this money is spent on efforts such as research and development, experiments and other related efforts in the end, the goal is to come together and create an environment where science and technology are made to thrive and succeed.

B. Flow of Investment: It is a fact that technology is very profitable. In the event that a tech company is able to stand on its feet and gain enough popularity add recognition, there is no doubt to the fact that they will make enough money going forward. The prospect of being on the groundwork of something big is one of the major tools which the creators of technology parks use to attract investment, and its goal usually pays off the long-run. The investment received helps to develop the park, and also go into other aspects of human endeavour.

C. Establishment of Companies and Jobs Creation: Technology parks also create enabling environments for start-ups and tech companies to come and set up nicely. Companies are able to comfortably pursue their goals and work towards achieving set objectives. A direct consequence of company establishment, jobs are created, and more people are able to get suitable jobs.

D. Development of an Area: Due to the concentration of companies and the attraction of investment, infrastructural development in the general area, where the technology park is located, is definitely assured. This is why technology parks are usually founded in areas where the advancement of infrastructure might not necessary be the best. People living near the technology park are able to get jobs, and this will definitely be a relief to the overall economy of the country.

12.10.4 Software Technology Parks (STPs) in India: India has earned itself a reputation of an information technology (IT) superpower. STPs in India have played a seminal role in accomplishing this status. Today, STPs of India across over the country are synonymous with excellent infrastructure and statutory support aimed at furthering growth of IT in the country.

Software Technology Parks of India, is an autonomous society set up by the Ministry of Electronics and Information Technology (MeitY), Government of India in 1991, with the objective of encouraging, promoting and boosting the software exports from India.

Software Technology Parks of India maintains internal engineering resources to provide consulting, training and implementation services. Services cover network design, system integration, installation, operations and maintenance of application networks and facilities in varied areas.

The objectives of software technology parks of India are as under:

1. To promote the development and export of software and software services including

IT-enabled services/Bio-IT.

2. To provide statutory and other promotional services to the exporters by implementing schemes pertaining to software technology parks and electronics and hardware technology parks and other such schemes which may be formulated by the Government from time-to-time.

3. To provide data communication services including value added services to IT/IT-enabled services related industries.

4. To promote micro, small and medium entrepreneurs by creating conducive environment for entrepreneurship in the field of IT/IT-enabled services.

13

Entrepreneurship and Innovations

13.1 Entrepreneur and Entrepreneurship

The growth and prosperity of all economies remains highly dependent on entrepreneurial activity. Entrepreneurs are the essence of economic growth as they provide a source of income and employment for themselves, create employment for others, produce new and innovative products or services, and drive greater upstream and downstream value-chain activities. Supportive environments are increasingly essential to successful entrepreneurship and these are evolving across the world. The ideal entrepreneurial environment has 5 pillars:

1. Access to funding.
2. Entrepreneurial culture.
3. Supportive regulatory and tax regimes.
4. Educational systems that support entrepreneurial mindsets.
5. A coordinated approach that links the public, private and voluntary sectors.

The face of entrepreneurship is also changing. Across the world, entrepreneurs are increasingly young and/or female due to increasing unemployment. The public and private sector each have an important role to play in creating entrepreneurial ecosystems that, in addition to funding, are essential to promoting entrepreneurial success.

Highlighting the diversity of the country, four kinds of entrepreneurial activities exist: (a) factor-driven entrepreneurship, (b) efficiency-driven entrepreneurship, (c) innovation-driven entrepreneurship, and (d) necessity-driven entrepreneurship.

Developed economies generate entrepreneurial opportunities as a result of their wealth and innovation capacity, yet they also offer more wage employment options to attract those that might otherwise become independent entrepreneurs. If these opportunities for entrepreneurship and innovation are to be captured, it is essential to create an enabling eco-system for entrepreneurship to thrive and instil a mindset and culture of opportunity and innovation-based motives and entrepreneurial incentives.

13.1.1 Who is an Entrepreneur? An entrepreneur is an individual who organizes and operates a business or businesses, taking on financial risk to do so. The entrepreneur is commonly seen as an innovator of new ideas, and business processes. Management skill and strong team building abilities are often perceived as essential leadership attributes for successful entrepreneurs. Leadership, management ability, and team-building are considered to be the essential qualities of an entrepreneur.

Psychological studies show that the psychological propensities for male and female entrepreneurs are more similar than different. A growing body of work shows that entrepreneurial behaviour is dependent on social and economic factors. For example, countries with healthy and diversified labour markets or stronger safety nets show a more favourable ratio of opportunity-driven rather than necessity-driven women entrepreneurs. Empirical studies suggest that male entrepreneurs possess strong negotiating skills and consensus-forming abilities.

Research studies that explore the characteristics and personality traits of, and influences on, the entrepreneur have come to differing conclusions. Most, however, agree on certain consistent entrepreneurial traits and environmental influences. Although certain entrepreneurial traits are required, entrepreneurial behaviours are also dynamic and influenced by environmental factors. The entrepreneur is solely concerned with opportunity recognition and exploitation, although the opportunity that is recognised depends on the type of entrepreneur.

Some of the most significant influences on an individual's decision to become an entrepreneur are workplace peers and the social composition of the workplace.

The ability of entrepreneurs to innovate is thought to relate to innate traits such as extroversion and a proclivity for risk-taking. The capabilities of innovating, introducing new technologies, increasing efficiency and productivity, or generating new products or services, are characteristic qualities of entrepreneurs. Entrepreneurs are catalysts for economic change, and researchers argue that entrepreneurs are highly creative individuals with a tendency to imagine new solutions by finding opportunities for profit or reward. It is widely maintained that entrepreneurs are unusual individuals. In line with this view, there is an emerging research tradition investigating the genetic factors that are perceived to make entrepreneurs so distinctive.

However, there are also critical perspectives that attribute these research attitudes to oversimplified methodological and/or philosophical assumptions. For example, it has been argued that entrepreneurs are not that distinctive, but that it is in essence unrealistic preconceptions about *non-entrepreneurs* that maintain laudatory portraits of *entrepreneurs*.

13.1.2 What is Entrepreneurship? In political economics, entrepreneurship is the quality of being an entrepreneur, i.e. one who *undertakes an enterprise*. The term puts emphasis on the risk and effort taken by individuals who both own and manage a business, and on the innovations resulting from their pursuit of economic success.

Entrepreneurship in this sense may result in new organizations or may be part of revitalizing mature organizations in response to a perceived opportunity. The most obvious form of entrepreneurship is that of starting new businesses (referred as a start-up company). In recent years, the term has been extended to include social and political forms of entrepreneurial activity. When entrepreneurship is describing activities within a firm or large organization it is referred to as intra-preneurship and may include corporate venturing, when large entities spin-off organizations.

Entrepreneurial activities are substantially different depending on the type of organization and creativity involved. Entrepreneurship ranges in scale from solo projects (even involving the entrepreneur only part-time) to major undertakings creating many job opportunities. Many high value entrepreneurial ventures seek venture capital or angel funding (seed money) in order to raise capital to build the business. Many kinds of organizations now exist to support would-be entrepreneurs including specialized government agencies, business incubators, science parks, and some NGOs. In more recent times, the term entrepreneurship has been extended to include elements not related necessarily to business formation activity such as conceptualizations of entrepreneurship as a specific mindset resulting in entrepreneurial initiatives e.g. in the form of social entrepreneurship, political entrepreneurship, or knowledge entrepreneurship have emerged.

The supposition that entrepreneurship leads to economic growth is an interpretation of the residual in endogenous growth theory and as such is hotly debated in academic economics. An alternate description suggests that the majority of innovations may be much more incremental improvements such as the replacement of paper with plastic in the construction of a drinking straw.

Entrepreneurship is about taking risk. The behaviour of the entrepreneur reflects a kind of person willing to put his or her career and financial security on the line and take risks in the name of an idea, spending much time as well as capital on an uncertain venture.

The acts of entrepreneurship are often associated with true uncertainty, particularly when it involves bringing something really novel to the world, whose market never exists.

13.1.3 Role and Importance of Entrepreneurs: Entrepreneurs play an important role in the economic development of a country. Successful entrepreneurs innovate, bring new products and concepts to the market, improve market efficiency, build wealth, create jobs, and enhance economic growth. The ability of entrepreneurs to create jobs is certainly relevant to India, given the need for incremental new jobs.

De novo firms that unleash creative destruction shift surpluses from rent-seeking large producers to consumers and broader society. Joseph Schumpeter, eminent American economist, put innovation at the heart of economic theory and capitalism. He proposed that innovation was the process by which economies were able to break out of their static mode and enter a path of dynamism. It was his theory of *creative destruction* that first highlighted the importance of innovators in revolutionizing the economic structure, leading to the creation of new products, services, and markets, and the decay of the old. Just as boosting entrepreneurship can lead to growth and job creation, failing to promote entrepreneurship can lead to stagnation, and social and economic inertia.

While India celebrates the success of several new ventures in e-commerce, information technology and mobile telephony, these are not sufficient to deliver aggregate growth expectations. The agricultural sector remains moribund, the rural economy neglected, and vast sectors starved of capital and talent, constrained as these are by collective under-investment in the requisite supporting institutions. Similar institutional inadequacy challenges bedevil investments in so-called social enterprises as well. India will have to encourage creation of new small and medium enterprises (SMEs) focused on manufacturing and innovation, while spurring rural innovation and growth. Hence, putting entrepreneurship at the forefront of the economic agenda is the need of the hour.

The ability of entrepreneurs to create jobs is particularly relevant to India given its employment crisis. India's *demographic dividend* [1] must be reaped. By 2020, 63 percent of India's population will be of working age. McKinsey estimates that India's working-age population will grow by 69 million between 2012 and 2022. Cashing in on this dividend will require India to create 69 million additional appropriate jobs, as well as jobs for those that are currently unemployed. Creation of new businesses will therefore be an important avenue for absorption of these workers. Therefore, developing and sustaining a vibrant entrepreneurial fabric is one policy option that should be part and parcel of any economic development plan.

13.2 Meaning and Importance of Innovations

Scientific research utilizes money to generate knowledge and, by providing solutions, innovation converts knowledge into wealth and/or value. Innovation thus implies S&T-based solutions that are successfully deployed in the economy or the society. It has assumed centre stage in the developmental goals of nations. Paradigms of innovation have become country and context specific.

Science has played a key role in enhancing the growth and development of society and generating access to new and improved goods and services. Science underpins most breakthrough initiatives, but beyond the domain of science, innovations play a critical role in enhancing delivery of services and enabling access to improved goods. In view of this, emerging economies need to stimulate and strengthen its entire formal scientific and industrial system as well as the innovation system to develop solutions for the country's agenda of faster, sustainable and more inclusive growth.

13.2.1 Meaning: Innovation is a process whereby people or groups of people with an entrepreneurial mindset (organizations, enterprises) develop new ideas or absorb and adapt existing ones. Together with institutions and policies that affect their behaviour and performance, they create new products, processes, and forms of organization. Innovation is not only about scientists in laboratories, theoretical science, or new discoveries. It is about building the capacity to find solutions to practical everyday development problems. So, an innovative economy is marked by ideas for new products or new ways of doing things and transforming them into profitable products or activities.

Joseph Schumpeter, an American economist, was one of the first academicians to study the idea of innovation. He developed a theory of economic and social change which focused on the importance of innovation and the factors influencing it. He suggested an important distinction between invention and innovation. According to him, invention is the first occurrence of the idea for a new product or process while innovation occurs when the idea is put into practice.

13.2.2 Importance of Innovations: Bringing about innovation has never been as important as today, as the global economy shifts away from the industrial economy towards the innovation economy. Traditional manufacturing is becoming increasingly commoditized while intellectual property is the need of the hour. What is heartening is that recent economic theory suggests that government investment in R&D, knowledge-creation, and technological progress does have a role to play in fuelling innovation, productivity, capital creation, and therefore growth. This thinking highlights the scope for appropriate government policy and investment to enable entrepreneurship and innovation.

Innovation can play a very important role in the development discourse, because it can offer a new approach to a system that is currently over-burdened by the multiple demands and has limited resources at its disposal. Enhanced focus on innovation can have an impact in diverse areas such as health and education delivery, governance, enterprise development and much more. Collectively, this can herald a generational change in the country and can lay out a chart for a more sustainable and inclusive growth paradigm.

For countries to make the next big move—from developing the right skills demanded by the market to dynamically improving the quality and quantity of that demand—developing an innovation system is critical.

13.2.3 Skills Required for Innovations: Innovations can come in various forms. They encompass the products, processes, and services that meet market needs. They may be developed and marketed in the manufacturing sector, but they may also apply to new ways of doing things in all sectors, including commerce and service delivery. And the innovative idea needs to be widely tested and applied by those who have the skills and financing to bring it to scale. This calls for engaging those with marketing and managerial skills and venture capital.

Research is important—but not always central—to innovation, which may also be realized through less technical experimentation and discovery. The use of cell phones to provide banking services across India is an example both of developing cheap handsets and communication networks and adapting the technology to non-traditional use.

Innovation—and thus growth—can be encouraged by three human development–related factors, and the accompanying policies that facilitate them. First, individuals need a range of skills. Second, these skills and the ideas flowing from them have to be connected to others. Third, productivity increases when innovative small business owners can grow with the aid of risk management tools or as innovative skilled workers enter the labour market. This three-part process is relevant to all individuals despite their starting points.

Three types of skills are necessary to unlock creative potential and take it to market.

1. The general skills are necessary to adapt existing technologies, compete in an innovation-driven economy, and manage the increasingly networked innovation process. These skills include basic literacy and numeracy, problem-solving, and social and interpersonal skills.

2. Creativity produces new ideas. Innovative thinkers are curious and persevering and have *divergent thinking*—imagining several responses to a single problem rather than converging to a single, right answer.

3. Entrepreneurial skills range from managerial skills in running a business to motivation. These are the skills to sort out good ideas from bad ones, find the resources and means to create a prototype, and take the idea through its growth phases. Education and training systems can teach individuals to be cognitively developed, creative, and entrepreneurial.

Both creativity and entrepreneurial skills can be incorporated into teaching methodologies at all points of the skill formation process. And education systems can encourage innovation-related specialties, such as math, science, and business and managerial skills. But these strategies will be successful only if education systems improve the quality of the basic mathematics and science skills for the majority of students. Without such a basis, efforts to instil risk-taking and entrepreneurial skills will be wasted.

Innovation cannot realize its full potential if innovators are isolated. The innovator needs other creative and skilled individuals to share ideas with and bring those ideas to market, capital to finance the realization of the idea, and an enabling environment that accepts new ideas.

In the knowledge economy, universities as a source of knowledge have become far more important than in the past. In recent years, they have acquired a crucial *third mission*, of contributing to economic development after teaching and research. Among the developed countries, the United States is feted for offering entrepreneurs many structural advantages, among them close linkages with universities. Many universities have incubators, technology parks, and venture funds within their sprawling campuses. Similarly, in Cambridge, UK, engagement of the faculty with industry has spawned many *millionaire dons*. The private sector can be tapped to fund research and development at universities.

Effective mechanisms of collaboration need to be created for universities and industry bodies so that research output and innovations can effectively be commercialized and transformed into marketable products and services for last mile benefits. A cluster-based approach to spur innovations at universities could be adopted wherein a minimum critical mass of universities is identified and efforts are made to create or strengthen the innovation system around them. The innovation universities could also provide a platform for experimenting with new models of universities where the above mentioned integration could be realized.

Collaborations can play a crucial role in stimulating innovations and fostering knowledge transfers which would foster interconnections that link intellectual, financial, human, and creative capital as well as unleash underutilized capital. Such enterprises could take the shape of physical or virtual clusters, which bring together research, business, risk capital, and creativity to turn ideas into products, processes, and services.

13.2.4 Innovations Need Incentives: Innovations are risky. New ideas need time and experimentation to develop, and if the idea fails, the individual has a negative return on his or her investment. So, in societies with few safety nets, innovation may be constrained. Policy can give a push to individual innovators by providing fall-back options. Risk management instruments, for example, can provide security to innovators so that they may expend resources on their new activities.

The poorest innovators need social safety nets to ensure that their families survive if the innovations fail. Since the greatest cost to these innovators is the time they spend on developing an innovation, general social safety nets insure against this income loss.

Those farther from the poverty line may need incentives to invest in innovation rather than more secure income generation activities. Innovation funds that provide grants to individuals to develop creative ideas are becoming more common. And for innovators across the poverty spectrum, policies that ensure a monopoly of returns from marketable innovations—patents, copyright laws—lower the income risk associated with developing non-rival ideas. While such legislation is outside the human development arena, its fair implementation and monitoring is crucial as individuals move through the process of implementing their ideas.

Incentives have long been used as a tool to encourage innovation in the developed world. Grand Challenges for instance, have a long history, dating all the way back to the 1700s, when the British Crown announced a *Grand Prize* for finding a way to measure longitude. In recent times, Grand Challenges have been on the rise after the Ansari X-Prize, which called for innovation in spaceflight, was introduced in the US in 1996. In 2014, the British Government announced Grand Challenges—to promote innovation in science and technology. More recently, in China, state-backed groups and institutes use the challenge-approach to widen the debate on innovation and find solutions to problems. China Association of Construction Enterprise Management, for instance, gives over 100 awards annually for innovation in construction. China's Ministry of Education oversees several national competitions in areas ranging from advertising to electric design to cloud computing. The US also has several reality TV shows that focus on business plan competitions.

Innovators need financial support at an early stage to develop and test their ideas in the marketplace. Venture funds are recognised globally as the most suitable form of providing risk capital for the growth of innovative technology and breakthrough ideas. While India is amongst the top recipients in Asia for venture funds and private equity funds, these investments are so far focused on relatively large and *safer* investments. Thus, despite the growth in the venture capital industry in India and some government schemes for supporting entrepreneurs, the seed funding stage in the innovation pipeline, where amounts required may be small but risks high, is severely constricted.

An extensive innovation ecosystem requires many lateral connections, often at local levels, between producers, sellers and financiers, and the facilitating government machinery. To induce a culture of innovation in the country, there is a need to offer encouragement through awards and challenges which mobilise people to engage and respond creatively and bring focus on neglected societal challenges.

To sum up, innovations can play a very important role in the development discourse, because they can offer a new approach to a system that is currently over-burdened by the multiple demands and has limited resources at its disposal. Enhanced focus on innovations can have an impact much beyond the realm of S&T in diverse areas such as health and education delivery, governance, enterprise development and much more. Collectively, this can herald a generational change in the country and can lay out a chart for a more sustainable and inclusive growth paradigm.

Innovation requires a financial system which is supportive and inclusive and which provides the necessary risk capital to spur innovations and enterprises. Venture funds are recognized globally as the most suitable form of providing risk capital for the growth of innovative technology and breakthrough ideas.

14

Domestic Industry and Foreign Direct Investment (FDI)

The wave of liberalisation and globalisation sweeping across the world has opened many national markets for international business. Global private investment, in most part, is now made by multinational corporations (MNCs) also referred to as transnational corporations (TNCs). Clearly, these transnational organisations play a major role in world trade and investments because of their demonstrated management skills, technology, financial resources and related advantages. Recent developments in the global market are indicative of the rapidly growing international business. The beginning of the 21st century has already marked a tremendous growth of international investments, trade and financial transactions along with the integration and openness of international markets.

Foreign investment is a subject of topical interest. Countries of the world, particularly developing economies, are vying with each other to attract foreign capital to boost their domestic rates of investment and also to acquire new technology and managerial skills. Intense competition is taking place among the fund-starved less developed countries to lure foreign investors by offering repatriation facilities, tax concessions and other incentives. However, foreign investment is not an unmixed blessing. Governments in developing countries have to be very careful while deciding the magnitude, pattern and conditions of private foreign investment.

14.1 Meaning of FDI

Investment in a country by individuals and organisations from other countries is an important aspect of international finance. This flow of international finance may take the form of direct investment (creation of productive facilities) or portfolio investment (acquisition of securities).

FDI is the outcome of the mutual interests of multinational firms and host countries. According to the International Monetary Fund (IMF), FDI is defined as "investment that is made to acquire a lasting interest in an enterprise operating in an economy other than that of the investor...the investor's purpose being to have an effective voice in the management of the enterprise". [1] The essence of FDI is the transmission to the host country of a package of capital, managerial, skill and technical knowledge. FDI is generally a form of long-term international capital movement, made for the purpose of productive activity and accompanied by the intention of managerial control or participation in the management of a foreign firm.

In India, FDI means investment by non-resident entity/person resident outside India in the capital of an Indian company under Schedule 1 of Foreign Exchange Management (Transfer or Issue of Security by a Person Resident Outside India) Regulations, 2000.

FDI is usually contrasted with portfolio investment which does not seek management control, but is motivated by profit. Portfolio investment occurs when individual investors invest, mostly through stockbrokers, in stocks of foreign companies in foreign land in search of profit opportunities.

However, the distinction between FDI and portfolio investment is not watertight because sometimes FDI policy and portfolio investments are intertwined.

14.2 Superiority of FDI over Other Forms of Capital Inflows

FDI is widely considered an essential element for achieving sustainable development. Even former critics of MNCs expect FDI to provide a stronger stimulus to income growth in host countries than other types of capital inflows. Developing countries are strongly advised to rely primarily on FDI, in order to supplement national savings by capital inflows and promote economic development.

FDI is perceived superior to other types of capital inflows for the following reasons:

1. FDI flows are usually preferred over other forms of external finance because they are non-debt creating, non-volatile and their returns depend on the performance of the projects financed by the investors. FDI also facilitates international trade and transfer of knowledge, skills and technology. In a world of increased competition and rapid technological change, their complimentary and catalytic role can be very valuable.

2. In contrast to foreign lenders and portfolio investors, foreign direct investors typically have a longer-term perspective when engaging in a host country. Hence, FDI inflows are less volatile and easier to sustain at times of crisis. A recent United Nations report has revealed that FDI flows are less volatile than portfolio flows. To quote, "FDI flows to developing and transition economies in 1998 declined by about 5 percent from the peak in 1997, a modest reduction in relation to the effects on other capital flows of the spread of the Asian financial crisis to global proportions. FDI flows are generally much less volatile than portfolio flows. The decline was modest in all regions, even in the Asian economies most affected by the financial crisis". [2]

3. While debt inflows may finance consumption rather than investment in the host country, FDI is more likely to be used productively.

4. FDI is expected to have relatively strong effects on economic growth, as FDI provides for more than just capital. FDI offers access to internationally available technologies and management know-how, and may render it easier to penetrate world markets.

5. The risk-sharing properties of FDI are undisputed. This suggests that FDI is the appropriate form of external financing for developing countries, which have less capacity than highly developed economies to absorb external shocks. Likewise, the evidence supports the predominant view that FDI is more stable than other types of capital inflows. It is noteworthy that the volatility of FDI remained exceptionally low in the 1990s, when several emerging economies were hit by financial crises.

However, positive growth effects of FDI cannot be taken for granted. The ambiguous, and sometimes contradictory, empirical findings indicate that FDI must no longer be considered to be a homogenous and universally applicable phenomenon in order to improve our understanding of the growth impact of FDI. In the ultimate analysis, it all depends on time-varying and location-specific factors whether FDI and growth are positively correlated or not. For example, opening up early to FDI inflows, combined with close integration into world trade, seems to have strengthened the FDI/growth nexus. The good news for small and less advanced economies is that they can benefit from positive growth effects of FDI as much as large and more advanced developing countries.

14.3 Resource-seeking, Market-seeking and Efficiency-seeking FDI

Three major types of FDI are typically differentiated: resource-seeking FDI, market-seeking FDI and efficiency-seeking FDI.

Resource-seeking FDI is motivated by the availability of natural resources in host countries. This type of FDI was historically important and remains a relevant source of FDI for various developing countries. However, on a world-wide scale, the relative importance of resource-seeking FDI has decreased significantly.

Regarding the history of FDI in developing countries, various empirical studies have shown that the size and growth of host country markets were among the most important FDI determinants. It is debatable, however, whether this is still true with ongoing globalisation.

Traditionally, FDI was the only reasonable means to penetrate local markets in various developing countries. For instance, exporting to Latin America was no promising alternative to investing there as local industries were heavily protected. FDI was used to circumvent import barriers. The situation has changed considerably in recent times. Many developing countries have liberalised their import regime, thereby enabling MNCs to choose between exporting or undertaking FDI. As a consequence, purely market-seeking FDI may decline. It is argued that one of the most important traditional FDI determinants, the size of national markets, has decreased in importance, even though conclusive empirical evidence is hard to come by.

The possible decline of market-seeking FDI is largely restricted to FDI in manufacturing industries. Market-seeking FDI received a major push by the opening of service industries to FDI. The bulk of FDI in services, which accounts for a rising share in overall FDI, is market-seeking almost by definition, as most services are not tradable in the sense of cross-border transactions.

Geographically dispersed manufacturing, slicing up the value chain and the combination of markets and resources through FDI and trade are becoming major characteristics of the world economy. Efficiency-seeking FDI, i.e. FDI motivated by creating new sources of competitiveness for firms and strengthening existing ones, may then emerge as the most important type of FDI. Accordingly, the competition for FDI would be based increasingly on cost differences between locations, the quality of infrastructure and business-related services, the ease of doing business and the availability of skills. Obviously, this scenario involves major challenges for developing countries, ranging from human capital formation to the provision of business-related services such as efficient communication and distribution systems.

14.4 Macroeconomic and Microeconomic Aspects of FDI

In judging the significance of FDI, especially from the viewpoint of developing countries, it is useful to make a distinction between macroeconomic and microeconomic effects. The former is connected with issues of domestic capital formation, balance of payments, and taking advantage of external markets for achieving faster growth, while the latter is connected with the issues of cost reduction, product quality improvement, making changes in industrial structure and developing global inter-firm linkages.

In this context, it needs to be recognised that FDI is an aggregate entity, the sum total of the investments made by many diverse multinationals, each with its own corporate strategy. The microeconomic effects of the investment made by one multinational may be quite different from that of another multinational even if the investments are made in the same industry. Also, what benefits the local economy will depend on the capabilities of the host country in regard to technology transfer and industrial restructuring.

14.5 Crowding-in and Crowding-out Impacts of FDI

Crowding-in is said to take place when foreign direct investment stimulates new investment in downstream or upstream production by other foreign or domestic producers. While investments in the export sector have the potential for encouraging downstream production, investments in infrastructure encourage upstream production. The MNCs may provide preferential opportunity for exports through access to large internal (inter-firm) markets, which is available only to affiliates set up in host countries. The capital-flow induced growth and the accompanying higher efficiency of the economy may, in turn, induce higher investments.

However, if FDI comes in sectors in which the domestic firms are themselves contemplating investment, the very act of foreign investment may take away the investment opportunities that were open to domestic enterprises. Moreover, if the MNCs raised funds for their expansion programmes from the host country, this might out-compete the domestic firms in the financial markets and thus compete them out. The decision of MNCs for acquisition of domestic firms might similarly lead to large inflow of foreign exchange, appreciating in the process the exchange rate. This might in turn make the host country's export less competitive and thus discourage domestic investment for export markets. All these imperatives may have crowding-out impact on domestic firms.

In view of the double edged nature of FDI, namely the crowding-out and crowding-in effects on domestic industries, the host economies especially the developing countries have been imposing some kind of *performance requirements* in regard to: (a) local content, (b) export commitment, (c) technology transfer, (d) dividend balancing and (e) foreign exchange neutrality.

These regulations are there to enhance the quality of FDI against the simple increase in the quantity of FDI inflow. Imposition of *performance criteria*, however, comes in the way of the relative openness of the trade regime and may make FDI less attractive for MNCs while deciding the location for their operations. In other words, a trade-off is involved between performance and openness.

14.6 Advantages of FDI for the Host Country

FDI can make up not only for deficiencies in the availability of savings and foreign exchange—which is true of all external flows—but also for weaknesses in domestic entrepreneurial capacity. In other words, the role of FDI in directly stimulating investment activity in the country can be of great significance. This is particularly important for India since there is a likelihood that corporate investment activity may not be dynamic enough to absorb the available resources, particularly in those areas which are being vacated by the public sector. In such a situation, the entrepreneurial function played by FDI can have the effect not only of bringing in additional resources, but also leading to better absorption of domestic savings.

Foreign investment takes place for private gain but it has the following potential benefits for less developed countries (LDCs).

14.6.1 Raising the Level of Investment: Foreign investment can fill the gap between desired investment and locally mobilised savings. Local capital markets are often not well developed. Thus, they cannot meet the capital requirements for large investment projects. Besides, access to the hard currency needed to purchase investment goods not available locally can be difficult. FDI solves both these problems because it is a direct source of external capital. It can fill the gap between desired foreign exchange requirements and those derived from net export earnings.

Foreign investment can stimulate domestic investment through forward and backward linkages. For example, output of a foreign firm can be an input of domestic industries. Similarly, output of the domestic industries can be inputs for the foreign firms. If this is so, foreign firms create demand for industries producing goods purchased by them.

14.6.2 Upgradation of Technology: Production units in developing countries use out-dated equipment and techniques that can reduce the productivity of workers and lead to the production of goods of a lower standard. The ability of domestic producers to compete abroad for export markets is reduced which, in turn, contributes to the difficulties of the developing countries to earn hard currencies. Foreign investment can supply a package of needed resources such as management experience, entrepreneurial abilities, organisational and technological skills. Foreign investment brings with it technological knowledge while transferring machinery and equipment to developing countries.

Similarly, as the foreign-owned enterprise comes into competition with the local firms, the latter category of enterprises are forced to improve their technology and standards of product quality. Further, the foreign-owned enterprises pressurise and assist the local support industries to improve the quality of their products and ensure greater reliability of delivery, both of which make it necessary for the support industries to upgrade their technology.

The indirect effects of FDI on development which arise from the diffusion of technology and other know-how are sometimes more important than the direct effects of FDI. Therefore, one should consider not only the actual transfer of technology but also the spread of better managerial practices and the contribution of FDI to enhancing competition in host country markets. The emphasis on the technology-related spill over effects of FDI is warranted in the light of the fact that most FDI originates from a small number of developed countries which play a dominant role in the development of new technology and that multinational enterprises from these countries dominate the demand and use of new technology. The overall positive effect of FDI in respect of technology is undeniable, whether these effects occur through actual transfers, licensing or through spill over.

With reference to the positive effects of FDI through technology spill over, it has been argued that it varies depending upon the characteristics and policies of host countries, and that the existence of a competitive environment and local technological capabilities is especially important in this regard.

14.6.3 Improvement in Export Competitiveness: FDI can help the host country improve its export performance. By raising the level of efficiency and the standards of product quality, FDI makes a positive impact on the host country's export competitiveness. Further, because of the international linkages of MNCs, FDI provides to the host country better access to foreign markets. Also, where the foreign investment has been made with the specific intention of sourcing parts/components (or even final products) from the host country to take advantage of low cost conditions, FDI contributes to exports directly. Enhanced export possibility contributes to the growth of the host economies by relaxing demand side constraints on growth. This is especially important for those countries which have a small domestic market and must increase exports vigorously to maintain their tempo of economic growth.

14.6.4 Employment Generation: Foreign investment can create employment in the modern sectors of developing countries. Recipients of FDI gain training of employees in the course of operating new enterprises, which contributes to human capital formation in the host country.

14.6.5 Benefits to Consumers: Consumers in developing countries stand to gain from FDI through new products, and improved quality of goods at competitive prices.

14.6.6 Resilience of FDI during Financial Crises: FDI is considered less prone to crisis because direct investors typically have a longer-term perspective when engaging in a host country. For instance, in East Asian countries, such investment was remarkably stable during the global financial crisis of 1997-98. In sharp contrast, other forms of private capital flows like portfolio equity and debt flows were subject to large reversals during the same crisis. The resilience of FDI during financial crisis was also evident during the Mexican crisis of 1994-95 and the Latin American debt crisis of the 1980s. This resilience has led many developing countries to favour FDI over other forms of capital flows to supplement national savings by capital inflows and promote economic development.

In addition to the risk-sharing properties of FDI, it is widely believed that FDI provides a stronger stimulus to economic growth in host countries than other types of capital inflows. FDI is more than just capital, as it offers access to internationally available technologies and management know-how.

14.6.7 Revenue to Government: Profits generated by FDI contribute to corporate tax revenues in the host country.

14.7 Disadvantages of FDI for the Host Country

FDI is not an unmixed blessing. Governments in developing countries have to be very careful while deciding the magnitude, pattern and conditions of private foreign investment. Possible adverse implications of foreign investment are the following:

1. When foreign investment is competitive with home investment, profits in domestic industries fall, leading to fall in domestic savings.

2. Contribution of foreign firms to public revenue through corporate taxes is comparatively less because of liberal tax concessions, investment allowances, disguised public subsidies and tariff protection provided by the host government.

3. Foreign firms reinforce dualistic socio-economic structure and increase income inequalities. They create a small number of highly paid modern sector executives. They divert resources away from priority sectors to the manufacture of sophisticated products for the consumption of the local elite. As they are located in urban areas, they create imbalances between rural and urban opportunities, accelerating flow of rural population to urban areas.

4. Foreign firms stimulate inappropriate consumption patterns through excessive advertising and monopolistic/oligopolistic market power. The products made by multinationals for the domestic market are not necessarily low in price and high in quality. Their technology is generally capital-intensive which does not suit the needs of a labour-surplus economy.

5. Foreign firms are able to extract sizeable economic and political concessions from competing governments of developing countries. Consequently, private profits of these companies may exceed social benefits.

6. Continual outflow of profits is too large in many cases, putting pressure on foreign exchange reserves. Foreign investors are very particular about profit repatriation facilities.

7. Foreign firms may influence political decisions in developing countries. In view of their large size and power, national sovereignty and control over economic policies may be jeopardised. In extreme cases, they (foreign firms) may bribe public officials at the highest levels to secure undue favours. Similarly, they may contribute to friendly political parties and subvert the political process of the host country.

Key question, therefore, is how host countries can minimise possible negative effects and maximise positive effects of FDI through appropriate policies.

14.8 Determinants of FDI

To understand the scale and direction of FDI flows, it is necessary to identify their major determinants. Factors influencing the destination of investment, i.e. the host-country determinants are explained below. The relative importance of FDI determinants varies not only between countries but also between different types of FDI. Furthermore, the relative importance of FDI determinants may change over time in a country. Traditionally, the determinants of FDI include the following.

14.8.1 Size of the Market: Large developing countries provide substantial markets where the consumers' demand for certain goods far exceeds the available supplies. This demand potential is a big draw for many foreign-owned enterprises. This explains the massive FDI flows into China since early 1980s. In many cases, the establishment of a low cost marketing operation represents the first step by a multinational into the market of the country. This establishes a presence in the market and provides important insights into the ways of doing business and possible opportunities in the country.

14.8.2 Political Stability: In many countries, the institutions of government are still evolving and there are unsettled political questions. Companies are unwilling to contribute large amounts of capital into an environment where some of the basic political questions have not yet been resolved.

14.8.3 Macroeconomic Environment: Instability in the level of prices and exchange rate enhances the level of uncertainty, making business planning difficult. This increases the perceived risk of making investments and therefore adversely affects the inflow of FDI.

14.8.4 Legal and Regulatory Framework: The transition to a market economy entails the establishment of a legal and regulatory framework that is compatible with private sector activities and the operation of foreign-owned companies. The relevant areas in this field include protection of property rights, ability to repatriate profits, and a free market for currency exchange. It is important that these rules and their administrative procedures are transparent and easily comprehensible.

14.8.5 Access to Basic Inputs: Many developing countries have large reserves of skilled and semi-skilled workers that are available for employment at wages significantly lower than in developed countries. This provides an opportunity for foreign firms to make investments in these countries to cater to the export market. Availability of natural resources—such as oil and gas, minerals and forestry products—also determines the extent of FDI.

14.9 World Bank Determinants of FDI

The motivation and determinants of FDI differ among countries and across economic sectors. These factors include the policy framework, economic determinants and the extent of business facilitation such as macroeconomic fundamentals and availability of infrastructure.

The World Investment Report, 1998 gave a comprehensive list of host country determinants of FDI. The same is reproduced below.

14.9.1 Policy Framework: It includes the following:

1. Economic, political and social stability.
2. Rules regarding entry and operations.
3. Standards of treatment of foreign affiliates.

4. Policies on functioning and structure of markets (especially competition, merger and acquisition policies).
5. International trade and investment agreements.
6. Privatisation policy.
7. Trade policy (tariffs and non-tariff barriers) and coherence of FDI and trade policies.
8. Tax policy.

14.9.2 Economic Determinants: These are as under:

A. Resource/Asset-seeking:

1. Raw materials.
2. Low-cost unskilled labour.
3. Skilled labour.
4. Technological, innovatory and other creative assets (i.e. brand names), including as embodied in individuals, firms and clusters.
5. Physical infrastructure (ports, roads, power, telecommunications).

B. Market-seeking:

1. Market size and per capita income.
2. Access to regional and global markets.
3. Country-specific consumer preferences.
4. Structure of markets.

C. Efficiency-seeking:

1. Cost of resources and assets, adjusted for productivity of labour resources.
2. Other input costs, e.g. transport and communications costs to/from and within host economy and costs of other intermediate products.
3. Membership of a regional integration agreement conducive to the establishment of regional corporate networks.

14.9.3 Business Facilitation: It includes the following:

1. Investment promotion (including image-building, investment-generating activities and investment facilitation services).
2. Investment incentives.
3. Hassle costs (corruption, administrative efficiency etc.).
4. Social amenities (bilingual schools, quality of life etc.).
5. Alternate investment services.

When competing for FDI, policymakers have to be aware that various measures intended to induce FDI are necessary and would lead to incremental investment, i.e. investment which will occur only if these measures are taken. In this respect, it becomes imperative to first study the determinants of FDI. These determinants enable policymakers to understand the scale and direction of FDI flows. It enables them in formulating a foreign investment policy that is most conducive to attracting FDI. They are able to concentrate on those factors or areas to which FDI is most sensitive. These normally include liberalisation of FDI regulations and various business facilitation measures.

Another reason to constantly study and review FDI determinants is that those determinants which were sufficient in the past, may prove to be less relevant in the future. The size of local markets appears to be the most important case in point. Similarly, tax incentives which were earlier considered a relatively minor consideration in most FDI decisions are now proven to have become an increasingly important factor in investment decisions. Globalisation and the resulting increase in capital mobility have created opportunities for tax competition among countries eager to attract FDI. In the process, tax incentives have assumed new and increasing importance. Globalisation can be expected to induce a shift from market-seeking FDI to efficiency-seeking FDI. International competitiveness of local production by foreign investors will then turn out to be a decisive factor shaping the distribution of future FDI. This, in turn, reinforces the role of skilled labour and business facilitation measures.

A study of FDI determinants can, therefore, help policymakers in developing nations to face the challenges arising out of capital inflows. In general terms, their task has various dimensions ranging from human capital formation and capacity-building to the provision of efficient business-related services.

14.10 FDI and Corporate Strategies

The transnational companies (TNCs) are the driving force behind foreign direct investment. They have large internal (inter-firm) markets, access to which is available only to affiliates. They also control large markets in unrelated parties having established brand names and distribution channels spread over several national locations. They can, thus, influence granting of trade privileges in their home (or in third) markets. In other words, they enjoy considerable advantages in creating an initial export base for new entrants.

While there are MNCs with sales turnover larger than the national incomes of many developing countries, there are also many new entrants, which are small and medium sized enterprises (SMEs). Many of these firms find it necessary to invest overseas to overcome lack of opportunities for growth at home, access skilled labour abroad and reduce cost. An increasing number of such firms are from developing countries. Some of these firms belong to economies in transition that previously had isolated themselves from international investment.

The changing context and the quest for location for manufacture and trade have brought about a change in corporate strategies. The following developments are particularly noteworthy:

1. A shift from stand-alone, relatively independent, foreign affiliates to *integrated international production systems* relying on specialised affiliates to service the entire MNC system. Within the framework of this international intra-firm division of labour, any part of the value-added chain of an enterprise can be located abroad while remaining fully integrated into a corporate network. Corporate strategies of this kind seek to exploit regional or global economies of scale and a higher degree of functional specialization.

2. This shift broadens the range of resources sought by MNCs in host countries, making firms more selective in their choices. However, it can also encourage FDI in countries that cannot provide a wide range of resources but have some specific assets

that are sought by MNCs (e.g. accounting or software skills).

3. A shift towards greater use of non-equity and co-operative relationships with other enterprises, such as alliances, partnerships, management contracts or sub-contracting arrangements. These arrangements serve a variety of corporate objectives. They can provide better access to technologies or other assets allowing firms to share the cost and risk of innovatory activities. They can reduce the production cost of labour-intensive products.

4. Emergence of a network type of organisation. This expands the scope of interactions between MNCs and enterprises from host countries, and also the forms of these interactions.

These changing corporate strategies bring a different pattern of international economic integration. Originally, this involved the integration of markets through arm's length trade-shadow integration. Integrated international production moves this integration to the level of production in all its aspects, i.e. deep integration. In the process, a significant part of international transactions becomes internalised, i.e. takes the form of transactions between various parts of transnational corporate systems located in different countries. The ability of firms to allocate their economic assets internationally and the international production system created in the process, have become themselves a part of the new context.

Endnotes

1. International Monetary Fund, *Balance of Payments Manual*, Washington, DC, 1977, p. 408.
2. United Nations, *World Economic and Social Survey*, 1999, p. 35.

15

Industry and Internet

With the commercialization of the internet, the nature of society has changed in many ways. In recent years, the economic power of internet has grown and further reconfigured the world we live in. Today, internet can be seen as a platform that assists in continuous technological innovations, encourages new business practices and changes the competitive landscape of various industry sectors. With technological innovations, internet has changed from *publishing-browsing-platform* to a *participation-interaction-platform*. It has enabled new business models and fostered changes in social life.

Researchers have clearly identified internet as a platform that cannot be overlooked or ignored by tourism organizations while forming their marketing mixes owing to its advantages such as global accessibility, convenience in updating, real time information service, interactive communication features and unique customization capabilities. Internet is successful in swift identification of customer needs and establishment of direct contact with consumers, offering them comprehensive, personalized and up-to-date information. Tourism suppliers can remotely control their servers to display information on products/services at an electronic speed. As far as the travellers are concerned, Internet allows them to communicate directly with tourism suppliers to seek information. It also empowers them to develop and purchase their own itineraries anytime and anywhere.

Internet services are regarded as catalyst in the growth of an economy. Since the information system of a country is interconnected, the development and deployment of information and communication technology is crucial for expanding knowledge base and increasing productivity. Development of technologies and improvement in telecommunications infrastructure has enabled loosely bound business entities to collaborate and provide a number of services, thus connecting more communities socially as well as technologically.

Broadband internet connection is a powerful tool for business enterprises as it provides connectivity to the global markets at a much lower cost than ever. It also acts as an enabling technology that allows them to adopt a number of valuable complimentary applications that may increase their efficiency.

15.1 Co-ordination of Productive Activities

The use of ICT enables businesses to reach distant employees and co-ordinate production activities more efficiently. Manufacturing sector benefits from the supply chain and customer management applications, whereas advanced communications applications are more useful for service sector firms. Some other applications like human resources, administration applications and management systems applications etc. are useful to most firms as these are not industry specific.

Gains from broadband on businesses can be classified into direct and indirect. Direct gains are due to increased efficiency which results in increased productivity. On the other hand, indirect gains result through positive externalities. Broadband has a positive impact on GDP and exports, which leads to increase in the intermediate demand and growth of support sectors.

Broadband technology improves productivity by facilitating the adoption of more efficient business processes. Also, extensive deployment of broadband accelerates innovation. Another way through which broadband brings in efficiency in the business is through a more efficient functional deployment of enterprises by maximizing their reach to labour pools, access to raw materials and consumers, streamlining of supply chains.

In addition to the impact on productivity, broadband technology also impacts business expansion, product innovation, and new business creation. Broadband has a positive impact on the development of new businesses. This results from the network effects of connectivity. When a large enough number of households are connected to broadband, the incentive to develop new businesses increases, especially around information search, advertising and e-commerce.

15.2 Consumer Centricity of Business

Stakeholder engagement has evolved with the changing role of corporations in the society. It has changed from being a reaction to customer problems to their greater participation in the value chain. The stakeholder engagement has benefited many companies through informed decision-making by generating business intelligence. It also brings diverse perspectives together for creativity and innovation.

Earlier, through traditional means of marketing, there used to be a monologue between customers and businesses and a wide range of advertisement was broadcasted. But the modern customer has less time to watch all these advertisements and therefore chooses the message he wishes to see. As internet facilitates interactions, customers want that companies should listen to them and respond. Technology is serving in a big way by helping companies get insights about their customers. Companies are offering customized products and services to their customers as they are no longer the passive players in the market. They already have a lot of information at their disposal. Therefore, being customer centric is the only way to survive in the modern day markets.

The concept of *digital customer engagement* emphasizes the dependence and reliability on customer generated content. Online modes of consumer engagement are gaining popularity as they involve internet marketing, social media marketing, blogs, web portals, crowd sourcing, e-mail campaigns etc. and have wide number of applications in different sectors. Many private companies are now using social media platforms, mobile devices and other technologies to get closer to their customers because of their volume and speed to reach customers.

Technology has also changed the way customers contact the companies. They seek automation, self-service and personalization. The technology also brings good prospects for the government and the jurisdiction of the country as it helps them to empower the citizens and gives them more access to the details through the use of location-based services. It helps in achieving long-term operational efficiencies.

As mobile phones (now mostly smart phones) have become an integral part of our day-to-day life, there is a need to change the way businesses reach and interact with its customers. Smart-phones act as primary internet devices and thus can be used for mass marketing to gain more participation. To ensure deeper reach, the focus must be on developing customer-centric applications. There is a need to make these applications available in different languages to avoid the gap that may be generated. Some touch points that can be of core importance for the businesses to engage with customers through mobiles are product discovery platforms, search engines, customer care portals, consumer grievance forums and digital payment mechanisms.

The proliferation of social media and the video invasion are instrumental for building strong relationships with customers. Videos ensure attention for longer duration and provide opportunities for emotional congruence. Social media relationships build on videos and social interaction results in self-efficacy and positive word of mouth. Social interactions and shared experiences increase the levels of commitment and engagement with the businesses. Increased interaction results in more satisfied customers and thereby positive actions. To attain higher levels of consumer engagement, businesses must integrate the digital channels with traditional brick and mortar.

Finally, to be a customer-centric company, a collective effort by different departments of the organization is an imperative practice. It is unlike product-centric approach where the functions are compartmentalized. Linkages have to be developed across the organization and a better understanding of customer needs has to be discovered at every level. These linkages are being made with the help of internet technologies. Even customers should be treated as business partners and their feedback and suggestions should be taken into consideration. E-tailers must first ask consumers what they want to buy rather than trying to push what they want to sell.

15.3 Marketing and Advertising

Companies use various marketing tools to increase customer engagement and participation. Internet has become much more user-friendly with the passage of time. Online business activities are a rapidly growing phenomenon. Internet has proved to be a powerful medium for obtaining and distributing information to help marketers take product decisions and devise appropriate marketing plans.

As the popularity of internet has increased, the popularity of sports has increased as well. Viewers are no more glued to their TV screens, wishing to watch only live shows. They want the convenience of watching their favourite matches whenever and wherever they want to. Digitization of media content, proliferation of IT-enabled devices and easy availability of high speed broadband connections has given birth to the phenomenon called *media convergence*—a phenomenon involving the interconnection of information and communications technologies, computer networks, and media content. Various forms of media such as TV, social platforms and even out-of-home (OoH) advertising, are being used by brands to bridge the gap between online and offline resources. It helps them to efficiently identify their target group of sports fans.

Sports fans are some of the most loyal customers because they are open to use the products of the brands, which are participating in their favourite games. Brands not only need to provide relevant content and enhanced experience to the sports fans, but also engage them sustainably with the brand. Programmatic technology is the need of the hour. Here, with the help of triggers, ads and content can be displayed to the viewers based on monitoring real time developments as the game progresses.

OoH advertising is an old form of advertising which was assumed to be restricted to hoardings and billboards on roadsides. They were more of a distraction rather than attention gainers. Now IT has shown the way to modernize the OoH advertising in the form of digitized and interactive billboards. OoH advertising has shown good results in the rural markets as well. In rural areas, people gather at public places such as bus stops or marketplaces, where many OoH exercises like permanent billboards are done. Even though the quality of those billboards is very basic, they have proven to be better communication tools than most others.

15.4 Online Shopping

Online shopping via mobile phones is gradually increasing in India.

15.4.1 Risk and Trust: Trust plays an important role in e-commerce activities. Trust is an important factor for the circulation and acceptance of e-commerce. There are two types of uncertainty, namely system-dependent and transaction specific. Online retailers are finding it increasingly difficult to sell their goods. Internet users are unwilling to shop online because of lack of faith that must exist between business and consumers. Trust is not only a short-term issue but the most important long-term barrier to realize the full potential of e-commerce. Consumers foresee numerous risks while buying on the internet as it does not involve simultaneous exchange of goods and money, because of the temporal separation between exchange partners.

System dependent uncertainties arise because of potential technological problems and lack of clear legal norms. On the other hand, transaction-specific uncertainties arise out of asymmetric distribution of information between the transaction partners. Trust plays a key role in buying process as consumers tend to look for experience in credence qualities of products and their sellers. Trust functions to lower the perceived risk of a transaction. On the other hand, there are some risks that come about during exchange of information via internet.

System-dependent uncertainty comprises of events that are beyond the direct influence of actors and can be characterized as environmental uncertainty. In the context of the internet, it relates to potential technological sources of errors and security gaps.

Technical safety gaps can emerge either in the data channel or on the final points of the process like the desktop system of the customer, the server of the internet retailer or the involved banks. Transaction specific uncertainty may arise out of decisions of economic actors and is caused by asymmetric distribution of information between the transaction partners. This primarily concerns the quality of products and services offered on the web because the quality assessment in electronic markets is much more difficult due to disappearance of the personal factors that are used in traditional modes of selling. This type of uncertainty can be reduced by application of concepts of search, experience and credence qualities. Online product evaluation is possible through performance-oriented information substitutes that relate to the seller and his reputation in the market or adequate indicators such as brand names or performance bonds.

Online retailers facilitate the evaluation of credence qualities by signalling trustworthiness like referring to a certificate of a trusted third party. Trust is a potentially important aspect for reducing uncertainty and complexity of online transactions and relationships. Trust is considerably useful in reaping economic benefits. Since in the near future trust will remain the decisive factor for success or failure of e-businesses, it is very important for internet companies to act in a way that engenders consumers' trust. Efforts to increase the security of e-commerce systems and trustworthy behaviour of online retailers will prove to be of advantage for both consumers and companies engaging in e-commerce.

15.4.2 Websites Shopping: There has been a phenomenal growth in the number of organizations using internet for marketing, promoting, and transacting products and services because of growth in B2C e-commerce. Firms and consumers have started using internet to gather information and for online shopping. The usefulness of a B2C site not only depends upon the content and design but also the navigation tools. There has been much technical advancement in internet security including cryptography, digital signatures, and certificates and authentication. Despite these advancements, consumers are apprehensive about online shopping. An effective B2C site provides quick access to information about product and services, information about the organization (the seller) and contact information.

A substantial number of customers experience problems while shopping online such as lost orders, service breakdowns, or inadequate handling of complaints. All these problems make the maintenance of the quality of e-service challenging.

Online shopping experience is different from offline shopping experience. There are many factors affecting online purchasing behaviour of consumer such as attitude towards technology, skills and experiences, people having greater internal control, knowledge of internet, willingness to adopt new technology or those who spend much of their time online, are more likely to shop online. Furthermore, those who are time starved are more likely to shop online. Other factors also influence the decision of shopping online or offline, such as type of product, customer mood and goal behind shopping. It is also found that website design, reliability and security/privacy serve as the basis of judgment for the quality of an online site. As more and more information and technological tools are available to customers, their preferences and experiences are likely to change.

15.4.3 Travelling Displacement: In the times of internet, the need for business travel may get eliminated. Internet allows business and people to call, e-mail, see and talk to counterparties without travelling to distant locations. Most of the business travel relates to management of foreign subsidiaries. The brain needs to move and not the bytes, primarily because:

- Brain has a capacity to absorb information, identify patterns and solve problems without us being aware of how it does it. It lets us understand facial expressions, body language, intonation and other subtle indicators that are gathered unconsciously and results in better evaluation.
- Brain is designed to work in parallel with other brains.

Thus, it is noted that the amount of travel is related to the amount of know-how that needs to be moved around. Thus, it is suggested that firms must try to move brains for key tasks and not just for relevant information to the brains.

E-commerce is also a major use, especially when making purchases, downloading software, financial transactions, placing product service requests, and downloading music are considered together.

Internet use leads to trip substitution as many use information technology instead of making trips to work, bookstores, other stores, and libraries. Information technology is also frequently used instead of making trips to clothing stores, music stores, friends' houses, government offices, and special interest organizations.

Internet is used to gather information to prompt trips to bookstores, other stores, government offices, movies, libraries, and other stores.

15.5 Electronic Commerce (E-commerce)

15.5.1 Types and Categories of E-commerce: E-commerce involves individuals and business organizations exchanging business information and instructions over electronic media using computers, telephones and other telecommunication equipments. Such form of doing business has been in existence ever since electronic mode of data/information exchange was developed, but its scope was limited only as a medium of exchange of information between entities with a pre-established contractual relationship. However, internet has changed the approach to e-commerce; it is no longer the same business with an additional channel for information exchange, but one with new strategy and models.

A business model generally focuses on: (a) where the business operates, i.e. the market, the competitors and the customers, (b) what it sells, i.e. its products and services, (c) the channels of distribution, i.e. the medium for sale and distribution of its products, and (d) the sources of revenue and expenditure and how these are affected. Internet has influenced all the four components of business model and thus has come to influence the business strategy in a profound way. The size of the market has grown enormously as one can access the products and services from any part of the world. So does the potential competition. The methods of reaching out to customers, receiving the response and offering services have a new, simpler and efficient alternative now, i.e. internet. The cost of advertisement, offer and delivery of services through internet has reduced considerably, forcing most companies to rework their strategies to remain in competition.

There are two types of e-commerce ventures in operation: (a) the old brick and mortar companies, who have adopted electronic medium, particularly internet, to enhance their existing products and services, and/or to offer new products and services, and (b) the pure e-ventures who have no visible physical presence. This difference has wider ramifications than mere visibility when it comes to issues like customer's trust, brand equity, ability to service the customers, adopting new business culture and cost.

Another way of classifying e-commerce is by the targeted counterpart of a business, viz. whether the counterpart is a final consumer or another business in the distribution chain. Accordingly, the two broad categories are: business-to-consumer (B2C) and business-to-business (B2B).

15.5.2 Business-to-Consumers (B2C): In the B2C category are included single e-shops, shopping malls, e-broking, e-auction, e-banking, service providers like travel related services, financial services, education, entertainment and any other form of business targeted at the final consumer. Some of the features, opportunities and concerns common to this category of business irrespective of the business segment, are the following.

A. Opportunities: Internet provides an ever-growing market both in terms of number of potential customers and geographical reach. Technological development has made access to internet both cheaper and faster. More and more people across the globe are accessing the net either through PCs or other devices. The purchasing power and need for quality service of this segment of consumers are considerable. Anybody accessing Internet is a potential customer irrespective of his or her location. Thus, any business targeting final consumers cannot ignore the business potential of Internet.

Internet offers a unique opportunity to register business presence in a global market. Its effectiveness in disseminating information about one's business at a relatively cost effective manner is tremendous. Time sensitive information can be updated faster than any other media. A properly designed website can convey a more accurate and focussed image of a product or service than any other media. Use of multimedia capabilities, i.e. sound, picture, movies etc. has made internet as an ideal medium for information dissemination. However, help of other media is necessary to draw the potential customers to the web site.

The quality of service is a key feature of any e-commerce venture. The ability to sell one's product at anytime and anywhere to the satisfaction of customers is essential for e-business to succeed. Internet offers such opportunity, since the business presence is not restricted by time zone and geographical limitations. Replying to customers' queries through e-mail, offering interactive help line, accepting customers' complaints online 24 hours a day and attending to the same etc. are some of the features of e-business which enhance the quality of service to the customers. It is of crucial importance for an e-venture to realize that just as it is easier to approach a customer through internet, it is equally easy to lose him. The customer has the same facility to move over to another site.

Cost is an important issue in an e-venture. It is generally accepted that the cost of overhead, servicing and distribution etc. through internet is less compared to the traditional way of doing business. Although the magnitude of difference varies depending on the type of business and the estimates made, but there is unanimity that internet provides a substantial cost advantage and this, in fact, is one of the major driving forces for more number of traditional business adopting to e-commerce and pure e-commerce firms to sprout.

Cost of communication through www is the least compared to any other medium. Many a time one's presence in the web may bring in international enquiries, which the business might not have targeted. The business should have proper plans to address such opportunities.

B. Concerns: There are various obstacles, which an e-commerce venture needs to overcome. Trust of customers in a web-venture is an important concern. Many customers hesitate to deal with a web venture as they are not sure of the type of products and services they will receive. This is particularly true in a B2C venture like e-shop, e-mall or e-auction site. Traditional business with well-established brands and goodwill and having a physical presence face less resistance from customers in this regard than a pure e-venture.

Many B2C ventures have ultimately to deliver a product or service in physical form to the customer for a deal contracted through internet. This needs proper logistics, an efficient distribution network, and control over quality of product or service delivered. These issues are not technology related and any let off in this area can drive the customer away to the competitor or from e-commerce.

The privacy of information on the customer's preferences, credit card and bank account details etc. and customers' faith in a system where such privacy is stated to be ensured are important issues to be addressed. These are mainly technological issues, but human factor is important both at the business and at the customers' end and also in building the trust in the system.

Security of a transaction, authenticity of a deal, identification of a customer etc. are important technological and systems issues, which are major sources of concern to e-commerce. Equally important are questions of repudiation of a deal, applicability of law, jurisdiction of tax laws etc. These are important to all forms of e-commerce, whether B2C or B2B and all segments of business, i.e. manufacturing, services and finance.

Accessibility to Internet by the consumers is an important issue in B2C domain. This is particularly so in countries like India where penetration of PCs and other devices to households for access to Internet is minimal. Also important are availability of bandwidth and other infrastructure for faster and easier access. Considering that e-commerce aims at global market, deficiencies of these kinds in the developing world are no longer concerns confined to these areas, but are global e-commerce concerns.

15.5.3 Business to Business (B2B): As opposed to B2C e-commerce, in B2B domain, the parties to a deal are at different points of the product supply chain. In a B2B type domain, a company, its suppliers, dealers and bankers are networked to finalize and settle all aspects of a deal online. Perhaps, only the goods in different stages of processing physically move from the supplier to the dealer. This scenario can be extended to include the shipper, providers of different ancillary services, IT service provider and the payment system gateway etc. depending on the degree of sophistication of the available systems.

Another important feature of a B2B domain, as distinct from B2C, is that business information/data is integrated to the back office systems of parties to a deal and the state of straight through processing (STP) or near STP is achieved. This is a very significant aspect of B2B model of e-commerce, which results in improved profits through lowering cost and reducing inventories.

For example, in a B2B environment, the back office system of a company controls inventory requirement with reference to the order book position updated regularly on the basis of orders received from dealers through internet. At the optimum level of inventory, it raises a purchase order with the supplier, whose system, in turn, processes the order and confirms supply. Buyer company's system issues debit instructions on its bank account for payment to the supplier. The buyer's bank credits seller's bank with the cost of sale though a payment gateway. Similar series of transaction processes are also initiated between the company and its dealers and their respective banks. Once e-commerce relationship is established between the firms, the transactions of the type shown above can be processed with minimal human intervention and on 24 hours a day and 7 day a week basis.

New business models are emerging in B2B domain. There are portals which offer a meeting ground to buyers and sellers of different products in supply chain, more like a buyer-seller meet in international business. This has enabled relatively smaller companies to enter the global market. Banks in the portal offer financial services for deals settled through the portal.

Technology and networking are important constituents of a B2B type of business domain. Earlier, only large firms could have access to such technology and they used private networks with interface to each other for information flow and transaction processing. A major concern used to be compatibility of EDI platforms across different B2B partners. Internet with www and other standard technology have offered opportunity to relatively smaller and medium sized firms to integrate their operations in B2B model and take advantage of the benefits it offers. It has also led to standardization of software platforms.

Other new forms of business models in B2B domain are application service providers (ASPs) and service integrators. ASPs offer application software online to e-commerce companies who pay for the same according to the use without owning it. Often entire back office processing is taken care of by ASPs and other service integrators. However, the utility of such service providers will to a large extent depend on the business strategy of the e-venture.

The concerns of B2B e-commerce are similar to those of B2C, discussed earlier. The security issues are more pronounced because of high value transfers taking place through the net. So also are the issues relating to privacy of information, law, tax repudiation etc. The other issues of importance to a B2B firm are the choice of appropriate technology, the issue of build or outsource, maintenance and training of personnel etc., since they involve large investments and are critical to success.

15.6 Internet Marketing

New forms of marketing also use the internet and are therefore called *internet marketing* or more generally *e-marketing, online marketing, digital marketing.* Internet marketing is sometimes considered to be broad in scope, because it not only refers to marketing on the internet, but also includes marketing done via e-mail, wireless media as well as driving audience from traditional marketing methods like radio and billboard to internet properties or landing page.

E-marketing (electronic marketing) can be described as the marketing of the company's products that occurs over the internet and mobile. The objective behind performing electronic marketing is to increase the awareness of a particular company amongst the consumer market. E-marketing is a novel form of marketing which has been developed in conjunction with the ever-growing popularity of the internet and website marketing. Being a relatively new form of marketing in India, majority of corporations continue to market themselves with use of the traditional methods of print magazine advertisements and television commercials.

Many companies, who are experts in website marketing and have been conducting business operations over the internet for a couple of years, are aware of electronic marketing and the amazing results in business success it can quickly and effortlessly achieve for them.

The growth of the internet during the past few years is undoubtedly the most important development in the history of commerce which shows no signs of abating in the future. Since the Industrial Revolution of the 19th century, no development has so dramatically altered human behaviour as the emergence of internet. Marketing has also been immensely influenced by the internet. Marketers have got a new medium for communicating and building long-term relationship with their customers at a fraction of cost they used to incur earlier. Various marketing activities can be performed more efficiently, effectively and smoothly than ever before with the help of internet. However, it is difficult to assess the potential of internet for business and foresee the probable threats brought by the new medium.

In India, the internet became available to the general public and the business in 1995. People have been mesmerized by the prowess of the internet, both as a communication tool and as an entertainment medium. The Indian corporate world was quick to realise the commercial potential of the web and embraced it as part of its business and marketing strategies. The Indian Government has also been providing the necessary infrastructural support for the internet. Worldwide, and in India also, empirical studies are being conducted to explore the possibilities of doing business on the internet, including growth in the volume of e-commerce, use of websites, on-line pricing and online advertising. However, what marketers in India think about the internet as a marketing tool and how they can use it for marketing purposes has not been attempted in a systematic manner.

16

Corporate Governance and Human Resources Management and Development

16.1 Corporate Governance

The concept of corporate governance has generated extensive debate during the last few years due to the fast changing economic scenario all over the world. The term corporate governance includes the policies and procedures adopted by a corporate entity in achieving its objectives in relation to shareholders, employees, customers, suppliers, regulatory authorities and the community at large. In general parlance, it means a code of corporate conduct in relation to all the stakeholders, whether internal or external. Corporate governance implies transparency of management systems and encompasses the entire mechanics of the functioning of the company. It provides a system by which corporate entities are directed and controlled, besides attempting to put in place a system of checks and balances between the shareholders, directors, auditors and the management.

16.1.1 Meaning of Corporate Governance: What constitutes corporate governance has been a subject of intense debate throughout the world with no concise, universally agreed upon, defined parameters. However, the concept has evolved in different ways in recent years depending upon the prevailing economic system.

As per some of the well-accepted definitions, corporate governance refers to the following:

1. System by which business corporations are directed and controlled.
2. Structure through which the company objectives are set, means of attaining those objectives and monitoring the performance.
3. Relationship among various participants in determining the direction and performance of corporations.
4. Balance between economic and social goals and between individual and communal goals.
5. Efficient use of resources and accountability for the stewardship of those resources.
6. Enhancement of the long-term shareholder value while at the same time protecting the interests of other stakeholders.

16.1.2 Models of Corporate Governance: Corporate governance clearly impinges upon the direction, goals and performance of a corporation. The belief that maximisation of shareholder value is the main purpose of modern business has been associated with the *Anglo-Saxon* agency model of the corporation. A clear separation between management control and shareholder ownership is the primary feature of this model. This contrasts with the *German* conception of the company as a social institution, wherein the majority shareholder is a part of the supervisory board along with other stakeholders like workers/employees. This is popularly known as *Insider System*.

In another model which has evolved in East Asian economies, the family controls the substantial shareholding and also actively participates in the management of the company. This is close to the corporate ownership structures in India where the family-run business groups still play a crucial role. Shareholdings in Indian companies are segregated mainly as promoter and non-promoter shareholding. The promoters usually have substantial shareholding.

The central corporate governance issue, irrespective of the economic model, is aligning the objectives of management with the objective of shareholder wealth maximisation. Companies are encouraged in most systems to take into consideration the interests of all the stakeholders while making their decisions. The idea is to emphasise that the board is responsible not only to shareholders but also to individuals or groups who have a stake in the actions and decisions of such an organisation.

The concepts of accountability, transparency and equality of treatment to all the shareholders occupy the centre-stage in corporate governance, irrespective of the economic system. Companies around the world are realising that better corporate governance adds considerable value to their operational performance.

16.2 Human Resources Management (HRM)

HRM relates to formulation of strategies by business entities concerning selection, training and rewarding of their personnel. The subject has assumed added significance in the wake of liberalization and globalization trends sweeping across the world. In the face of intense competition unleashed by market-oriented reforms, firms are vying with each other to acquire competitive advantage to prosper in business and in many cases to survive in business. Every possible strategy is being applied to achieve the explicit and implicit objectives of the firm. HRM has emerged as an important ingredient of the policy mix to score points over the existing and potential competitors.

Human resources are of critical importance for the growth of knowledge and technology, value addition and improvement of competitiveness in manufacturing through processes of continuous improvement. In fact, the human resources are the only *appreciating resources* in a manufacturing system. They are the only resources that have the motivation and ability to increase their value if suitable conditions are provided, whereas all other resources—machines, building, materials and so on—depreciate in value with time. The best enterprises view their people as their prime asset and the source of their competitive advantage. Nations that have achieved sustainable competitiveness in manufacturing even when they do not have required raw materials, such as Japan and South Korea, have created systems for the continuous improvement of the capabilities of their human resources.

Human beings are the heartbeat of an organization. They are the brains trust and think tanks of future strategies. Intangible assets, like human capital, decide the use of tangible and material resources innovatively to fulfil the objectives of any business entity. Vision sharing with employees with adequate empowerment constitutes an essential element of HRM strategy. A system of fair compensation for performance and provision of a good *work-life balance* and succession planning become important in the context of the *war for talent*, rising salaries and growing levels of attrition, particularly in developing economies like India.

HRM is a dynamic process of bringing people and organizations together so that the goals of each other are met. Since people constitute the most significant resource of any organization, management of human resources becomes critical for the success of the organization.

With the rapid changes in the business scenario in the recent past, organizations are forced to reorient themselves to meet the new challenges. Technological advances, global competition, demographic changes, information revolution and trends towards service society have changed the rules of the game significantly.

In such a scenario, organizations with similar set of resources can gain competitive advantage only through effective and efficient management of resources. HRM is no more an administrative function but a growth-oriented professional function. Human resources managers have to face a number of challenges for managing the modern knowledge-oriented organizations. In the light of these, several new issues have emerged including talent management, outsourcing, performance management, online recruitment, emotional intelligence, team management and impact of information technology and communications.

The premise that people provide organizations with an important source of sustainable competitive advantage is established. The effective management of human capital as a determinant of organizational performance is thus accepted. Competition, technology, management and the rise of the new economy, has forced organizations to look for innovative strategies to gain the competitive edge. The role of HRM in organizations has assumed significance in this context and has been evolving dramatically in recent years. The successful organizations are using human resources as a strategic partner, investing them with far-reaching transformational roles and responsibilities. This activity involves making the function of managing people the most prioritized activity in the organization and integrating all policies/programmes pertaining to human resources within the framework of a company's strategy. Indian organizations are increasingly turning to HRM techniques to face the emerging challenges posed by liberalization and globalization.

The HRM strategy highlights issues like talent identification, retention and engagement of employees. It has also brought out the need for a *gap analysis* and measures to fill the gaps in knowledge, talent, productivity and strategy leading to competence building and better position-person fit. A watch has to be kept on demand-supply mismatches and in-house development of multi-skilled personnel to enable companies to diversify, integrate and carry on multiple businesses. These issues call for taking new initiatives in the area of training, imparting skills and empowerment, competence mapping and career development.

Hitherto, companies in India looked at HRM as a segmented strategy. In the present context of increasing global competition, high customer expectations and emergence of novel business models, time has come when one has to revisit HRM strategy and look at it as a vital input for business. This approach involves aligning of HRM practices with business strategy and harnessing of human capital for business success. Human capital has to be deployed to secure predictable, sustainable and desirable long-term competitive advantage.

With the growing complexity of technology, customer expectations and competitive challenges, there is need for closer industry-academia interaction and more purposeful linkage of theory and practice. Companies have to accord high priority to development of people for the development of the company. This calls for aligning aspirations of the employees with the objectives of the company.

India must invest in and build its human resources capabilities to catch up with other countries that have moved ahead and thereafter sustained competitive advantages in manufacturing. Indeed the contentious debate of *labour* versus *capital* in the enterprise, could be reframed if employees are seen as assets, with value that can appreciate, rather than as labour costs. Human resources should be managed as a source of sustainable competitive advantage.

16.3 Human Resources Development (HRD)

HRD aims at improving human resources. HRD is concerned with the development of competencies and effectiveness of people working in the organization. The design of HRD system should strengthens corporate planning, production processes, marketing strategies, and budgeting and finance.

Different roles in an organization should be integrated using different mechanisms, e.g. manpower planning inputs should be available to line managers so that they can do career planning. A systematic way to monitor the progress and to identify the level of effectiveness of the system is required.

HRD managers are expected to know everything about organizational efficiency and for this they should work closely with different departmental heads in the organization. It is one of their roles to design, develop and implement the evaluation of programmes. They should assess the needs of training and development of employees, analyze the data obtained and organize further programmes for their career development.

As HRD managers are concerned about the development of their organization, it becomes their role to identify the threats and opportunities provided by the external environment, e.g. there is a strong need to bring advancement in technology based on the study of external environment. Identifying the threats and opportunities helps an organization to survive and further it helps in achieving objectives efficiently.

To manage learning is one of the most significant roles performed by HRD manager. They should communicate the results obtained from respective decision-makers so that they can take corrective action on time. It is expected that HRD managers should clearly understand the importance of career development and when it can be brought into the system of learning.

HRD managers also act as marketing specialists. They are actively involved in management function. Ultimately, their aim is to make and maintain favourable internal and external environment relations for smooth conduct of the business.

16.3.1 Skill Development: Skills and knowledge are the driving forces of economic growth and social development for any country. Countries with higher levels of skills adjust more effectively to the challenges and opportunities in domestic and international job markets. As India moves progressively towards becoming a global knowledge economy, it must meet the rising aspirations of its youth. This can be partially achieved through focus on advancement of skills that are relevant to the emerging economic environment. Government of India has recently taken a number of initiatives to empower all individuals through improved skills and knowledge to gain access to decent employment and ensure India's competitiveness in the global market.

India must invest in and build its human resources capabilities to catch up with other countries that have moved ahead and thereafter sustained competitive advantages in manufacturing. Indeed the contentious debate of *labour* versus *capital* in the enterprise, could be reframed if employees are seen as assets, with value that can appreciate, rather than as labour costs. Human resources should be managed as a source of sustainable competitive advantage.

Equal access to skill development is essential for all social groups particularly women and disadvantaged section of society, to help them in securing decent employment and moving out of poverty. Removing barriers to access and addressing their specific needs are key elements in achieving inclusive growth. Entry barriers such as educational qualification, transportation, loss of wages, language etc. should be addressed. While enhancing the opportunity of skill development for all, entry assessments should be deployed to channelize people with different profiles and needs into appropriate skill development programmes. Effort should be combined with a major initiative in raising awareness among the target groups about the benefit of skill development, employment and learning opportunities and also about support schemes that enable them to participate in training. In addition to vocational skills, the provision of soft (or life) skills—including basic literacy, numeracy, occupational safety and health, hygiene, basic labour rights, team work and confidence building—should be made as an integral component of the curricula. This will also help in empowerment of vulnerable groups.

17

Corporate Social Responsibility (CSR)

A movement is growing around the world, within businesses themselves, to develop frameworks of accountability that go beyond the responsibility of business towards investors and customers to responsibility towards citizens and society. Business organisations are expected to report for public scrutiny the impact of their business activities on the environment and communities. Leading Indian companies are part of this international movement.

This voluntary movement for accountability must be strengthened. It must spread beyond the few leading firms. Business organizations do not want more government control of their activities. They resent government imposed reporting requirements, especially those that are tedious and costly to implement. However, reporting standards developed by business associations themselves, as the new frameworks are, should be acceptable. Government could work with industry associations and put pressure for the wider adoption of such standards. They should not be footnotes to financial accounts. They must be front and centre where they are noticed.

Private business enterprises are the principal engines of industrialisation in India. Government is no longer promoting public sector enterprises in industry. Its principal role in industry today is to enable and regulate the activity of business enterprises in the private sector to ensure that they may profit and grow, and meet societal needs too. Therefore, Government must induce private enterprises to pay more attention to societal concerns of inclusion and environmental sustainability.

17.1 What is CSR?

Corporate social responsibility (also called corporate conscience, corporate citizenship, social performance, sustainable responsible business) is a form of corporate self-regulation integrated into a business model. CSR policy functions as a built-in, self-regulating mechanism whereby a business monitors and ensures its active compliance with the spirit of the law, ethical standards, and international norms. In some models, a firm's implementation of CSR goes beyond compliance and engages in "actions that appear to further some social good, beyond the interests of the firm and that which is required by law". CSR is a process with the aim to embrace responsibility for the company's actions and encourage a positive impact through its activities on the environment, consumers, employees, communities, stakeholders and all other members of the public sphere who may also be considered as stakeholders.

CSR is a concept, accepted the world over, whereby corporates integrate social and environmental concerns in their business operations and in the interactions with their stakeholders on a voluntary basis. The three keys to an effective CSR are commitment, clarity and congruence with corporate values. Clarity is all important because each corporate entity has to frame its CSR initiatives based on the environment of the activities being carried out. Congruence is about ensuring the corporate attitude to its responsibilities towards society. CSR should also be consistent with own values and culture of the company.

CSR encompasses a wide spectrum of issues ranging from business ethics, corporate governance and socially responsible investing (SRI) to environmental sustainability and community investment. CSR is about the behaviour of businesses over and above what is ordinarily required by regulatory bodies and legal requirements.

Presently, there is an increasing awareness about CSR the world over. Consequently, there is a concerted effort among all types of organizations, to ensure that sustainable development is not lost sight of, in the pursuit of their respective goals—profit-making, social service, philanthropy etc. CSR entails the integration of social and environmental concerns by companies in their business operations as also in interactions with their stakeholders.

17.2 Main Features of CSR

These are as under:

1. CSR is behaviour by businesses over and above legal requirements, voluntarily adopted because businesses deem it to be in their long-term interest.
2. CSR is intrinsically linked to the concept of sustainable development. Businesses need to integrate the economic, social and environmental impact in their operations.
3. CSR is not an optional *add-on* to core activities of business but about the way in which business is managed.
4. CSR is the alignment of business operations with social values. It takes into account the interests of stakeholders in the company's business policies and actions.
5. CSR focuses on the social, environmental, and financial success of a company—the so-called *triple bottom line*—with the aim to achieve social development while achieving business success.

17.3 Origins of CSR

The concept of corporate social responsibility was formally coined in 1953 by Howard Bowen in his publication *Social Responsibilities of Businessmen*. Bowen defined CSR as the obligations of businessmen to pursue those policies, to make those decisions, or to follow those lines of action which are desirable in terms of the objectives and values of society. The concept received academic attention in 1980s and 1990s and became an issue of debate and discussion among academic circles.

The term *corporate social responsibility* came into common use in the late 1960s and early 1970s after many multinational corporations formed the term stakeholder, meaning those on whom an organization's activities have an impact. It was used to describe corporate owners beyond shareholders as a result of an influential book by R.

Edward Freeman, *Strategic Management: A Stakeholder Approach* in 1984.

The first company to implement CSR was Shell in 1998. Although, the literature on CSR has been developed in all countries, its practical application is more profuse in the developed countries, mainly the US and some European nations. The concept of social responsibility has been interpreted by different authors from different corporate perspectives. A number of concepts and issues are subsumed under the heading of CSR, including human rights, environmental perspective, diversity management, environmental sustainability and philanthropy.

Thus, it can be said that the concept of CSR is complex in nature. Numerous studies have investigated the link between CSR and financial performance through a theoretical as well as an empirical lens. In particular, research rooted in neo-classical economics argued that CSR unnecessarily raises a firm's costs, putting the firm in a position of competitive disadvantage vis-à-vis its competitors. Predominantly based on agency theory, some studies have argued that employing valuable resources of a firm to engage in CSR results in significant managerial benefits rather than financial benefits to the firm's shareholders.

17.4 Approaches to CSR

Many global frameworks and standards for CSR have been developed that are meant to help companies conform to principles and practices that go beyond compliance with the law.

CSR is titled to aid an organization's mission as well as a guide to what the company stands for and will uphold to its consumers. Development business ethics is one of the forms of applied ethics that examines ethical principles and moral or ethical problems that can arise in a business environment. ISO 26000 is the recognized international standard for CSR.

A more common approach to CSR is corporate philanthropy. This includes monetary donations and aid given to local and non-local non-profit organizations and communities, including donations in areas such as the arts, education, housing, health, social welfare, and the environment, among others, but excluding political contributions and commercial sponsorship of events. Some organizations do not like a philanthropy-based approach as it might not help build on the skills of local populations, whereas community-based development generally leads to more sustainable development.

Another approach is garnering increasing corporate responsibility interest. This is called creating shared value (CSV). The shared value model is based on the idea that corporate success and social welfare are interdependent. A business needs a healthy and educated workforce, and sustainable resources to compete effectively. For society to thrive, profitable and competitive businesses must be developed and supported to create income, wealth, tax revenues, and opportunities for philanthropy.

Various approaches to CSR pit businesses against society, emphasizing the costs and limitations of compliance with externally imposed social and environmental standards. CSV acknowledges trade-offs between short-term profitability and social or environmental goals, but focuses more on the opportunities for competitive advantage from building a social value proposition into corporate strategy. CSV has a limitation in that it gives the impression that only two stakeholders are important—shareholders and consumers—and belies the multi-stakeholder approach of most CSR advocates.

Many companies use the strategy of benchmarking to compete within their respective industries in CSR policy, implementation, and effectiveness. Benchmarking involves reviewing CSR initiatives of the competitor, as well as measuring and evaluating the impact that those policies have on society and the environment, and how customers perceive competitor's CSR strategy. After a comprehensive study of competitor's strategy and an internal policy review, a comparison can be drawn and a strategy developed for competition with CSR initiatives.

17.4.1 Cost-benefit Analysis with a Resource-based View: In competitive markets the cost-benefit analysis regarding positive financial outcomes upon implementing a CSR-based strategy, can be examined with a lens of the resource-based-view (RBV) of sustainable competitive advantage. A firm can conduct a cost-benefit analysis through a RBV-based lens to determine the optimal and appropriate level of investment in CSR, as it would with any other investments. A firm introducing a CSR-based strategy might only sustain high returns on their investment if their CSR-based strategy were inimitable by their competitors. In competitive markets, a firm introducing a CSR-based strategy might only sustain high returns on their investment and there may only be a short-lived strategic competitive advantage to implementing CSR as their competitors may adopt similar strategies. There is, however, a long-term advantage in that competitors may also imitate CSR-based strategies in a socially responsible way. Even if a firm chooses CSR for strategic financial gain, the firm is also acting responsibly. Attention to CSR as an element in corporate strategy leads to examining CSR activities through the lens of the resource-based-view (RBV) of the firm. RBV presumes that firms are bundles of heterogeneous resources and capabilities that are imperfectly mobile across firms. Accordingly, the imperfect mobility of heterogeneous resources can result in competitive advantages for firms that have superior resources or capabilities.

17.4.2 Social Accounting, Auditing, and Reporting: Social accounting emphasizes the notion of corporate accountability. It is an approach to reporting a firm's activities which stresses the need for the identification of socially relevant behaviour, the determination of those to whom the company is accountable for its social performance and the development of appropriate measures and reporting techniques.

17.4.3 Social License: Social license generally refers to a local community's acceptance or approval of a company's project or ongoing presence in an area. It is increasingly recognized by various stakeholders and communities as a prerequisite to development. The development of social license occurs outside of formal permitting or regulatory processes, and requires sustained investment by proponents to acquire and maintain social capital within the context of trust-based relationships. Often intangible and informal, social license can nevertheless be realized through a robust suite of actions cantered on timely and effective communication, meaningful dialogue, and ethical and responsible behaviour.

Local conditions, needs, and customs vary considerably and are often opaque, but have a significant impact on the likely success of various approaches to building social capital and trust. These regional and cultural differences demand a flexible and responsive approach and must be understood early in order to enable the development and implementation of an effective strategy to earn and maintain social license. Governments could facilitate the necessary stakeholder mapping in regions for which they are responsible and provide a regulatory framework that sets companies on the right path for engagement with communities and stakeholders.

Social media tools empower stakeholders and communities to access and share information on company behaviours, technologies, and projects as they are implemented around the world. Understanding and managing this reality will be important for companies seeking social license. Voluntary measures integral to corporate-responsibility frameworks contribute to achieving social license, particularly through enhancing a company's reputation and strengthening its capacity for effective communication, engagement, and collaboration. However, such measures do not obviate the need for project-specific action to earn and maintain social license.

17.5 Principle of Triple Bottom Line (TBL)

People, planet, profit (also known as the *triple bottom line*) are words that should be used and practiced in every move an organization makes. People relates to fair and beneficial business practices toward labour, the community and region where corporation conducts its business. Planet refers to sustainable environmental practices. A triple bottom line company does not produce harmful or destructive products such as weapons, toxic chemicals or batteries containing dangerous heavy metals. Profit is the economic value created by the organization after deducting the cost of all inputs, including the cost of the capital tied up. It therefore differs from traditional accounting definitions of profit.

The main principles involving corporate social responsibility involve economic, legal, ethical and discretionary aspects. A corporation needs to generate profits, while operating within the laws of the state. The corporation also needs to be ethical, but has the right to be discretional about the decisions it makes. Levels of corporate social responsiveness to an issue include being reactive, defensive, responsive and interactive. All these terms are useful in management issues. Selecting when and how to act can make a difference in the outcome of the action taken.

Increasingly, corporations are motivated to become more socially responsible because their most important stakeholders expect them to understand and address the social and community issues that are relevant to them. Understanding what causes are important to employees is usually the first priority because of the many interrelated business benefits that can be derived from increased employee engagement (i.e. more loyalty, improved recruitment, increased retention, higher productivity, and so on). Key external stakeholders include customers, investors (particularly institutional investors), communities in the areas where the corporation operates its facilities, regulators, academics, and the media.

17.6 Potential Business Benefits of CSR

The definition of CSR used within an organization can vary from the strict *stakeholder impacts* definition used by many CSR advocates and will often include charitable efforts and volunteering. CSR may be based within the human resources, business development or public relations departments of an organisation, or may be given a separate unit reporting to the CEO or in some cases directly to the board. Some companies may implement CSR-type values without a clearly defined team or programme.

The scale and nature of the benefits of CSR for an organization can vary depending on the nature of the enterprise, and are difficult to quantify, though there is a large body of literature exhorting business to adopt measures beyond financial ones.

17.6.1 Human Resources: A CSR programme can be an aid to recruitment and retention, particularly within the competitive graduate student market. Potential recruits often ask about a firm's CSR policy during an interview, and having a comprehensive policy can give an advantage. CSR can also help improve the perception of a company among its staff, particularly when staff can become involved through payroll giving, fundraising activities or community volunteering. CSR has been found to encourage customer orientation among frontline employees.

17.6.2 Risk Management: Managing risk is a central part of many corporate strategies. Reputations that take decades to build up can be ruined in hours through incidents such as corruption scandals or environmental accidents. These can also draw unwanted attention from regulators, courts, governments and media. Building a genuine culture of *doing the right thing* within a corporation can offset these risks.

The desire of enterprises to improve their risk management is a powerful factor behind CSR. Enterprises generally agree that CSR helps them in managing their risks, their intangible assets, their internal processes, and their relations with internal and external stakeholders. Although most businesses support the assumption of a positive impact of CSR on competitiveness, particularly in the long term, they are however not able to quantify this effect.

17.6.3 Brand Differentiation: In crowded marketplaces, companies strive for a unique selling proposition that can separate them from the competition in the minds of consumers. CSR can play a role in building customer loyalty based on distinctive ethical values.

17.6.4 Relationship between Enterprises and Society: The potential of CSR policies to strengthen the symbiotic relationship between enterprises and society needs to be tapped in areas such as sustainable growth, education and social cohesion. CSR can support the creation of an atmosphere of trust within companies, which leads to a stronger commitment of employees and higher innovation performance. A similar atmosphere of trust in co-operation among other stakeholders (business partners, suppliers, and consumers) can increase the external innovation performance. Consumer confidence fostered through CSR can be a major contributor to economic growth. More specifically, through CSR practices, enterprises can play an important role in preventing and combating corruption and bribery, and discouraging the use of enterprises for money laundering and criminal activities financing.

CSR policies can also boost the societal benefit that enterprises create with regard to innovation. Innovative practices aiming at better jobs, safer and employee-friendly workplaces, gender mainstreaming and the innovation or technology transfer to local communities and developing countries, leading to a more equitable economic and social development, are further examples of societal benefits created by innovative enterprises. Indeed, CSR can play a positive role in fostering development by helping to establish a dialogue among public authorities, social partners, civil society and companies.

17.6.5 Business-to-business Good Practices: The exchange of experience and good practices about CSR between companies, can serve as an important tool to develop the concept further. It can help businesses to acquaint themselves with the concept, to benchmark their position against competitors and to build up a consensus about its instruments, such as reporting standards or verification procedures. These exchanges could be particularly beneficial at sectoral level, where they can play an important role is identifying common challenges and options for co-operation among competitors. Such co-operation could reduce the costs of adopting CSR and help to create a level-playing field.

17.6.6 Developing Management Skills: The importance of education and training of managers, employees, and other actors to promote CSR cannot be undermined. The education system, at all levels, has a crucial role to play in the fostering of social responsibility in citizens, including those who are working—or will work—in the world of business or outside it. It can fulfil this role by enabling citizens to understand and appreciate social, environmental and ethical values and equipping them to take informed decisions. Education and training in the field of business administration have particular relevance to CSR in this context, and the encouragement of an effective dialogue between the worlds of business and education on this subject can contribute to the promotion of CSR principles and practices.

17.6.7 Cleaner Technologies: One of the fundamental objectives under CSR includes sound and progressive environmental principles. Experience shows that undertakings, which follow sound environmental standards are, in medium and long-term, more competitive on the international market, as environmental standards promote innovation and modernisation of processes and products and lead to cleaner technologies. Conversely it may also be that internationally competitive firms are better able to invest in newer, more efficient and cleaner technologies.

The importance of environmental technologies, and their ability to contribute both to the profitability of individual firms and to the competitiveness of the economy has been highly stressed. In particular, the use of cleaner 'integrated' technologies are often associated with improved process efficiency and can provide savings for the firm thanks to improved resource efficiency, reduced waste etc. This provides clear guidance for action by enterprises willing to improve their environmental performance.

CSR has partly evolved in response to consumer demands and expectations. Consumers, in their purchasing behaviour, increasingly require information and reassurance that their wider interests, such as environmental and social concerns, are being taken into account. Enterprises are increasingly sensitive to these demands both to retain existing customers and to attract new customers.

Consumers and their representative organisations have therefore an important role to play in the evolution of CSR. If CSR is to continue to serve its purpose, strong lines of communication between enterprises and consumers need to be created.

17.6.8 Other Benefits: In addition to the above-mentioned, an organization can reap the following benefits out of CSR:

1. It can enhanced brand image and reputation.
2. There have been enough instances where CSR has added new customers to companies. Typical example would be health awareness programmes which generate need for related products.
3. CSR not only adds to the reputation of the brand but also gives confidence to the customers that they are dealing with responsible, long-term institutions and not short-term operators.
4. CSR can forge partnerships with other organizations

Thus, an increasing number of firms have embraced a culture of CSR. Only competitive and profitable enterprises are able to make a long-term contribution to sustainable development by generating wealth and jobs without compromising the social and environmental needs of society. In fact, only profitable firms are sustainable and have better chances to adopt/develop responsible practices.

The role of enterprise policy is to help create a business environment, which supports sustainable economic growth. Its objective is to ensure a balanced approach to sustainable development, which maximises synergies between its economic, social and environmental dimensions. Another key element is to support businesses in enhancing their competitiveness and in meeting the challenges of the transition to the knowledge economy.

17.7 Pressure for CSR

Now-a-days across the globe, companies are under massive pressure from their shareholders, investors, media, NGOs as well as their customers to carry out business in a responsible and ethical manner. Recently, several initiatives have been initiated to promote CSR practices around the globe. For instance, United Nations Environment Programme-Finance Initiative (UNEP-FI) was launched in 1990s to promote sustainable development within the framework of market mechanisms. Likewise, Bank Tract Network was formed by global coalition of NGOs to promote sustainable finance. State regulatory bodies, media, NGOs, customers have significantly addressed social responsibility issues in banking sector.

Likewise, international organization such as the World Bank also frequently exert pressures on banks to analyse social and environmental risks involved in projects to be financed. In addition to this, CSR practices of an organization have significant impact on its reputation and resultant profitability. Many researchers have found positive correlation between CSR and financial performance of the organization. Some researchers have also proved a negative impact of socially irresponsible operation on share prices and brand reputation of a bank. Around the globe, banking industry is showing a good commitment to CSR principles. Banks have exhibited conscious efforts to comply with the relevant provisions to reduce the regulatory action through depicting a good environmental citizen's image.

17.7.1 Public Policies: CSR has inspired national governments to include CSR issues into their national public policy agendas. The increased importance driven by CSR, has prompted governments to promote socially and environmentally responsible corporate practices. Over the years, governments have considered CSR as a public issue that requires national governmental involvement to address the very issues relevant to CSR. The heightened role of government in CSR has facilitated the development of numerous CSR programmes and policies.

While the interests of shareholders and the actions of managers of any business enterprise have to be governed by the laws of economics, requiring an adequate financial return on investments made, in reality the operations of an enterprise need to be driven by a much larger set of objectives that are today being defined under the term CSR.

The broad rationale for a new set of ethics for corporate decision-making, which clearly constructs and upholds a company's social responsibility arises from the fact that a business enterprise derives several benefits from society, which must, therefore, require the enterprise to provide returns to society as well. Of course, the system of taxation in most countries does ensure that basic services provided by government—such as a system of law and order, provision of infrastructure that includes assets such as roads, transportation facilities, the benefits received from the apparatus of society for respecting and enforcing property rights etc.—are paid for through taxation on economic goods and services produced and consumed. However, there are other aspects of services provided by society that have now become even more important than traditional relationship between government and business. These go far beyond what was the case a few decades ago.

17.8 Convergence and Transparency of CSR Practices and Tools

The need for transparent and proactive communication of CSR is a key issue of concern. Much of the demand for CSR disclosure may be viewed as the result of public desire for information on which to base an opinion about whether or not a corporation is appropriate or right and proper, i.e. to evaluate corporate legitimacy. Many corporations voluntarily disclose social information. These disclosures may take the form of management discussion in annual reports, or separate disclosures in social, sustainability or environmental reports. Largely, the format, content and detail of such disclosures are unregulated.

CSR relates to a very wide range of company activities. This is particularly the case when an enterprise operates in several countries and has to adapt its activities to the specific situations in these countries. This diversity has helped to create an impressive richness of voluntary enterprise initiatives, which often include innovative elements, but also implies challenges, namely the lack of transparency and comparability.

Transparency is a key element of the CSR debate as it helps businesses to improve their practices and behaviour. Transparency also enables businesses and third parties to measure the results achieved. CSR benchmarks against which the social and environmental performance of businesses can be measured and compared are useful to provide transparency and facilitate an effective and credible benchmarking. The interest in benchmarks has resulted in an increase of guidelines, principles and codes in recent years.

Several market-driven international multi-stakeholder initiatives are emerging, which work towards convergence and transparency in the area of CSR. The areas where initiatives have been taken to promote CSR are as under:

1. Codes of conduct.
2. Management standards.
3. Socially responsible investment.

17.8.1 Codes of Conduct: The increasing public interest in the social and environmental impact and ethical standards of industry has moved many companies, in particular those of the consumer goods sector, to adopt codes of conduct relating to labour issues, human rights and the environment.

Codes of conduct are innovative and important instruments for the promotion of fundamental human, labour and environmental rights, and anti-corruption practices, especially in countries where public authorities fail to enforce minimum standards.

The biggest challenge related to codes is to ensure that they are effectively implemented, monitored and verified. Special attention should be given to implementing codes in respect of workers in the informal sector and sub-contractors and in the free-trade zones.

The codes of conducts should include appropriate mechanisms for evaluation and verification of their implementation, as well as a system of compliance.

17.8.2 Management Standards: Faced with a widening range of complex issues in areas such as labour practices and supplier relations, businesses, regardless of sector, size, structure or maturity, would benefit from the inclusion of social and environmental issues into their daily operations. In this context, CSR management systems—like Total Quality Management systems—could allow enterprises to have a clear picture of their social and environmental impacts, and help them to target the significant ones and manage them well.

The Eco-management and Audit Scheme (EMAS), for example, allows voluntary participation in an environmental management scheme. It is a scheme for companies and other organisations that are willing to commit themselves to evaluate, manage and improve their environmental and economic performance. In addition, active involvement of employees is a driving force for EMAS and a contribution to the social management of organisations.

17.8.3 Socially Responsible Investment (SRI): For SRI to contribute to the promotion of CSR, the development by rating organisations of criteria and indicators which identify the factors of competitive advantage and business success of socially responsible enterprises is essential.

Registration statements and prospectuses issued at the time of an IPO (initial public offering), can be another useful source of information on social and environmental risks allowing the prospective investor to assess the overall risks associated with a business.

Deeply-rooted societal changes such as increasing participation of women in the labour market should be reflected in CSR, adapting structural changes and changing the work environment in order to create more balanced conditions for both genders acknowledging the valuable contribution of women as strategies which will benefit the society as well as the enterprise itself.

SRI has come to stay with the creation of many funds that invest only on companies that exhibit socially responsible behaviour and preliminary evidence suggests that such funds are providing excellent returns to their customers.

Recently, institutions like the Global Reporting Initiative have come out with elaborate guidelines for preparing social or sustainability reports. These guidelines have been taken up by many organizations as a framework to build their social reports. In Asia, Japan has made significant strides in building such corporate social reporting initiatives, but other countries like India and China have a very limited number of companies, and that too in select industries like oil, chemicals and steel, providing social reporting. However, the contents of such reporting, particularly in countries like India, remain relatively understudied. Many aspects of CSR reporting in these countries still remain unintelligible. In most of the studies, the areas of social responsibility have been identified as environment, equal opportunity, community involvement and development and each one of these areas has been further sub-divided into specific indicators.

CSR-oriented financial institutions have robust stakeholder engagement programmes to solve complex sustainability challenges, provide input into business strategy, and keep abreast of stakeholder concerns. While the debate starts to gather steam over the degree to which financial institutions have a responsibility to advance sustainability, best practice CSR financial institutions are playing a lead role to promote sustainable practices within their operations, and to their consumers and the public at large. Best practice CSR financial institutions are treating sustainability as a business strategy and opportunity—not as an add-on, feel-good charitable endeavour.

They are developing strategic CSR policies and programmes across a range of social and environmental areas to reduce or offset their negative, and boost their positive, direct and indirect impacts.

17.9 Challenges in Promoting CSR

The challenges to CSR practices among enterprises stem from insufficient knowledge about the relationship between CSR and business performance. Also, there is lack of consensus among various parties involved on an adequate concept taking account of the global dimension of CSR, in particular the diversity in domestic policy frameworks in the world. Besides, there is lack of teaching and training about the role of CSR, especially in commercial and management schools.

Focussing the strategy on the following areas would help in wider diffusion of CSR:
1. Increasing knowledge about the positive impact of CSR on business and societies.
2. Developing the exchange of experience and good practices on CSR between enterprises.
3. Promoting the development of CSR management skills.

4. Facilitating convergence and transparency of CSR practices and tools.
5. Integrating CSR into community policies.

CSR has found recognition among enterprises, policy-makers and other stakeholders, as an important element of new and emerging forms of governance, which can help them to respond to the following fundamental changes:

1. Globalisation has created new opportunities for enterprises, but it has also increased their organisational complexity and the increasing extension of business activities abroad has led to new responsibilities on a global scale, particularly in developing countries.
2. Considerations of image and reputation play an increasingly important role in the business competitive environment, as consumers and NGOs ask for more information about the conditions in which products and services are generated and the sustainability impact thereof, and tend to reward, with their behaviour, socially and environmentally responsible firms.
3. Partly as a consequence of this, financial stakeholders ask for the disclosure of information going beyond traditional financial reporting so as to allow them to better identify the success and risk factors inherent in a company and its responsiveness to public opinion.
4. As knowledge and innovation become increasingly important for competitiveness, enterprises have a higher interest in retaining highly skilled and competent personnel.

17.10 Criticisms and Concerns

Critics of CSR as well as proponents debate a number of concerns related to it. These include relationship of CSR to the fundamental purpose and nature of business and questionable motives for engaging in CSR, including concerns about insincerity and hypocrisy.

Proponents argue that corporations make more long-term profits by operating with a perspective, while critics argue that CSR distracts from the economic role of businesses. Some argue that CSR is merely window-dressing, or an attempt to pre-empt the role of governments as a watchdog over powerful multinational corporations.

It is argued that a corporation's purpose is to maximize returns to its shareholders. Corporations are only responsible to their shareholders and not to society as a whole. Some people perceive CSR as incongruent with the very nature and purpose of business, and indeed a hindrance to free trade.

Critics of this argument perceive free market as opposed to the well-being of society and a hindrance to human freedom. They claim that the type of capitalism practiced in many developing countries is a form of economic and cultural imperialism, noting that these countries usually have fewer labour protections, and thus their citizens are at a higher risk of exploitation by multinational corporations.

Critics concerned with corporate hypocrisy and insincerity generally suggest that better governmental and international regulation and enforcement, rather than voluntary measures, are necessary to ensure that companies behave in a socially responsible manner.

17.11 CSR in India

CSR developed very slowly in India though it was started a long time ago. CSR has been assuming greater importance in the corporate world, including the banking sector. There is a visible trend in the financial sector of promoting environment- friendly and socially responsible lending and investment practices.

Presently, there is a growing perception among enterprises that sustainable business success and shareholder value cannot be achieved solely through maximising short-term profits, but instead through market-oriented yet responsible behaviour. Companies are aware that they can contribute to sustainable development by managing the operations in such a way as to enhance economic growth and increase competitiveness while ensuring environmental protection and promoting social responsibility, including consumer interests.

The increasing relevance of CSR in India has stemmed from the fact that a business cannot succeed by ignoring the human and social needs of society. In this age of widespread communication and growing emphasis on transparency, customers of any product or service are unlikely to feel satisfied in buying from a company that is seen to violate the expectations of ethical and socially responsible behaviour.

Therefore, companies that pay genuine attention to the principles of socially responsible behaviour are favoured by the public and preferred for their goods and services. In the Indian context, protection of the environment and country's natural resources would certainly be of paramount importance in understanding this concept with regards to sustainable development. Nevertheless, what would be equally important is the need to ensure that society does not suffer from disparities of income and provision of basic services like health care, education and literacy.

Consequently, if corporate actions are to target the most fundamental problems (poverty, illiteracy etc.) become guideposts for corporate social strategy and action.

It is important to mention here that the progress and welfare of society is not merely the responsibility of governments alone. In an effective sense it involves appropriate actions by all stakeholders, of which the corporate sector is extremely important. Hence, actions to address some of these basic challenges also become important for leaders of business and industry.

The objectives of sustainable development rest within the principles of CSR, because unless the needs of society, both present and future, are served, sustainable development would remain only a myth. And the most significant step in pursuing CSR is to proactively protect the environment.

CSR in India is still characterized mainly by philanthropic and community development activities and Indian companies and stakeholders have begun to adopt some aspects of the mainstream agenda, such as the integration of CSR into their business processes and engagement in multi-stakeholder dialogues. Companies Act, 2013 makes an effort to introduce the culture of corporate social responsibility (CSR) in Indian corporates by requiring companies to formulate a corporate social responsibility policy and at least incur a given minimum expenditure on social activities.

18

Industrial Pollution and Environmental Protection

Productivity of an economic system depends, to a large extent, on the supply and quality of its natural resources. In fact, natural and environmental resources are the basis of all economic activities. Soil, forests, mines, water, air and other natural resources are productive assets of an economy. Poor quality of water and air adversely affects the health of population, causing reduced labour productivity and premature mortality. Similarly, soil degradation and erosion leads to reduced and inferior quality of agricultural output.

18.1 Conflict between Development and Environment

Economic development often depends on the utilisation and conversion of natural resources into useful goods and services. This process of consumption and conversion uses energy, minerals and other natural resources such as air, water, land and biodiversity. It also produces wastes which are released into environment with adverse impacts.

Economic activities, in turn, affect the quantity and quality of natural and environmental resources. Mining, lumbering, manufacturing, fishing and a host of other economic activities change the stock of natural resources which calls for appropriate trade-off between the needs of present and future generations.

Increase in economic activities—due to growing population and/or enhanced consumption levels—often impacts environment negatively. Degradation of natural resources and losses in environmental quality adversely affect people at large. As a consequence of high level of economic activities, emissions, effluents and waste discharges exceed the carrying capacity of different resources. Economic growth without environmental considerations can cause serious damage to the quality of life of the present and future generations. It is in this context that economists distinguish between economic growth and economic development. Economic growth means sustained increase in per capita real income. Economic development is a much wider term. It includes economic growth and at the same time encompasses questions regarding patterns of production, distribution of national income, consumption behaviour of the people and concern for environment.

Economic progress improves our standard of living and makes our life more comfortable. On the other hand, it is this very progress that can lead to degradation of the environment. Any increase in national income would arise only from increased production of goods and services involving greater consumption of resources such as land, forest, fuels etc. whose supply is, essentially, limited. While some of these resources may be renewable, others get depleted and, ultimately, exhausted with continuous use. Any attempt to preserve the non-renewable resources might require compromising on the growth rates.

The conflict between economic development and environment is, essentially, a conflict between short- and long-run priorities, between the interests of current and future generations. Large exploitation of natural resources today, while increasing the economic growth for the current generations, would lead to gradual exhaustion and degradation of these resources, thereby reducing their availability to our future generations and adversely affecting their output, income and living standards.

18.1.1 Environmental Pollution: Demographic expansion, over exploitation of natural resources, mega development projects—with least concern for `sustainability and conservation—have greatly affected the environment. The magnitude and alterations that humanity can make to environment, threaten to undermine the basic natural process that sustains biosphere. The process of economic development necessarily entails exploitations of natural resources. However, when such exploitation becomes indiscriminate and is undertaken without adequate environmental safeguards, the consequences can be disastrous.

Pollution can be defined as an undesirable change in the physical, chemical, or biological characteristics of the air, water or land that can harmfully affect health, survival or activities of human beings or other living organisms. Pollution refers essentially to a process by which a resource is rendered unfit for some beneficial use. Of the various kinds of pollution (air, water, land, noise, radiation and odour) that affect the quality of life in India, water pollution is by far the most serious in its implications for the health and well-being of the people.

Environmental pollution is one of the major problems faced by the world community, especially in the cities of the developing countries which have experienced unbridled growth of population, urbanization and industrialization. Municipal services—such as water supply and sanitation, drainage of storm water, management of solid and hazardous wastes, supply of adequate and safe food and housing—are unable to keep pace with urban growth. The unplanned location of industries in and around urban areas and volume of traffic have caused serious pollution problems. All these factors have led to deteriorating environmental conditions, adversely impacting the health of the people.

Pollution has become a major threat to the very existence of mankind on this earth. Pollution of various resources has gone to such an extent that people are unable to breathe fresh air and drink fresh water. True, advancements in science and technology have added to human comforts by way of automobiles, electrical appliances, supersonic jets, modern medicines, communications and entertainment. However, these blessings have been diluted by serious problems posed by ecological imbalances and climate changes.

Environmental degradation not only affects us but also has repercussions for future generations. Globally, the need for sustainable development is being emphasized. Sustainable development attempts to strike a balance between the demands of economic development and the need for protection of our natural environment.

18.21 Mining Activities and Ecological Balance

Minerals are valuable natural resources being finite and non-renewable. They constitute the vital raw materials for many basic industries and are a major resource for development. The metallurgical and mineral industries constitute the core of the industrial sector as they provide the basic raw material for most of the industries. The metallurgical industries are highly capital-intensive. They are also energy-intensive and highly polluting, and make large demands on the infrastructural sector in terms of coal, power and railway transportation. The efficiency of use of various inputs in the metallurgical industries is, therefore, of paramount importance as it has a significant impact on the rate of growth of the economy. Due attention should be paid to adopting more effective measures for environmental protection and restoring ecological balance.

Sustainable development has become a global agenda. Like other development-related activities, mineral exploration and exploitation also adversely affect the environment. For sustainable development, the key issue is managing natural resources including minerals optimally without disturbing the ecological balance and containing natural hazards.

The role of earth scientists has, therefore, become important, especially since environment problems cannot be resolved in isolation through engineering solutions only or even through legal and administrative actions. In the domain of environment and earth system studies, one of the goals will have to be continued updating of the geo-scientific database.

Mineral development is one of a number of competing land uses. Due to lack of planning and other frameworks to balance and manage possible uses there are problems and disagreements in the matter of control, use, and management of land. Exploration and mining pose significant challenges in terms of land access and management. The most appropriate use of land is best decided within an integrated land planning framework that balances competing interests such as between national and local levels or between mining and conservation. There are trade-offs that may be made in order to generate benefits in one domain, but decisions on these should not be taken without inclusion of and negotiation with all those likely to be directly affected. A broad consensus must be achieved on the management of protected areas (e.g. forests) and the trade-offs involved. The local stake in the success of protected areas and resources available to manage them needs to be ensured.

The decision whether or not to mine a certain area should be undertaken through a democratic decision-making process and should be based on an integrated assessment of ecological, environmental, economic, and social impacts. The planning process will be more effective in the presence of equitable and inclusive rules of tenure, compensation schemes for those affected, and strong governance, including mechanisms for arbitration where necessary.

Mitigation of natural hazards, including landslides, is one area where geo-scientists can play an effective role. For this, gathering of base-line geological data and related information, its critical analysis and monitoring will be the key to understanding the basic physical processes which cause the phenomenon, its area of influence and the magnitude of impact.

18.3 Sustainable Development: The Balancing Act

The concept of sustainable development is inextricably linked with environment protection. It is a strategy for improving the quality of human life while living within the carrying capacity of supporting eco system. It is clear from the above definition that sustainable development entails commitment, protection and preservation.

Sustainable development is that which meets the needs of the present without compromising the ability of future generations. The heaviest burden in international economic adjustment has been carried by the world's poorest population. The consequence has been the considerable increase in human distress and over exploitation of land and water resources to ensure survival in the short term. Further, the desire to solve all social and human problems at one stroke has influenced the pace of development. Its reaction is visible in the atmosphere and in natural, physical and social environment. Awareness regarding the consequences of this event has developed into a consensus referred to as ecological concern.

Sustainable development advocates economic progress in an environmentally responsible manner. Sustainable development attempts to strike a balance between the requirements of economic development and the need for protection of the environment. It seeks to combine the elements of economic efficiency, inter-generational equity, social concerns and environmental protection. Although, the term sustainable development has many interpretations, it generally refers to non-declining human well-being over time.

Economic growth and development have to be guided by the compulsion of sustainability, because no country can afford to ignore the economic as well as the environmental threat that a fast-deteriorating ecosystem poses to its economy. No country is immune to the reality of climate change, ecological degradation, depletion of the ozone layer and contamination of freshwater.

Sustainable development is a difficult balancing act in countries with low incomes. Society has to simultaneously accomplish three things with trade-offs: improve economic well-being with social justice for the present generation, yet manage with more restrained use of land, air, forest, energy, and water resources, and protect future generations. The choices are more difficult in developing countries because they affect people's livelihoods. Such a 'stewardship' to succeed therefore needs to respond to people's needs, share information on choices and costs, and ensure participation and ownership.

18.3.1 Environmental Economics: Environmental economics is a branch of economics which deals with the inter-relationships between environment and development. Environmental economics examines the interface between economic agents and environment. Economic activities of human beings have a profound impact on natural environment. Hence, use/abuse of natural resources has raised many moral, legal and practical questions for present and future generations. There has been a gradual shift in many developed countries from command and control type of policy approach to environmental policy goals. Presently, many governments require cost-benefit analysis of policy options with regard to changes in environmental legislations by resetting environmental standards and introducing new policy instruments for environmental protection. Environmental economics has also made significant contributions to valuation techniques and design of new policy instruments for pollution control and management.

It is often said that gross domestic product (GDP) is not the best way of measuring the true well-being of nations, because the pursuit of growth can be at the cost of the environment. Conventional ways of measuring GDP in terms of production do not take into account the environmental damage caused by production of goods and services. Only after GDP is adjusted for environmental costs that growth of adjusted GDP can be called a measure of the increase in total production in the economy. There is obviously a two-way relationship between environment and economic growth. Natural resources and raw materials such as water, timber and minerals directly provide inputs for the production of goods and services.

18.3.2 Environmental Management: Due to its cross-cutting nature, and wide local and global stakeholder base, environmental governance needs to be strategic. An ideal framework should be anticipative, technically oriented, cognizant of legal issues, geo-politically relevant and forward-looking, capable of maximising national interests and progressive enough to make a social impact. Most importantly, management of the environment should include progressively adapting/changing actions that rely on sound scientific, technological, human-cognitive and collaborative principles.

18.3.3 Green Growth: Green growth involves rethinking growth strategies with regard to their impact on environmental sustainability and the environmental resources available to poor and vulnerable groups. It is significant to note that many stimulus packages announced globally to combat recession incorporated a green component. International experience is that green growth promotes inclusivity. Further, the renewable energy sector is relatively labour-intensive, with the potential for generating more jobs than the oil and gas industries.

Environment must not be considered as just another sector of national development. It should form a crucial guiding dimension for plans and programmes in each sector. This becomes clear only if the concern for environmental protection is understood in its proper context. Ecological degradation compromises the quality of life in the long-run.

A. Requirements of Green Growth: Low-carbon green growth is a pattern of development that decouples economic growth from carbon emissions, pollution and resource use, and promotes growth through the creation of new environment-friendly products, industries and business models that also improve people's quality of life. Thus, low-carbon green growth entails the following:

1. Using less energy, improving the efficiency with which resources are used and moving to low-carbon energy sources.
2. Protecting and promoting the sustainable use of natural resources such as forests and peat lands.
3. Designing and disseminating low-carbon technologies and business models to reinvigorate local economies.
4. Implementing policies and incentives which discourage carbon intensive practices.

Green growth is not anti-growth. Rather, it represents a change in how we manage economies to reflect a broader conception of what constitutes effective and sustainable growth. Environmental assets—water, land, air, ecosystems and the services they provide—represent a significant share of a country's wealth. Just like physical and human capital, natural capital requires investment, maintenance, and good management if it is to be productive and fully contribute to prosperity.

Green growth requires policies that are on their own terms good for growth, as well as for the environment, such as reforming energy subsidies or trade barriers that protect pollution-intensive sectors. It entails politically difficult reforms in the patterns of pricing, regulation, and public investment, and it calls for complex changes in behaviours and social norms. Importantly, green growth requires knowing when to go for the politically expedient rather than the economically optimal.

B. Advantages of Green Growth: The amount of CO_2 a country emits into the atmosphere depends on a wide range of factors, including the size of its economy, the level of industrialization, and the efficiency of its energy use, as well as population, lifestyle choices and land use changes. As a consequence of rapid and carbon-intensive growth, the Asian region has been fast becoming a major source of greenhouse gas emissions. The transition to a low-carbon economy will benefit emerging Asia in the following ways:

1. Many low-carbon interventions have important co-benefits for Asia at different levels, including the enhanced energy security associated with energy efficiency (on both the supply and demand side) and renewable energy projects. Human health benefits from interventions that reduce air pollutants, such as those from transport; and the environmental benefits that can be achieved through forestry and agricultural management, waste reduction programmes and employment programmes.

2. Interventions, which have positive economic rates of return and short pay-back time and should be undertaken irrespective of climate change considerations, can contribute substantially to the economic development of emerging Asian countries.

3. Asian countries that pursue low-carbon development, including the transfer of financial resources through the carbon market and new public programmes that support the reduction of emissions are likely to reap strategic and competitive advantage at the regional and international levels.

4. Emerging countries of Asia are likely to suffer disproportionately from the impacts of climate change (drought, increased severity of tropical storms, sea level rise, etc). Asia has a strong interest in becoming a leading participant in global efforts on both emissions reduction and adaptation.

5. Low-carbon green growth will become more important as countries seek to take a pro-poor, pro-employment economic development path based on innovation.

6. Emerging Asia will have real social gains in the low-carbon green growth process by involving local communities to promote equity and fairness, along with improved air quality and other eco-system services.

7. Emerging Asia will become a leader in key green technologies and business models, and an important destination for the commercialization of key low-carbon technologies, green products and services.

8. Emerging Asia will be able to sweep away the short-term developmental thinking

that has plagued the past several decades and replace it with paths delivering development that flourishes within ecological limits.

Low-carbon green growth is a unique opportunity to invest in change. Many analysts believe that the sooner emerging Asian countries take advantage of low-carbon green growth, the better it will be for their long-term development prospects, economic restructuring and their quest to find new drivers of growth. Even though the transition to a low-carbon green growth paradigm is a long-term process, the following years are crucial for Asia to seize the economic, social and environmental opportunities, gain competitive advantage and show global leadership through regional cooperation.

18.3.4 Inclusive Green Growth: Sustainable development has three pillars: economic, environmental, and social sustainability. We cannot presume that green growth is inherently inclusive. Green growth policies must be carefully designed to maximize benefits for, and minimize costs to, the poor and most vulnerable, and policies and actions with irreversible negative impacts must be avoided.

Rapid growth is necessary to meet the urgent development needs of the world's poor. However, growth will be unsustainable in the long-run unless it is both socially inclusive and green—the latter by ensuring that the earth's natural assets are able to adequately provide the resources and environmental services on which humans depend. Inclusive green growth requires tackling political economy constraints, overcoming deeply entrenched behaviours and social norms, and developing innovative financing instruments to change incentives and promote innovation, and thus address the market, policy, and institutional failures that lead to the overuse of natural assets. Greener growth is necessary, efficient, and affordable. It should focus on what needs to happen in the next 20 to 30 years to avoid getting locked into unsustainable paths and causing irreversible environmental damage.

Economic and social sustainability, on the one hand, and social and environmental sustainability, on the other, have been found to be not only compatible, but also largely complementary. Not so with economic and environmental sustainability, as growth has come largely at the expense of the environment which is why green growth aims to ensure that economic and environmental sustainability are compatible.

18.4 Economic Instruments for Promoting Sustainable Development

The role of economic instruments in financing and promoting sustainable development is well recognised. The following economic instruments can help achieve sustainable development through their influence on behavioural patterns leading to sustainable consumption and production in the economy:

18.4.1 Environmental Taxes: An environment or green tax is imposed on a product that damages the environment, in an attempt to reduce its production or consumption. Well-designed environmental taxes and other economic instruments can play an important role in ensuring that prices reflect environmental costs, in line with the *polluter pays principle*. Environmental taxes can be simple and efficient financial instruments for improving the productivity of natural resources. Environmental taxes on water and fossil fuels need not be part of the general revenues of the Government. Rather they should be directly ploughed back into environmentally sustainable action on these fronts. Coal Cess is a good example of environment tax imposed by Government of India in recent times, whose proceeds are channelled to the National Clean Energy Fund. Some benefits of environment taxation are enumerated below:

1. They provide incentives for measures that protect the environment, and deter actions that lead to environmental damage.
2. Economic instruments such as taxes can enable environmental goals to be achieved at the lowest cost, and in the most efficient way.
3. By internalizing environmental costs into prices, they help signal the structural economic changes needed to move to a more sustainable economy.
4. They can encourage innovation and development of new technology.
5. The revenue raised by environmental taxes can be used to reduce the level of other taxes. This could help reduce distortions, while raising the efficiency with which resources are used in the economy.

18.4.2 Subsidies: There has been a growing recognition of fiscal and environmental implications of the subsidy policies in energy, water and agriculture sectors. Most of these subsidies pose a threat to the environment. For example, in India the subsidy on diesel has distorted the use of energy in transport and industrial sectors, and worsened the problem of hazardous air pollution. Similarly, excessive use of nitrogenous fertilizers and over-drawing of water, backed by subsidies at both Centre and State levels, is playing havoc with the sustainability of soil and water ecosystem.

18.4.3 Non-monetary Incentives: Non-monetary incentives are policy instruments that typically do not have a monetary value, but definitely have a financial impact that promotes sustainability. These incentives can be used as a bargaining tool by the Government to encourage conservation of resources in an economy. Activities such as those encouraging judicious use of water, planting trees, car pooling and avoiding use of plastic bags can be rewarded so that it encourages the practice, and acts as an example for others. Through the initiation of innovative policies and awards, the Government can provide recognition, which will encourage sustainable development amongst the citizens and the firms.

18.4.4 Eco-Industrial Hubs: An eco-industrial park (EIP) or estate is a community of manufacturing and service businesses located together on a common property. Member businesses seek enhanced environmental, economic and social performance through collaboration in managing environmental and resource issues. By working together, the community of businesses seeks a collective benefit that is greater than the sum of individual benefits each company would realise by only optimizing its individual performance.

The goal of an EIP is to improve the economic performance of the participating companies while minimizing their environmental impacts. Components of this approach include green design of the park infrastructure (new or retrofitted); cleaner production; prevention of pollution; energy efficiency and inter-company partnering. An EIP also seeks benefits for neighbouring communities to assure the net impact of its development is positive.

To sum up, sustainable development is a pattern of social and structured economic transformations (i.e. development) which optimizes the economic and social benefits available at present, without jeopardizing the likely potential for similar benefits in the future. The primary goal of sustainable development is to achieve a reasonable and equitable distribution level of economic well being that can be perpetuated continually for the future human generations.

Sustainability is about meeting the needs of the present without compromising the ability of future generations to meet their needs. It is about preserving the environment and biodiversity for future generations, and about being cautious with our natural resources and climate. But sustainability is also about guaranteeing human rights and a life in dignity, free from want and poverty for all people living today.

Developing countries have options other than to *grow dirty and clean up later*. Much that is useful can be done now. Clean air and water and solid waste management are basic needs, and many environmental policies enhance productivity and poverty alleviation. So while poor countries should focus on meeting basic needs and expanding opportunities for growth, they need not do so at the expense of unsustainable environmental degradation. Further, environmental performance does not automatically improve with income, so policy action is needed anyway. Finally, it may be impossible or prohibitively expensive to *clean up later*, either because of the irreversibility of environmental damages like the loss of biodiversity, or because "lock-in" will make subsequent shifts to more environmentally benign structures and processes extremely costly.

Part II
Industrialization in India

19

Indian Industry in Historical Perspective

Prior to Independence in 1947, India was a dependency of the United Kingdom. It consisted of British India, and the Princely States. It encompassed the entire area which now forms the four countries of India, Pakistan, Myanmar, and Bangladesh.

The British came to India as merchants in the middle of the 17th century. After gaining foothold on the coastline, they spread to every corner of the Indian peninsula. They gained political supremacy around the middle of the 18th century. After winning the Battle of Plassey in 1757 and the Battle of Buxer in 1764, they established themselves firmly as the rulers of India and ruled it till 1947 to sub-serve their economic interests.

19.1 Pre-Independence Period

Prior to the colonisation of India, the country had reached significant fineness in the production of luxury products in the form of handicrafts. These luxury goods consisted of cotton, silk, and ivory which had a significant market in Europe. Before mercantilism, these products were exported to the European market and these products were considered very significant in bringing gold, silver and other valuable exchange items into India. During the period of mercantilism, the link between European markets and Indian sub-continent became more direct and trade became easier. The rising import of Indian cotton into Europe created significant competition for the British industry.

The major products exported to Europe included indigo, cotton textiles, spices, silk and pepper. The wealthiest province of Bengal was prominent in textile manufacturing, especially muslin trade. Indian farmers began extensive cultivation of maize and tobacco with increased yields due to improvements in the irrigation system.

At the time of the arrival of the British, Indian economy was, by and large, self-sufficient, possessing a fine balance between agriculture and industry. A large proportion of population, about three-fourths, depended on agriculture which was a subsistence occupation. Agricultural activities were mainly devoted to food crops like paddy, wheat and millets. Most of the food produced in the village was consumed by the village population itself. The raw materials produced fed the handicrafts.

Apart from agriculturists, there were other classes of people in rural areas like weavers, carpenters, potters, oilmen, washer men, cobblers and barbers. All these occupations were hereditary and passed from father to son by tradition. The people engaged in these occupations got paid out of the crops at the time of harvest for the services rendered by them.

There were three distinct classes in the village: (a) agriculturists, (b) village artisans and menials, and (c) village officials. Most of the villages had their *panchayats* (bodies of village elders to settle local disputes). The villages were isolated and self-contained production units, appropriately called by economic historians as *small republics.*

Urban areas were centres of excellence in different crafts, and craftsmen were organised into guilds. There was considerable degree of division of labour and territorial specialisation. The towns were either places of pilgrimage (Allahabad, Benaras, Puri) or seat of a court (Delhi, Lahore, Tanjore) or trading and commercial centres (Mirzapur, Bangalore, Hubli). The muslin of Dhaka, the calicos of Bengal, the *sarees* of Benaras were known even to the foreigners. Urban areas were also well-known for their artistic industries like marble work, jewellery, brass, copper and wood carving works.

19.1.1 Consequences of British Rule: The British rule in India can be divided into two periods: (a) the rule of the East India Company from 1757 to 1858, and (b) the rule of the British Government from 1858 to 1947.

The British interests in India were governed by the requirements of the Industrial Revolution which started in Britain in the middle of the 18th century and then spread to other regions of Europe. These were two-fold: (a) to secure raw materials from India for factories in Britain, and (b) to ensure permanent market in India for the British manufactures. To fulfil these objectives, they adopted the following measures which proved disastrous for the Indian economy.

The British pursued a trade policy which encouraged exports of raw materials and imports of manufactured goods. The farmers were forced, through *zamindars* (landlords) and British agents to switch over from food crops (wheat, paddy, millets) to cash crops (cotton, jute, tobacco, indigo) and sell the latter for exports to Britain. The process of commercialisation of agriculture was intensified by the development of railways. The new land revenue system (explained below) and the commercialisation of agriculture proved suicidal for the Indian economy. The switch over from food crops to cash crops disturbed the balance between the demand and supply of foodgrains, resulting into famines and scarcities.

Prior to Industrial Revolution in Britain, the East India Company concentrated on the export of Indian spices and other manufactured goods like textiles. However, the start of Industrial Revolution reversed the character of India's foreign trade. Due to the policies of the British rulers, India became an exporter of raw materials and importer of manufactured goods.

India's indigenous handicrafts could not stand competition from imported machine-made goods which were relatively cheaper and attractive. The development of roads, railways and communications intensified the competition between indigenous and foreign goods. The opening of Suez Canal in 1869 reduced the transport cost and made the exploitation of the Indian market easier. This led to the decline of handicrafts.

There were other reasons also for the decline of handicrafts. These handicrafts enjoyed patronage from princes, *nawabs,* and *rajas* who gradually lost power to the British. Thus, the disappearance of princely courts proved a set back for handicrafts. Similarly, there grew a class in India which was influenced by western style of living. This led to a change in the pattern of demand. Indigenous goods went out of fashion and the demand for European goods increased.

The destruction of Indian handicrafts had far reaching economic consequences. The artisans lost their hereditary occupation and fell back on agriculture in the absence of any alternative source of employment. They became landless agricultural labourers. The increased pressure of population on land led to progressive sub-division and fragmentation of holdings and high land rents.

19.1.2 Modern Factory System: Though the British were responsible for the decline of handicrafts, they may be credited with the start of modern factory system in India. The period 1850-55 witnessed the establishment of the first cotton mill, first jute mill, and the first railway line in India. By the end of the 19th century there were 194 cotton mills, and 36 jute mills. Mining activities had also picked up. For example, coal production had risen to over 6 million tonnes per annum. In 1905, the *Swadeshi* movement was started which encouraged Indian industries. Between 1890 and 1914, some 70 cotton mills and 30 jute mills were set up in the country. The foundation of iron and steel industry was also laid during this period. The pattern of industrialisation ending with the outbreak of First World War was characterised mainly by the production of export goods like jute and tea in which India enjoyed natural advantage.

The responsibility for promoting modern commerce and industry came to be concentrated in the hands of certain classes in the urban areas, and up to the end of the 19th century the only major large-scale industries which had taken root in the country were cotton and jute textiles. Little attention was paid to improvement of agriculture or to the needs of the rural areas.

While it is true that industries on modern lines were started by the British beginning the middle of the 19th century, the pace of industrialisation was not only slow but lop-sided.

19.1.3 Swadeshi Movement: During the second half of the 19th century, modern industry began to take root in India but its progress remained very slow. Initially, this development was confined to the setting up of cotton and jute textile mills. The cotton textile mills, mainly dominated by Indians, were located in the western parts of the country, namely Maharashtra and Gujarat, while the jute mills dominated by the foreigners were mainly concentrated in Bengal. Subsequently, the iron and steel industries began coming up in the beginning of the 20th century. Tata Iron and Steel Company (TISCO) was incorporated in 1907.

As the National Movement picked up, there was deliberate boycott of foreign goods by the people. At that time many industries were set up to meet the requirements of the people. An example is the Swadeshi Mill, started by Jamshedji Tata after the partition of Bengal in 1905. There was a unity of purpose between the political leaders and the entrepreneurs during the Swadeshi movement. The Swadeshi movement enabled much money to be mobilized and invested in industrial ventures under the control of indigenous management. As the environment became relatively favourable for proper investment, many of the industries proved to be successful and the native trading communities were drawn into industrial enterprises.

19.1.4 First World War (1914-18): Up to the First World War, the opposition of the British Government to industrial development in India was open and unconcealed. However, the war proved to be an eye-opener to them. When the war broke out in 1914, imports from foreign countries had completely ceased and this brought home the need for developing India industrially.

Moreover, it became necessary for the British rulers to make certain political and economic concessions and promises of concessions to secure the co-operation of the Indian people during the war and in the disturbed period following the war.

The outbreak of the First World War exposed the weakness of Britain's strategic position in the East as India had been deprived to develop the most elementary basis of modern industry. In order to impress upon the Indian people and the (industrial) bourgeoisie, Britain granted some political and economic concessions, particularly future industrialisation during the War and immediately after the War.

As the issue of tariff protection crept into the heads of Indians, the British Government appointed the Industrial Commission in 1916 and assured that industrialisation efforts would henceforth continue with utmost sincerity. Unfortunately, industrialisation scheme as prepared by the Industrial Commission ultimately came to nothing.

However, during the war-period, industries like cotton and jute made much headway. Steel industry also experienced substantial growth. Consumer goods industries like chemicals, cement, fertilisers, mineral acids, etc., for which India depended on foreign countries, also progressed during the War.

The war created enormous demand for factory goods in India. Imports from Britain and other foreign countries fell substantially. Besides, the government demand for war-purposes increased considerably. Consequently, production increased in such industries as iron and steel, jute, leather goods, cotton and woollen textiles. Indian mills and factories were working to full capacity. However, the expansion of industries was handicapped in the absence of heavy and machine tool industry.

19.1.5 Inter-War Period: After First World War, it came to be recognised that without rapid industrialisation, significant economic development was not possible. Inter-War period witnessed the establishment and growth of several industries in the country. A more positive government policy and a change in the terms of trade in favour of the producers of manufactured goods and against the primary producers in the period of the depression materially assisted capital formation in the industrial sector. There was, however, little overall economic improvement as conditions in the agricultural sector deteriorated sharply.

In 1921, the Indian Fiscal Commission was appointed to examine the tariff policy of the Government of India. It submitted its report in 1922.

The recommendations of the Fiscal Commission were debated in the Legislative Assembly in February 1923 and a resolution was passed accepting in principle the need to tailor India's tariff policy for encouraging Indian industries. As suggested by the Fiscal Commission, a Tariff Board was set up which investigated the claims of a number of industries for protective duties. Following the recommendations of the Tariff Board, the government adopted what came to be called the policy of *discriminatory protection* under which tariff protection was granted to select industries against foreign competition.

The industries which benefited from the policy of discriminating protection included, *inter alia,* iron and steel, cement, textiles, sugar, paper, matches, and jute.

The worldwide depression of 1930s had little direct impact on India, with only slight impact on the modern secondary sector. The government did little to alleviate distress, and was focused mostly on shipping gold to Britain. The worst consequences involved deflation, which increased the burden of the debt on villagers while lowering the cost of living. Falling prices for jute (and also wheat) hurt larger growers. The worst hit sector was jute, based in Bengal, which was an important element in overseas trade. It had prospered in the 1920s but was hard hit in the 1930s. The discontent of farmers manifested itself in rebellions and riots. The Salt Satyagraha of 1930 was one of the measures undertaken as a response to heavy taxation during the depression.

In terms of employment, there was some decline, while agriculture and small-scale industry exhibited gains. The most successful new industry was sugar, which had meteoric growth in the 1930s.

In short, during the period between the two World Wars, there was a marked change in the industrial activity in India. There was diversification of industrial activity in many new directions while the traditional industries like jute and others maintained a comparatively slow pace of growth.

19.1.6 Second World War (1939-45): The War created conditions for the maximum utilisation of existing capacity in Indian industries. Cotton, jute and steel remained the principal items of war procurement though large orders for ammunition shells gave engineering factories and railway workshops some useful experience of mass production.

Conditions were, however, not favourable for the setting up of large scale equipment and plant for new industries. Several industries such as ferroalloys, non-ferrous metals like aluminium and antimony, diesel engines, pumps, bicycles and sewing machines were started on a modest scale during this period. Some stray efforts were also made in the field of chemicals like soda ash, caustic soda, chlorine and super phosphate, and certain types of machine tools and simple machinery. However, the major impetus of the war was felt in the medium and small industries sectors such as light engineering, pharmaceuticals, medicines and drugs, cutlery etc.

Capital equipment was exposed to considerable wear and tear. Maintenance and replacement were neglected. Coal and transport bottlenecks remained a serious threat to output expansion throughout the war.

19.1.7 Post-War Period: In the immediate post-war years, there was considerable new investment activity leading to the establishment of industries like rayon, automobiles, ball and roller bearings, carding engines, ring frames and locomotives. Several new units were started and existing units expanded in industries like fertilizers, cement, sheet glass, and the manufacture of caustic soda and sulphuric acid.

Industrial development during the War and the post-War period was influenced largely by the prevailing inflationary conditions and scarcities, with the result that long-term factors such as the most advantageous location or scale of operation, the availability of raw materials, the size of the market and the adequacy of the financial and technical organisation for successful operation under competitive conditions did not receive the attention they deserved.

The immediate problem for industry after the War was to make up the damage caused by excessive wear and tear and lack of maintenance. A worldwide shortage of machinery and shipping, and political disturbances made it difficult to launch any major industrial expansion after the War. The partition of the country in 1947 left India with nearly the entire industry of undivided India.

19.1.8 Critical Appraisal: India was a typical backward economy in terms of industrialization at the time of Independence. The arrested industrial development during the 19th century and the first half of the 20th century was more a consequence of India's political dependency to Britain rather than of her own cultural heritage.

The Indian economy registered limited and partial development during the British rule. Judged in terms of per capita incomes and standards of well-being, the economy, on the whole, remained more or less stagnant. This was primarily because the basic conditions under which an economy can continuously expand were lacking.

The major emphasis in industrial development in India was on consumer goods industries, while the development of basic capital goods industries lagged behind. The output of consumer goods industries such as cotton textiles, sugar, soap, matches and salt was on the whole sufficient to meet the existing low level of demand in the country. In the case of capital goods industries and industries manufacturing intermediate products, the available capacity in the country was in most cases inadequate. The production of iron and steel in the country was hardly 50 percent of the existing volume of demand.

The British rule resulted into colonisation and systematic exploitation of the Indian economy. In their efforts to convert India into a market for their manufactures, the British systematically destroyed India's own manufacturing industry. Liberal imports of machine-made goods led to the decline of domestic handicrafts, causing unemployment and misery for the native craftsmen. India was gradually transformed into an agrarian society with emphasis on cash crops and plantations. The result of this colonial policy was suicidal for the native Indians. Economy remained stagnant, masses suffered appalling poverty, and famines occurred frequently. This was in sharp contrast to the ancient glory of India as a leading manufacturing country of the world. Historians have recorded the skills of Indians in the production of delicate woven fabrics, metallurgy, chemical substances, and arts. Mummies in Egyptian tombs have been found wrapped in Indian muslin of the finest quality.

In short, India inherited a dismal economy from the British rulers at the time of Independence. Owing to poor technological and scientific capabilities, industrialization was limited and lop-sided. Agricultural sector exhibited features of feudal and semi-feudal institutions, resulting into low productivity.

19.2 Post-Independence Period

After Independence in 1947, India followed the mixed economy framework by combining the advantages of the capitalist economic system with those of the socialist economic system. Over the years, this policy resulted in the establishment of a variety of rules and laws, which were aimed at controlling and regulating the economy.

19.2.1 Industrial Policy Resolution, 1948: The Government of India's industrial policy after Independence was shaped broadly in terms of the Industrial Policy Resolution of April 1948. That Resolution emphasised clearly the responsibility of Government in the matter of promoting, assisting and regulating the development of industry in the national interest. It envisaged for the public sector an increasingly active role. While it reiterated the inherent right of the State to acquire any industrial undertaking whenever the public interest requires it, it laid down, in view of the circumstances then existing, a certain demarcation of fields for the public and private sectors.

The 1948 Resolution envisaged a mixed economy for India. It declared that public sector would play an effective and dominant role in the future economic development of India. This role was to be particularly significant in the establishment and development of heavy and basic industries. Certain crucial sectors for industrial development were reserved for Government initiative.

In terms of this Resolution, the principle of Government ownership and control was accepted in regard to a segment of the economy comprising arms and ammunition, atomic energy and railways. It was also stated that in regard to certain key industries like coal, iron and steel, aircraft manufacture, ship-building, manufacture of telephone, telegraph and wireless apparatus etc., the State was to be responsible for further expansion except to the extent that it considers the cooperation of private enterprise necessary for the purpose. In the rest of the industrial field the initiative for development and the responsibility for management would rest on private enterprise. Government had, however, the right to acquire any undertaking in the public interest and to intervene in cases where the conduct of industry under private enterprise was not satisfactory. Central regulation and control was envisaged for 18 specified industries of special importance from the points of view of the investment and technical skill involved.

19.2.2 Industrial Policy Resolution, 1956: The Industrial Policy Resolution of 1948 was reviewed in the light of experience gained, and in accordance with the goal of the state controlling the commanding heights of the economy, the Industrial Policy Resolution of 1956 was placed before the Parliament (and adopted) by Prime Minister Jawaharlal Nehru on April 30, 1956. The 1956 Resolution, launched on the eve of the Second Five Year Plan (1956-61), and called by some as the economic constitution of India, observed, "The adoption of the socialistic pattern of society as well as the need for planned and rapid development require that all industries of basic and strategic importance or in the nature of public utility services should be in the public sector".

The most important feature of the 1956 Industrial Policy Resolution was the classification of all industries into the following three categories, having regard to the part which the state would play in each of them.

1. **Schedule A Industries:** This Schedule listed 17 industries which included, *inter alia,* arms and ammunition, atomic energy, iron and steel, heavy electricals, coal, mineral oils, air transport, railways, and generation and distribution of electricity.

These industries were reserved for exclusive development in the public sector.

2. **Schedule B Industries:** These included industries which were to be progressively owned by the Government and in which the Government would generally set up new enterprises. However, private sector was expected to supplement the efforts of the Government. This list included 12 industries, the leading ones being aluminium, machine tools, fertilisers, road transport, and sea transport.

3. **Schedule C Industries:** These contained the rest of the industries which were left to the care of the private sector but under the general control of the Government.

These categories were not intended to be rigid or watertight In the industries listed in Schedule A, for instance, the expansion of existing privately owned units was not precluded, and the State was free to secure the cooperation of private enterprise in the establishment of new units when the national interest so required, subject to the proviso that while securing such cooperation, it would ensure, through majority participation in the capital of the undertaking or otherwise, that it had the requisite powers to guide the policy and control the operations of the undertaking.

Schedule B related to what may be called the mixed sector, a sector in which the State would enter progressively and enlarge its operations, but private enterprise would, at the same time, have the opportunity to develop, either on its own or with state participation.

In the rest of the field, development would ordinarily be undertaken through the initiative and enterprise of the private sector, but it would be open to the State to start any industry even in this field.

The prime consideration determining State policy over the whole industrial field was rapid development in keeping with the overall objectives defined. The public sector had to grow and the private sector had to conform to the requirements of the national priorities.

19.2.3 Industrial Policy Statement, 1991: The process of economic reforms initiated in 1985 got a big boost when the Government of Prime Minister Narsimha Rao announced a new industrial policy in the Indian Parliament on July 24, 1991. The new policy introduced radical changes "to unshackle the Indian industrial economy from the cobwebs of unnecessary bureaucratic controls". Some of the provisions of the new policy were as follows:

1. It abolished industrial licenses for all projects, except for a short list of 18 specified industries related to: (a) security and strategic areas, (b) hazardous chemicals, (c) items of elitist consumption (d) environmental concerns and (e) social reasons. After further delicensing, there are, presently, only 5 industries under compulsory industrial licensing. These are the following: (a) distillation and brewing of alcoholic drinks, (b) cigars and cigarettes of tobacco and manufactured tobacco substitute, (c) electronic aerospace and defence equipment, all types, (d) industrial explosives including detonating fuses, safety fuses, gunpowder, nitrocellulose and matches, and (e) specified hazardous chemicals.

2. It removed the asset limits for MRTP totally. The MRTP Act is now used for controlling and regulating monopolistic, restrictive, and unfair trade practices. The MRTP Commission was given powers to initiate investigations suo moto or on

complaints received from individual consumers or classes of consumers about monopolistic, restrictive, and unfair trade practices.

3. It raised the limit for foreign equity holding from 40 percent to 51 percent. The automatic clearance for direct foreign investment up to 51 percent in high priority areas was a clear signal that the foreign investment was welcome. The new policy also announced automatic permission for foreign technology agreements in high priority industries. Moreover, the policy made liberal provisions for hiring foreign technicians, and foreign testing of indigenously developed technology.

4. With a view to raise resources and ensure wider participation, the new policy announced disinvestment in public sector undertakings in favour of mutual funds, financial institutions, workers, and the general public. While reservation of industries for the public sector was retained, the bar for opening such areas to the private sector was to be selectively removed. The July 1991 policy statement reduced the list of industries reserved for public sector from 17 included in the Industrial Policy Resolution of 1956 to only 8. Subsequently, 6 more items were de-reserved. Thus, at present there are only 2 industries reserved for the public sector. These are: (a) atomic energy (production, separation or enrichment of special fissionable materials and substances and operation of the facilities) and (b) railway transport.

5. According to the new policy, chronically sick public sector units were to be referred to the Board for Industrial and Financial Reconstruction.

6. Industries reserved for the small-scale sector would continue to be so reserved.

7. The new policy promised social security mechanism to protect workers' interest in affected public sector enterprises. It also promised to promote workers' participation in management and proposed workers' co-operatives to make sick units healthy.

In short, the thrust of the new industrial policy announced in July 1991 was on removing bureaucratic controls that thwarted industrial development and opening up a large number of industries to the private sector. The location policy for industries was substantially simplified and liberalized. These relaxations of the regulatory apparatus governing domestic industrial activity certainly eased the barriers to entry in the industrial sector. It helped to make the industrial sector more competitive both domestically and internationally. The new policy was generally welcomed for ensuring competitive and market economy in place of the outmoded command and controlled economy. Many saw it as a reversal of the 1956 Industrial Policy Resolution.

Since then, successive Governments have carried forward the reforms in industrial sector, financial sector, fiscal sector and external sector. It is liberalisation, privatisation and globalisation all the way, though some believe the reforms are taking place at a slow speed.

Government is continuing the process of liberalising the economy to give more freedom to entrepreneurial energy. The benefits of this approach are being realised in the faster growth of the economy at rates that are now amongst the highest in the world. Meanwhile societal concerns with the condition of the environment and climate change are increasing. Though India is continuing on its path of industrial liberalisation and progressive dismantling of government controls yet regulation of business conduct in some form cannot be avoided. If voluntary regulation is not effective, governments worldwide are pressed to step in. The more effective the industry is at self-regulation, and the more credible its actions are, the less will be the societal pressure on government to control the industry.

To sum up, the process of industrial liberalisation is continuing in the Indian economy. Private sector has been invited to invest in oil exploration and refining which are otherwise reserved for public sector. Similarly, power sector is now open to both domestic and foreign private investment. Government has also allowed private sector activities in the mining industry.

One of the principal objectives of the Government of India's industrial policy is to have a balance in industrial development between different regions of the country by addressing the problem of industrial development of backward areas. For stimulating industrial development of backward areas, the Union Government has been supplementing the efforts of state governments through various policies, schemes and packages of incentives.

Poor infrastructure, inadequate power supply, and the plethora of inspectors and permissions required are some of the obstacles in the path of industry in India. The lesson from all Asian countries, that have rapidly-grown strong industries in recent years, is that policy-makers must work closely with industrial managers to solve problems in the production sphere. In a world in which companies and countries are rated on their competitiveness by international agencies, the only sustainable source of competitive advantage can be a company's or country's ability to learn, change, and improve faster than any potential competition. Therefore, a country's competitive ability lies in the capability of the collaborative process between producers and policy-makers to produce effective policies and not on any particular policy.

India cannot simply copy the collaborative process used by Japan, Korea, or more recently China. Its circumstances are different and times have changed. Nevertheless, Indian policy-makers must find ways to improve competitiveness and growth of Indian industry. The processes that will enable policy-makers to do so should include consultation not only with large domestic companies but also with those who represent labour rights, land owners, environmentalists and small-scale producers.

20

Important Laws to Regulate Industry and Business

Various legislations have been enacted to regulate industrial and business activities in India. Select legislations in this regard are explained below.

20.1 Competition Act, 2002

The main objectives of the Act are the following:

1. To provide for the establishment of a Commission to prevent practices having adverse effect on competition.
2. To promote and sustain competition in markets in India.
3. To protect the interests of consumers.
4. To ensure freedom of trade carried on by participants in markets in India and for related matters.

Even though Competition Act, 2002 was enacted on January 13, 2003, its enforcement was delayed because of certain legal issues raised in courts of law. The Act was amended by Competition (Amendment) Act, 2007 to address the issues raised. The amended Act provides for appeal against the decision of the Commission to a newly created Competition Appellate Tribunal (CAT). Appeals against CAT can be made to the Supreme Court.

The Act is divided into 9 chapters. Chapter I covers short title, extent and commencement, as also definitions. Chapter II relates to prohibition of certain types of agreements and abuse of dominant position. It also covers regulation of combinations. Combination includes mergers, amalgamations, acquisitions and acquisition of control. Chapters III and IV deal with the establishment, composition etc. of the Commission, its duties, powers and functions and the duties of the Director General. Competition Commission of India is an autonomous body with the Chairperson and every other Member a person of ability, integrity and standing and who has special knowledge (and professional experience of not less than 15 years), of international economics, business, commerce, law, finance, accountancy, management, industry, public affairs or competition matters, including competition law and policy, which in the opinion of the Central Government, may be useful to the Commission. Chapter V relates to duties of the Director General. Chapter VI relates to penalties. (It is noteworthy that MRTP Act did not have penalty provisions, which made it toothless and ineffective. This, along with the absence of definition of cartels made the MRTP Act very ineffective in dealing with cartels). Chapter VII mandates competition advocacy, which is a salient feature of Competition Act, 2002. Chapter VIII envisages the creation of the Competition Appellate Tribunal, its role, procedures etc. Chapter IX deals with miscellaneous provisions which include the power of the Central Government to exempt, issue directions to the Commission, supersede the Commission under certain circumstances etc.

While the Act covers all types of enterprises, including government departments (except when such acts are in the discharge of sovereign function), the Central Government has the power to exempt enterprises from the application of the Act, or any provision thereof, and for such time period as it may specify.

Competition Act, 2002 is an economic law and the Commission is an expert body which is expected to take decisions based on a number of factors, most of which are of economic nature. The decision-making process, as far as the law is concerned, would involve considerable extent of economic analysis.

20.1.1 Competition Commission of India (CCI): Competition Act, 2002 provided for the establishment of a Competition Commission of India which was established on October 14, 2003. CCI is entrusted with the task to: (a) eliminate practices having adverse effect on competition, (b) promote and sustain competition in markets, (c) protect the interest of consumers and (d) ensure freedom of trade carried on by other participants.

CCI has been given, under the Act, the mandate to generate public awareness about competition issues. Its efforts in this area may be further strengthened. CCI should formulate, publish and post in the public domain guidelines covering various dimensions related to competition law for enhancing public awareness. Such guidelines will help enterprises by bringing greater clarity about the provisions of the competition law and the manner of its enforcement.

20.1.2 Competition Appellate Tribunal: The Competition (Amendment) Act, 2007 passed by the Parliament in September 2007 incorporated some changes in the Competition Act, 2002 including the establishment of a Competition Appellate Tribunal to hear appeals from the orders of the CCI.

20.2 Limited Liability Partnership (LLP) Act, 2008

Unlike limited liability entities, where the liability of the shareholder is limited to the extent of the contribution made or due from him, in proprietorships or partnerships there is no separation of personal and business liability. When a business fails, not only do the assets of the business but the entrepreneur's personal assets also get attached to pay off business dues. Further, all guarantors which are drawn from the critical social safety net of the small entrepreneur, get personally involved and in the eventuality of failure they also get implicated and the whole safety net crumbles.

Insolvency of corporate entities such as companies is governed by the Companies Act, 1956. Insolvency in proprietorship or partnership firms, on the other hand, is governed by the Provincial Insolvency Act, 1920, which has largely remained static. Here, the focus is not revival followed by structured exit in case of failure, but of recovery of outstanding dues through a court driven process. The relevant courts under the Act are district courts which take their own time adjudicating the petitions and are apt to enforce the processes of seizing debtor estates, appointing receivers and punitive remedies against the debtor including imprisonment rather than enabling any revival or turnaround. Indeed adjudicatory order on an insolvency petition under this Act lays the entrepreneur open to action including arrest and detention in a civil prison as if business failure were a criminal act. The provisions for arrangements under this act are also aimed at composition of debt due rather than rehabilitation. During the interim period when the insolvency petition is pending for disposal, there is no absolute stay against the proceedings initiated under different acts such as for recovery of statutory dues.

In many countries reforms have taken place that allows insolvency of businesses to be dealt with in a comprehensive manner that enables revival or rescue before liquidation and winding up. Insolvency is treated as a commercial phenomenon requiring to be dealt with in accordance with commercial principles in a framework of fairness and equity. There is an independent institutionalized process of providing a grace period for businesses to deal with distress. This is intended to enable a revival plan if the business is inherently viable, puts all creditors on hold pending revival, gets business out of holding period if it revives or takes action on winding up if the business is non-revivable. Both personal as well as business insolvency are dealt with on the basis of similar principles with ease of filing for bankruptcy and securing of certain protection from creditor action once this is done.

LLP Act, 2008 provides for a flexible governance structure to be determined by the partners themselves by mutual agreement, easy compliance requirements in comparison to companies, combined with limitation of liability to the extent of the partner's contribution.

The salient features of the LLP Act, 2008 are as under:

1. LLP shall be a body corporate and a legal entity separate from its partners. It will have perpetual succession. Indian Partnership Act, 1932 shall not be applicable to LLPs, since LLP shall be in the form of a body corporate.
2. An LLP has to be incorporated with a minimum of two persons. The Act does not restrict the benefit of LLP structure to certain classes of professionals only and would be available for use by any enterprise which fulfils the requirements of the Act.
3. The LLP will be an alternative corporate business vehicle that would give the benefits of limited liability but would allow its members the flexibility of organizing their internal structure as a partnership based on an agreement.
4. On registration, LLP shall be capable of: (a) suing and being sued and (b) acquiring, owning, holding and developing or disposing off property.
5. A person may cease to be a partner of a LLP in accordance with an agreement with the other partners or in absence of agreement with the other partners, by giving a notice in writing of not less than 30 days of his intention to resign as partner.
6. In the event of an act carried out by a LLP, or any of its partners, with intend to defraud creditors of the LLP or any other person or for any fraudulent purpose, the liability of the LLP and partners, who acted with intend to defraud creditors or for any fraudulent purpose shall be unlimited for all or any of the debts or other liabilities of the LLP.
7. A contribution of a partner may consist of tangible, movable or immovable or intangible property or other benefits to the LLP including money, promissory notes, other

agreements to contribute cash or property, and contracts for services performed or to be performed.

8. While the LLP will be a separate legal entity, liable to the full extent of its assets, the liability of the partners would be limited to their agreed contribution in the LLP. Further, no partner would be liable on account of the independent or unauthorized actions of other partners, thus allowing individual partners to be shielded from joint liability created by another partner's wrongful business decisions or misconduct.

9. An LLP shall be under obligation to maintain annual accounts reflecting true and fair view of its state of affairs.

10. Provisions have been made in the Act for corporate actions like mergers, amalgamations etc.

11. There is a provision of voluntary winding up as well as winding up by the Tribunal.

12. There are provisions for inter conversion of LLP into private company etc.

The LLP Act has paved the way for greater corporatisation of the small and medium enterprises, thereby enhancing their access to equity and funds from the market.

20.3 Companies Act, 2013

20.3.1 Background: The Companies Act, 1956 was in need of a substantial revamp for quite some time, to make it more contemporary and relevant to corporates, regulators and other stakeholders in India. While several unsuccessful attempts were made in the past to revise the 1956 Act, the most recent attempt was the Companies Bill, 2009 which was introduced in the Lok Sabha on August 3, 2009. This Companies Bill, 2009 was referred to the Parliamentary Standing Committee on Finance, which submitted its report on August 31, 2010 and was withdrawn after the introduction of the Companies Bill, 2011. The Companies Bill, 2011 was also considered by the Parliamentary Standing Committee on Finance which submitted its report on June 26, 2012. Subsequently, the Bill was considered and approved by the Lok Sabha on December 18, 2012 as the Companies Bill, 2012. The Bill was then considered and approved by the Rajya Sabha too on August 8, 2013. After having obtained the assent of the President of India on August 29, 2013, it came into effect from April 1, 2014.

20.3.2 Significance: The 2013 Act introduces significant changes in the provisions related to governance, e-management, compliance and enforcement, disclosure norms, auditors and mergers and acquisitions. Also, new concepts such as one-person company, small companies, dormant company, class action suits, registered valuers and corporate social responsibility have been included.

An attempt has been made to reduce the content of the substantive portion of the related law in the Companies Act, 2013 as compared to the Companies Act, 1956. In the process, much of the aforesaid content has been left, *to be prescribed*, in the Rules which are yet to be finalised and notified.

The changes in the 2013 Act have far-reaching implications that are set to significantly change the manner in which corporates operate in India. The 2013 Act has introduced several new concepts and has also tried to streamline many of the requirements by introducing new definitions.

20.3.3 Main Provisions:

A. Types of Companies:

1. **One-person Company:** The 2013 Act introduces a new type of entity to the existing list i.e. apart from forming a public or private limited company, the 2013 Act enables the formation of a new entity a 'one-person company' (OPC). An OPC means a company with only one person as its member [Section 3(1) of 2013 Act].

2. **Private Company:** The 2013 Act introduces a change in the definition for a private company, *inter alia*, the new requirement increases the limit of the number of members from 50 to 200 [Section 2(68) of 2013 Act].

3. **Small Company:** A small company has been defined as a company, other than a public company.

- Paid-up share capital of which does not exceed ₹ 50 lakh or such higher amount as may be prescribed which shall not be more than ₹ 5 crore.
- Turnover of which as per its last profit-and-loss account does not exceed ₹ 2 crore INR or such higher amount as may be prescribed which shall not be more than ₹ 20 crore:

   As set out in the 2013 Act, this section will not be applicable to the following: (a) a holding company or a subsidiary company, (b) a company registered under section 8 and (c) a company or body corporate governed by any special Act [Section 2(85) of 2013 Act].

4. **Dormant Company:** The 2013 Act states that a company can be classified as dormant when it is formed and registered under this 2013 Act for a future project or to hold an asset or intellectual property and has no significant accounting transaction. Such a company or an inactive one may apply to the ROC in such manner as may be prescribed for obtaining the status of a dormant company [Section 455 of 2013 Act].

B. Mergers and Acquisitions: The 2013 Act features some new provisions in the area of mergers and acquisitions, apart from making certain changes from the existing provisions. While the changes are aimed at simplifying and rationalising the procedures involved, the new provisions are also aimed at ensuring higher accountability for the company and majority shareholders and increasing flexibility for corporates. The 2013 Act has streamlined as well as introduced concepts such as reverse mergers (merger of foreign companies with Indian companies) and squeeze-out provisions, which are significant. The 2013 Act has also introduced the requirement for valuations in several cases, including mergers and acquisitions, by registered valuers.

C. Prohibition of Association or Partnership of Persons Exceeding Certain Number: The 2013 Act puts a restriction on the number of partners that can be admitted to a partnership at 100. To be specific, the 2013 Act states that no association or partnership consisting of more than the given number of persons as may be prescribed shall be formed for the purpose of carrying on any business that has for its object the acquisition of gain by the association or partnership or by the individual members thereof, unless it is registered as a company under this 1956 Act or is formed under any other law for the time being in force.

As an exception, the aforesaid restriction would not apply to the following: (a) A Hindu undivided family carrying on any business and (b) an association or partnership, if it is formed by professionals who are governed by special acts like the Chartered Accountants Act etc. [Section 464 of 2013 Act].

D. Insider Trading and Prohibition on Forward Dealings: The 2013 Act for the first time defines insider trading and price-sensitive information and prohibits any person including the director or key managerial person from entering into insider trading [Section 195 of 2013 Act]. Further, the Act also prohibits directors and key managerial personnel from forward dealings in the company or its holding, subsidiary or associate company [Section 194 of 2013 Act].

E. Corporate Governance: The 2013 Act intends to improve corporate governance by requiring disclosure of nature of concern or interest of every director, manager, any other key managerial personnel and relatives of such a director, manager or any other key managerial personnel and reduction in threshold of disclosure from 20 percent to 2 percent. The term 'key managerial personnel' has now been defined in the 2013 Act and means the chief executive officer, managing director, manager, company secretary, whole-time director, chief financial officer and any such other officer as may be prescribed.

F. Accounts and Audit: The 2013 Act has introduced certain significant amendments in this chapter. It has also introduced several additional requirements such as preparation of consolidated financial statements, additional reporting requirements for the directors in their report such as the development and implementation of the risk management policy, disclosures in respect of voting rights not exercised directly by the employees in respect of shares to which the scheme relates, etc., in comparison with the requirements of the 1956 Act.

The 2013 Act features extensive changes within the area of audit and auditors with a view to enhance audit effectiveness and accountability of the auditors. These changes undoubtedly, have a considerable impact on the audit profession. However, it needs to be noted that these changes will also have a considerable impact on the company in terms of time, efforts and expectations involved. Apart from introducing new concepts such as rotation of audit firms and class action suits, the 2013 Act also increases the auditor's liability substantially in comparison with the 1956 Act.

Unlike the appointment process at each annual general meeting under the 1956 Act, the auditor will now be appointed for a period of 5 years, with a requirement to ratify such an appointment at each annual general meeting [Section 139(1) of 2013 Act].

G. Dividend: The 2013 Act proposes to introduce significant changes to the existing provisions of the 1956 Act in respect of declaration of dividend. The changes are likely to affect the existing practices followed by companies with regard to the declaration of dividend.

The existing provisions of the 1956 Act in relation to the transfer of a specified percentage of profit to reserve is no longer applicable and thus, companies will be free to transfer any or no amount to its reserves.

H. Revival and Rehabilitation of Sick Companies: Chapter XIX of the 2013 Act lays down the provisions for the revival and rehabilitation of sick companies. The chapter describes the circumstances which determine the declaration of a company as a sick company, and also includes the rehabilitation process of the same. Although it aims to provide comprehensive provisions for the revival and rehabilitation of sick companies, the fact that several provisions such as particulars, documents as well as content of the draft scheme in respect of application for revival and rehabilitation, etc. have been left to substantive enactment, leaves scope for interpretation.

The coverage of this chapter is no longer restricted to industrial companies, and the determination of the net worth would not be relevant for assessing whether a company is a sick company.

I. Corporate Social Responsibility: The 2013 Act makes an effort to introduce the culture of corporate social responsibility (CSR) in Indian corporates by requiring companies to formulate a corporate social responsibility policy and at least incur a given minimum expenditure on social activities.

It may be recalled that the Ministry of Corporate Affairs (MCA) had introduced the Corporate Social Responsibility Voluntary Guidelines in 2009. These guidelines have now been incorporated within the 2013 Act and have obtained legal sanctity. Section 135 of the 2013 Act, seeks to provide that every company having a net worth of ₹ 500 crore, or more or a turnover of ₹ 1,000 crore or more, or a net profit of ₹ 5 crore or more, during any financial year shall constitute the corporate social responsibility committee of the board. This committee needs to comprise of three or more directors, out of which, at least one director should be an independent director. The composition of the committee shall be included in the board's report. The committee shall formulate the policy, including activities specified in Schedule VII, which are as follows:

1. Eradicating extreme hunger and poverty.
2. Promotion of education.
3. Promoting gender equality and empowering women.
4. Reducing child mortality and improving maternal health.
5. Combating human immunodeficiency virus, acquired immune deficiency syndrome, malaria and other diseases.
6. Ensuring environmental sustainability.
7. Employment enhancing vocational skills.
8. Social business projects.
9. Contribution to the Prime Minister's National Relief Fund or any other fund set-up by the central government or the state governments for socio-economic development and relief, and funds for the welfare of the scheduled castes and Tribes, other backward classes, minorities and women.
10. Such other matters as may be prescribed.

There have been mixed reactions to the introduction of the 'spend or explain' approach taken by the MCA with respect to CSR. It may take a while before all of Corporate India imbibes CSR as a culture.

However, activities specified in the Schedule are not elaborate or detailed enough to indicate the kind of projects that could be undertaken, for example, environment sustainability or social business projects could encompass a wide range of activities.

The committee will also need to recommend the amount of expenditure to be incurred and monitor the policy from a time-to-time. The board shall disclose the contents of the policy in its report, and place it on the website, if any, of the company. The 2013 Act mandates that these companies would be required to spend at least 2 percent of the average net-profits of the immediately preceding three years on CSR activities, and if not spent, explanation for the reasons thereof would need to be given in the director's report (Section 135 of the 2013 Act).

In short, Companies Act, 2013, is a landmark legislation with far-reaching consequences on all companies incorporated in India. Corporate India continues to evolve at a fast pace leading to the emergence of a diverse set of stakeholders. The growth has led to a surge in consequences such as risk and default that seem to be visibly impacting the virtues of governance, which is precisely the area on which the Act promises to substantively raise the bar. The Act is also quite outward looking and in several areas attempts to harmonize with international requirements. The Act in a comprehensive form purports to deal with various aspects of corporate India and Indian companies will have to closely examine these developments to develop a clear strategy at ensuring compliance per the new requirements.

20.4 Insolvency and Bankruptcy Code (IBC), 2016

There can be many reasons why an enterprise needs to close down—voluntary or forced by circumstances. The ease of closing down business is crucial for a good entrepreneurship ecosystem.

20.4.1 Need for Entrepreneur-friendly Bankruptcy Laws: With globalisation and competition, the possibility of a large number of manufacturing enterprises not getting business, and having to close, has to be particularly catered to. The experimental character of entrepreneurship and the risks involved need to be understood so that an entrepreneur gets another chance in which he/she may do better. The business environment can be strengthened by reducing the bankruptcy stigma and facilitating re-starts. Unfortunately, a great deal of emphasis is placed on stigmatizing failure. The underlying message is that if an entrepreneur has failed once, he would not be given a second chance. A policy change is needed here. Unless there has been wilful default, surreptitious draining of resources etc., a failed entrepreneur may have actually learnt from his mistakes and become a good investment bet.

At a broader level, the bankruptcy laws should be designed to help viable companies in distress, and make closing and re-starting easier. Enterprises need insolvency procedures which recognise that viable businesses can suffer from temporary problems, e.g. an economy-wide recession. Such procedures should facilitate the necessary internal reorganisation and restructuring of debt. A key objective of the bankruptcy laws should be to help viable companies survive while safeguarding the interests of the creditors. This requires being able to distinguish quickly and at low cost between firms to restructure and firms to close.

The policies and institutions of an economy should provide adequate freedom to every person to enable him to pursue his economic interests meaningfully. Inclusive economies provide such freedom to pursue vocation, create a level playing field for good ideas to replace obsolete ones, and encourage scarce resources to pursue the most productive avenues. Such economies unleash and realize full potential of every person and thereby develop faster.

Business plans entail informed risk taking to compete and succeed. Either incumbents are displaced by new businesses or new businesses fail to carve out a competitive space for themselves. Either way, failure of some businesses is integral to a market economy. When a business fails, it needs to be resolved at the earliest and expeditiously. Any undue delay in commencement or conclusion of resolution may lead to exodus of key stakeholders and aggravate the failure, sometimes beyond repair. If the resolution is not possible, an orderly exit mechanism should allow stakeholders to recover their dues from liquidation proceeds of the business and free-up resources for reallocation.

In many countries reforms have taken place that allow insolvency of businesses to be dealt with in a comprehensive manner that enables revival or rescue before liquidation and winding up. Insolvency is treated as a commercial phenomenon requiring to be dealt with in accordance with commercial principles in a framework of fairness and equity. There is an independent institutionalized process of providing a grace period for businesses to deal with distress. This is intended to enable a revival plan if the business is inherently viable, puts all creditors on hold pending revival, gets business out of holding period if it revives or takes action on winding up if the business is non-revivable. Both personal as well as business insolvency are dealt with on the basis of similar principles with ease of filing for bankruptcy and securing of certain protection from creditor action once this is done.

20.4.2 Situation Prior to IBC, 2016: Unlike limited liability entities, where the liability of the shareholder is limited to the extent of the contribution made or due from him, in proprietorships or partnerships there is no separation of personal and business liability. When a business fails, not only do the assets of the business but the entrepreneur's personal assets also get attached to pay off business dues. Further, all guarantors of the small entrepreneur get personally involved and in the eventuality of failure they also get implicated.

Prior to the implementation of IBC, 2016, insolvency of business entities was governed by a host of outdated legislations. The focus in these laws was not revival followed by structured exit in case of failure, but on recovery of outstanding dues through a court-driven process. The relevant courts under the statutes were district courts which took their own time adjudicating the petitions and were apt to enforce the processes of seizing debtor's estates, appointing receivers and punitive remedies against the debtor including imprisonment rather than enabling any revival or turnaround. Indeed adjudicatory order on an insolvency petition under these statutes laid the entrepreneur open to action including arrest and detention in a civil prison as if business failure was a criminal act.

The existing legal framework for insolvency and bankruptcy was spread across multiple statutes and was found to be inadequate resulting in undue delays in resolution and thus rendering it ineffective, at times. In an economy growing at a rapid pace not only the credit delivery mechanism but also the economic culture surrounding it needs to be as per best global practice. Thus there was need for an effective statutory framework to deal with insolvency and bankruptcy to facilitate development of credit markets in the country, encourage entrepreneurship, improving ease of doing business, facilitate investments, create more employment opportunities leading to higher economic growth and development.

A closure of an enterprise required, *inter alia*, legal compliances related to labour laws, taxation laws, power utility, water utility, municipal body, creditors, financial institutions etc. Even when the laws were clear enough on the requirements to be fulfilled, the implementation of the same was problematic for micro, small and medium enterprise (MSMEs).

There was no mechanism that rescued failed firms or released resources from failed firms to alternate firms. The resources did not move seamlessly from less competitive firms to more competitive firms continuously. This deterred optimal utilization of resources and dampened entrepreneurship.

The promoters stayed in control of the company even after default. The creditors were ineffectual in recovering their dues. There was, thus, a need to streamline the procedures, reduce discretion and intermediation.

20.4.3 Bankruptcy Law Reforms Committee (BLRC): BLRC (Chairman: T.K. Viswanathan) was set up on August 22, 2014 for providing an entrepreneur-friendly legal bankruptcy framework, as announced in the Budget Speech of the Finance Minister for the year 2014-15. BLRC submitted its Report and Draft Bill to the Finance Minister on November 4, 2015. Based on this, a Draft Bill, namely The Insolvency and Bankruptcy Code, 2015 was introduced in the Lok Sabha on December 21, 2015.

20.4.4 Insolvency and Bankruptcy Code (IBC), 2016: IBC, 2016 is the bankruptcy law of India which consolidated the existing framework by creating a single law for insolvency and bankruptcy.

IBC, 2016 is a one-stop solution for resolving insolvencies. A strong insolvency framework—where the cost and time incurred are minimal in attaining liquidation—was long overdue in India. IBC, 2016 is intended to protect the interests of small investors and make the process of doing business a less cumbersome process.

Insolvency and Bankruptcy Code, 2015 was introduced in the Lok Sabha on December 21, 2015 by late Finance Minister Arun Jaitley. It was referred to a Joint Committee of Parliament on December 23, 2015, which recommended it on April 28, 2016. The Code was passed by the Lok Sabha on May 5, 2016 and by the Rajya Sabha on May 11, 2016. The Code received assent from President Pranab Mukherjee on May 28, 2016 and was notified in The Gazette of India on May 28, 2016. It became effective in December 2016. It repealed the Presidency Towns Insolvency Act, 1909 and Sick Industrial Companies (Special Provisions) Repeal Act, 2003, among others.

A. Key Features: These are as under:

1. **Insolvency Resolution**: IBC, 2016 outlines separate insolvency resolution processes for individuals, companies and partnership firms. The process may be initiated by either the debtor or the creditors. A maximum time limit, for completion of the insolvency resolution process, has been set for corporates and individuals. For companies, the process will have to be completed in 180 days, which may be extended by 90 days, if a majority of the creditors agree. For start-ups (other than partnership firms), small companies and other companies (with asset less than ₹ 1 crore), resolution process would be completed within 90 days of initiation of request which may be extended by 45 days.

2. **Insolvency Regulator**: Insolvency and Bankruptcy Board of India (IBBI) has been established under IBC, 2016 to oversee the insolvency proceedings in the country and regulate the entities registered under it. IBBI will have 10 members, including representatives from the Ministries of Finance and Law, and the Reserve Bank of India.

3. **Insolvency Professionals**: The insolvency process will be managed by licensed professionals. These professionals will also control the assets of the debtor during the insolvency process.

4. **Bankruptcy and Insolvency Adjudicator**: IBC, 2016 proposes two separate tribunals to oversee the process of insolvency resolution, for individuals and companies: (a) National Company Law Tribunal for companies and limited liability partnership firms and (b) Debt Recovery Tribunal for individuals and partnerships.

5. **Procedure:** A plea for insolvency is submitted to the adjudicating authority (NCLT in case of corporate debtors) by financial or operation creditors or the corporate debtor itself. The maximum time allowed to either accept or reject the plea is 14 days. If the plea is accepted, the tribunal has to appoint an insolvency resolution professional (IRP) to draft a resolution plan within 180 days (extendable by 90 days), following which the corporate insolvency resolution process (CIRP) is initiated by the court. For the said period, the board of directors of the company stands suspended, and the promoters do not have a say in the management of the company. The IRP, if required, can seek the support of the company's management for day-to-day operations. If the CIRP fails in reviving the company the liquidation process is initiated.

20.4.5 Amendments: IBC, 2016 was amended in 2017 to prohibit certain persons from submitting a resolution plan in case of defaults, and to prohibit the sale of property of a defaulter to such persons during liquidation.

20.4.6 Insolvency and Bankruptcy Board of India (IBBI): IBBI was set up on October 1, 2016 under the Insolvency and Bankruptcy Code, 2016. It has regulatory oversight over the insolvency professionals, insolvency professional agencies and information utilities. It writes and enforces rules for transactions, namely corporate insolvency resolution, corporate liquidation, individual insolvency resolution and individual bankruptcy under IBC, 2016. It is a key pillar of the ecosystem responsible for implementation of IBC, 2016.

In short, IBC, 2016 consolidates and amends the laws relating to reorganization and insolvency resolution of corporate persons, partnership firms and individuals in a time bound manner for maximization of the value of assets of such persons, to promote entrepreneurship, availability of credit and balance the interests of all the stakeholders.

IBC, 2016 enables a firm to get in and get out of business with ease, keep striving for resurrection and new pursuits, undeterred by honest business failures. It reduces incidence of failure in two ways. First, the inevitable consequence of default in terms of insolvency proceedings prompts behavioural changes on the part of debtor to try hard to prevent business failure. Second, it reduces failure by setting in motion a process that rehabilitates failing but viable businesses. If rehabilitation is not possible, IBC, 2016 facilitates closure of businesses with the least cost and disruptions. It thus addresses business failures by reducing the chances of failure, rescuing failing businesses where possible and releasing resources from businesses, where rehabilitation is not possible and thereby promotes entrepreneurship. It improves availability of credit by: (a) preventing default, (b) recovering default from future earnings of the firm, post resolution and (c) recovering default from sale of liquidation assets.

It enables the optimum utilization of resources, all the time, either by: (a) preventing use of resources below the optimum potential, (b) ensuring efficient resource use within the firm through resolution of insolvency or (c) releasing unutilized or under-utilized resources for efficient uses through closure of the firm.

By liberating the resources stuck up in inefficient and defunct firms for continuous recycling, the IBC, 2016, has completed the circle of freedom to enter, started by economic reforms since 1991, with freedom to exit.

20.5 Industry-related Ministries

Industry in India is looked after by various Ministries of the Government of India, the important ones being the following:
1. Ministry of Commerce and Industry.
2. Ministry of Heavy Industry and Public Enterprises.
3. Ministry of Micro, Small and Medium Enterprises.

20.5.1 Ministry of Commerce and Industry: It has two departments: (a) Department of Commerce and (b) Department of Promotion of Industry and Internal Trade (DPIIT).

The mandate of the Department of Commerce is regulation, development and promotion of India's international trade and commerce. Goals are realized through the formulation of appropriate international trade and commercial policy and its effective implementation. The long-term vision is to make India a major player in world trade by 2020, and assume a role of leadership in international trade organizations commensurate with India's growing importance.

The Department formulates, implements and monitors the Foreign Trade Policy which provides the basic framework of policy and strategy to be followed for promoting exports and trade. Foreign Trade Policy is periodically reviewed to incorporate changes necessary to take care of emerging economic scenarios, both in the domestic and international economy. Besides, the Department is also entrusted with responsibilities relating to multilateral and bilateral commercial relations, special economic zones (SEZs), state trading, export promotion and trade facilitation, and development and regulation of certain export-oriented industries and commodities.

The basic role of the Department is to facilitate the creation of an enabling environment and infrastructure for accelerated growth of international trade.

The role of DPIIT is to promote the industrial sector in India and facilitate balanced development of industries.

The broad objectives of DPIIT in line with its defined role as above are as follows:

1. Accelerating industrial growth by providing financial, infrastructural and other support.
2. Facilitating foreign investment in industries and coordinating faster implementation of investment approvals.
3. Facilitating development of industries in North-East and other special category states.
4. Improving intellectual property rights regime consistent with the country's international commitments and increase output and efficiency in trademark and patent offices.
5. Maintaining a sound information base of macroeconomic indicators of industrial production and prices.
6. Initiating measures towards procedural changes to make functioning of the department more transparent and responsive.

Over the years, the role of DPIIT has evolved from being a regulator and administrator of the industrial sector to that of a facilitator of new technology, and of foreign direct investment (FDI) flows into the country.

20.5.2 Ministry of Heavy Industry and Public Enterprises: It comprises of the Department of Heavy Industry (DHI) and the Department of Public Enterprises (DPE).

DHI is concerned with the development of the engineering industry, viz. machine tools, heavy electrical, industrial machinery and auto industry. DHI maintains a constant dialogue with various industry associations and encourages initiatives for the growth of industry. It also assists the industry in the achievement of their growth plans through policy initiatives, suitable interventions for restructuring of tariffs and trade, promotion of technological collaboration and up-gradation, and research and development activities.

DPE acts as a nodal agency for all public sector enterprises (PSEs) and assists in policy formulation pertaining to the role of PSEs in the economy as also in laying down policy guidelines on performance improvement and evaluation, financial accounting, personnel management and in related areas. It also collects, evaluates and maintains information on several areas in respect of PSEs. DPE also provides an interface between the Administrative Ministries and the PSEs. In fulfilling its role, it associates itself with other Ministries and organisations as also premier management institutes in the country.

20.5.3 Ministry of Micro, Small and Medium Enterprises (MoMSMEs): This Ministry designs policies and promotes/facilitates programmes, projects and schemes and monitors their implementation with a view to assisting MSMEs and help them scale up. MoMSMEs has a wide network of institutes and training centres to discharge above-mentioned functions.

The schemes/programmes undertaken by MoMSMEs and its organizations seek to facilitate/provide:

1. Adequate flow of credit from financial institutions/banks.
2. Support for technology upgradation and modernization.
3. Integrated infrastructural facilities.
4. Modern testing facilities and quality certification.
5. Access to modern management practices.
6. Entrepreneurship development and skill upgradation through appropriate training facilities.
7. Support for product development, design intervention and packaging.
8. Welfare of artisans and workers and assistance for better access to domestic and export markets.
9. Cluster-wise measures to promote capacity-building and empowerment of the units and their collectives.

The primary responsibility of promotion and development of MSMEs is of the State Governments. However, the Government of India, supplements the efforts of State Governments through different initiatives. The role of MoMSMEs and its organisations is to assist the States in their efforts to encourage entrepreneurship, employment and livelihood opportunities and enhance the competitiveness of MSMEs in the changed economic scenario.

21

Public Sector Enterprises (PSEs)

Prior to Independence in 1947, public sector activities in India were restricted to certain utility services like irrigation, railways, posts and telegraph, and ports.

After Independence the thrust of economic policy was to direct the available resources to priority sectors and to control and regulate economic activity in line with certain stated objectives of policy. The 1948 Resolution laid down the future pattern of industrialisation in the country, with a number of key industries being reserved for the State. The 1948 Resolution envisaged a mixed economy for India. It declared that public sector would play an effective and dominant role in the future economic development of India. This role was to be particularly significant in the establishment and development of heavy and basic industries. Certain crucial sectors for industrial development were reserved for Government initiative.

The 1948 Resolution was reviewed in the light of experience gained, and the new Industrial Policy Resolution was placed before Parliament by the Prime Minister on April 30, 1956.

The Industrial Policy Resolution, 1956, launched on the eve of the Second Five Year Plan (1956-61), and called by some as the economic constitution of India, observed, "The adoption of the socialistic pattern of society as well as the need for planned and rapid development require that all industries of basic and strategic importance or in the nature of public utility services should be in the public sector".

21.1 Expansion of Public Sector

From 1956 onwards, it was public sector all the way, through new units and through nationalisation of existing units. Private sector was subjected to strict rules and regulations. The expansion of public sector started in right earnest with the launching of the Second Five Year Plan (1956-61) which was virtually a plan for the establishment of heavy and key industries. Three new steel plants, each of 1 million tonne capacity, were set up in the public sector and foundations were laid for heavy electricals, heavy machine tools, and heavy engineering industries.

There were 5 CPSEs owned by the Central Government at the beginning of the First Five Year Plan on April 1, 1951 with a total investment of ₹ 29 crore. By the end of the Seventh Five Year Plan in 1990, the number of CPSEs had increased to 244 with a total investment of ₹ 99,329 crore. Thereafter, though the capital invested increased to ₹ 3,93,057 crore in 2005-06, the number of CPSEs declined to 239.

Nationalisation of existing enterprises also contributed to the expansion of public sector. Government nationalised the life insurance business in September 1956 and the general insurance business in January 1973. In July 1969, Government acquired the ownership and control of 14 major commercial banks in the country. In April 1980, six more commercial banks were nationalised, making banking business a near-monopoly of the public sector.

In another move, the Government nationalised the coking mines in 1972 and the non-coking coal mines in 1973, with the result that coal production in the country came almost completely under the public sector. Similarly, a large number of sick units, mainly in the textile sector, were nationalised from time to time.

Presently, public sector presence is predominant in public utilities and infrastructure. Railways, post and telegraph, ports, airports and power are dominated by CPSEs or department-owned enterprises. In the roads sector, while some roads are owned and maintained by the private sector, publicly-owned and maintained roads dominate. Road freight capacity is almost entirely private, while road passenger traffic capacity is also significantly privately-owned and managed. In telecom, the public sector continues to be dominant in the provision of fixed line telephone services, while private licences are operating in some urban areas. Mobile services are predominantly private, particularly in urban areas, while inter- state and international linking services are significantly privately managed and owned.

In the tradable goods sector, the public sector is dominant in coal; and oil and gas (exploration, development, extraction and transportation), though nearly one-third of oil refining capacity is now owned by the private sector. The public sector is also a significant player in steel, fertilizer, aluminium and copper. In the engineering industry, the public sector has been losing market share except in electrical machinery, where BHEL is a significant player. In construction and project services, the public sector is a minor player. The bulk of the remaining tradable sector is privately-owned and managed.

21.2 Objectives of Public Sector Enterprises

The need for public sector investment was felt to achieve the following objectives.

21.2.1 Development of Infrastructure: Public sector was needed in those areas of industrial activities which required long-term investment, advanced technology, and secrecy of operations (defence production). In other words, direct participation by the Government was required in areas where private sector was either incapable or unwilling or undesirable. By laying a strong infrastructure, public sector was expected to create congenial conditions for investment initiatives by the private sector.

21.2.2 Balanced Regional Development: The pre-Independence industrialisation was concentrated at a few port cities like Bombay, Madras and Calcutta. The post-Independence industrial policy of the Government stressed the need for the development of backward regions of the country. In promoting regional balanced development, public sector was assigned an important role and many public enterprises were located in most backward areas of the country. They were expected to benefit these areas in terms of development of infrastructure, employment opportunities and development of ancillary industries.

21.2.3 Employment Generation: Public sector enterprises employ 2.3 million workers at present mainly in such areas as iron and steel, coal, textiles, and heavy engineering. The working conditions of these workers are on the average much better than those employed in the private sector.

21.2.4 Promotion of Competitive Conditions: Public sector enterprises were expected to provide stiff competition to private sector industries in various fields like automobiles, iron and steel, road transport, pharmaceuticals, and food processing industries.

21.2.5 Check on Concentration of Economic Power: The massive capital base of public enterprises and their turnover was expected to prevent the growth of monopolies and undue concentration of economic resources of the country in few hands.

To ensure the attainment of these objectives, governmental intervention was inevitable, particularly in view of the limitations of private sector in terms of financial resources, managerial and technical skills, and entrepreneurial initiative to undertake long-gestation investments.

21.3 Organisation of Public Sector

In India, public sector enterprises have been organised in a variety of form. These enterprises may be classified into departmental enterprises and non-departmental enterprises. Non-departmental public enterprises constitute the following: (a) Government companies and (b) statutory corporations set up under special enactments of Parliament and State Legislatures. Non-departmental enterprises comprise both financial and non-financial enterprises.

21.3.1 Departmental Undertakings: Departmental enterprises such as railways are unincorporated enterprises owned and operated directly by the Government. They are run on commercial lines and their working is assessed by financial performance, a criterion which distinguishes them from administrative activities of the Government.

A departmental undertaking is directly subordinate to a Ministry of the Government. It is financed by annual appropriations from the treasury and its revenues are paid into the treasury. It is subject to the budget accounting and audit controls applicable to Government activities. The employees of a departmental undertaking are civil servants and their conditions of recruitment and service are the same as for other civil servants. It can be sued only by following the procedure prescribed for filing suits against the government.

The departmental form of organisation is considered more suitable in areas of strategic importance, requiring secrecy of operations. The ordnance factories, e.g. the Gun Carriage Factory, are under the charge of the Ministry of Defence. This form of organisation is preferred also for undertakings which provide services affecting the totality of the community or the security of the country. Thus, Indian Railways come under the charge of a full-fledged Ministry of Railways. Similarly, the operations connected with post and telegraphs are managed by a separate ministry.

The departmental system of organisation and management ensures effective Government control but suffers from the disadvantages of too much political interference, bureaucratic delays, and lack of initiative in decision-making.

21.3.2 Government Companies: A Government company is a body corporate created under the general law, viz. Indian Companies Act 1956. It embodies features of a private limited company with whole of the capital stock or 51 percent or more owned by the Government. When the whole of the capital stock is not owned by the Government, the enterprise is sometimes described as joint company, provided the share of the Government is not less than 51 percent of the stock capital. Hindustan Shipyard Limited is a case in point. The directors are appointed by the Government and the employees of the company are not civil servants. It can sue and be sued. It is generally exempt from the personnel, budget, accounting and auditing laws and procedures applicable to Government departments.

Company form of organisation is considered advantageous because it allows flexibility and autonomy necessary for the successful operation of a commercial enterprise. However, in actual practice, most of the functions of a public sector company are vested in the Government and therefore the law regulating limited companies becomes a mere fiction.

21.3.3 Public Corporations: A public corporation is created by a special law defining its objectives, powers, and privileges. Except for appropriations to provide capital or to cover losses, it is usually independently financed. It derives revenues from the sale of goods and services and can also borrow from the Government and from the public. Employees of public corporation are not civil servants.

21.3.4 Holding Companies: It is a public authority entrusted with the task of general development and running of undertakings in a particular sector of industry. For example, Steel Authority of India Limited (SAIL) is a holding company.

21.4 Poor Performance of Public Sector

Started with great fanfare after Independence, public enterprises have been afflicted with various ills over the years. Their poor performance, at least in financial terms, is reflected in low profits and in some cases mounting losses year after year. Profit-making enterprises generally enjoy monopoly status and therefore their profits are not reflective of their operational efficiency. The unsatisfactory performance of the public sector is mainly attributable to the following factors.

1. Lack of technological upgradation.
2. Inadequate attention to research and development.
3. Delays in completion and consequently increase in costs of public projects.
4. Over-staffing.
5. Labour indiscipline.
6. Under-utilisation of installed capacity.
7. Excessive political interference.
8. Bureaucratic instead of professional management.
9. Undue emphasis on capital-intensive technology.

Losses of public enterprises upset fiscal balance of the Government because these losses are eventually met from budgetary resources. If the government can get rid of these losses, it can reduce, or even wipe out, budgetary deficit.

Public sector was assigned the job of providing infrastructural facilities from the very beginning. However, its performance has been unsatisfactory. It is abundantly clear from chronic power shortages in different parts of the country which adversely affect industrial and agricultural output. Similarly, shortage of railway wagons, bad roads, congestion at sea ports and inefficient telecommunication systems have seriously hampered the growth of private industry and trade. These infrastructural bottlenecks continue to this day. Government is now soliciting the participation of private sector to augment and improve infrastructural facilities in the economy.

Regretting the performance of public sector enterprises, the Eighth Five Year Plan (1992-97) observed, "The public sector, as envisaged by Jawahar Lal Nehru, was to contribute to the growth and development of the nation by providing surplus reinvestible resources. This has not happened as it should have. Many PSUs make substantial losses and have become a continuing drain on the exchequer, absorbing resources which are withdrawn from sectors where these are desperately needed to achieve other developmental goals. Apart from the fact that the present fiscal situation does not permit any more accumulation of unsustainable losses, there is also the fact that many loss making PSUs do not serve the goal for which they were set up". [1]

21.5 Industrial Policy Statement, 1991 on Public Sector

The growing problems of the public sector enterprises in terms of low productivity, lack of technological upgradation, inadequate attention to research and development and overstaffing led to the adoption of a new approach towards the public sector. Regretting the poor performance of public sector enterprise, the Industrial Policy Statement, 1991 observed, "After the initial exuberance of the public sector entering new areas of industrial and technical competence, a number of problems have begun to manifest themselves in many of the public enterprises. Serious problems are observed in the insufficient growth in productivity, poor project management, over-manning, lack of continuous technological upgradation, and inadequate attention to R&D and human resource development. In addition, public enterprises have shown a very low rate of return on the capital investment. This has inhibited their ability to re-generate themselves in terms of new investments as well as in technology development. The result is that many of the public enterprises have become a burden rather than being an asset to the Government". [2]

The Industrial Policy Statement, 1991 had the following decisions as regards public sector enterprises.
1. Portfolio of public sector investments will be reviewed with a view to focus the public sector on strategic, high-tech and essential infrastructure. Whereas some reservation for the public sector is being retained there would be no bar for areas of exclusivity to be opened up to the private sector selectively. Similarly, the public sector will also be allowed entry in areas not reserved for it.
2. Public enterprises which are chronically sick and which are unlikely to be turned around will, for the formulation of revival/rehabilitation schemes, be referred to the Board for Industrial and Financial Reconstruction (BIFR), or other similar high level

institutions created for the purpose. A social security mechanism will be created to protect the interests of workers likely to be affected by such rehabilitation packages.

3. In order to raise resources and encourage wider public participation, a part of the Government's share-holding in the public sector would be offered to mutual funds, financial institutions, general public and workers.

4. Boards of public sector companies would be made more professional and given greater powers.

5. There will be a greater thrust on performance improvement through the Memoranda of Understanding (MoU) system through which management would be granted greater autonomy and will be held accountable. Technical expertise on the part of the Government would be upgraded to make the MoU negotiation and implementation more effective.

6. To facilitate fuller discussion on performance, the MoU signed between Government and the public enterprises would be placed in Parliament. While focusing on major management issues, this would also help place matters on day-to-day operations of public enterprises in their correct perspective.

As already noted, the July 1991 policy statement reduced the list of industries reserved for public sector from 17 included in the Industrial Policy Resolution of 1956 to only 8. Subsequently, 4 more items were de-reserved.

The Industrial Policy Statement of July 1991 marked a turning point in the public sector policy of the Government. Broadly speaking, the new policy favoured that the State should leave industry and commerce to the private sector and concentrate on those areas where it had a special or unique responsibility.

21.6 New Economic Realities and Public Sector Enterprises

Some public enterprises were established at a time when private capital was not forthcoming. However, the private sector has, in recent years, developed the capacity to invest and operate in a globally competitive manner. The private sector is now permitted in many sectors, including those which were once the exclusive preserve of the public enterprises.

With global integration of the Indian economy, many commodities and even services are imported and exported liberally and the regime is bound by obligations to the World Trade Organization (WTO). Thus, the strategic role of public enterprises in the national economy has to be considered in the context of a relatively open economy. With a liberalised environment of global trade, India is importing goods and services manufactured by the private sector from other countries. These include defence equipment as well. In such a situation, the private sector in India can legitimately expect to occupy the same space without any detriment to public interest. The dynamism of the Indian private sector has been globally acknowledged and hence its comparative advantage relative to India's public sector should be recognised. If India aspires to be a global economic power, as it should, then domestic industry has to be internationally competitive in terms of quality and range of choice available to the consumers, both at home and abroad.

Technological developments have changed the nature and range of natural monopolies (water and electricity supply). Erstwhile natural monopolies have been unbundled and several areas have since been opened for the private sector and competition. In terms of global practices, interests of consumers are better protected through effective regulation and competition than public ownership of enterprises.

Public enterprises were started with the objective of leveraging resources for development and if these enterprises are not generating assured resources for the government, there is no justification for their continued existence.

There may be a compelling need for the presence of public enterprises in specific activities from a strategic perspective, but what constitutes strategic perspective demanding the presence of public enterprises does vary from time to time. What is strategic and what is non-strategic is time-specific. Landline telephone instruments and telephone cables were considered sensitive and hence items of strategic importance in the famous Industrial Policy, 1956. Under that policy, these items were included in the list of 17 items reserved for exclusive production by government-owned enterprises. Today, transmitting and receiving video calls on a smart phone is an ordinary thing.

Likewise, what is of strategic importance presently (e.g. atomic energy) may become non-strategic a few decades from hence. In addition to nuclear-powered aircraft carriers and submarines, we may have nuclear-powered aeroplanes, railway engines and even motor cars.

Budgetary support to these loss making PSEs has been a recurring feature over the last several years. Increased competitive pressures have adversely affected some PSEs which were earlier profitable. Growing financial stringency will reduce the capacity of government to support them. Loss making PSUs are a drain on the budget unless a viable policy of disinvestment is evolved and implemented for them.

These new realities must be recognised in order to shape and develop a comprehensive public sector enterprise policy with adequate focus on the fiscal costs and benefits.

21.7 Present Policy on Public Sector

Policy of the present government regarding public sector was well articulated by Finance Minister Nirmala Sitharaman in her Budget Speech to the Parliament on February 1, 2021. It has the following objectives:

1. Minimizing presence of Central Public Sector Enterprises (CPSEs) including financial institutions and creating new investment space for private sector.
2. Post-disinvestment, economic growth of CPSEs/financial institutions will be through infusion of private capital, technology and best management practices to contribute to economic growth and new jobs.
3. Disinvestment proceeds to be used to finance various social sector and developmental programmes of the government.

Government's disinvestment policy has the following features:

1. Policy covers existing CPSEs, public sector banks and public sector insurance companies.
2. Various sectors will be classified as strategic and non-strategic sectors.

3. Strategic sectors are: (a) atomic energy, space and defence, (b) transport and telecommunications, (c) power, petroleum, coal and other minerals, and (d) banking, insurance and financial services.

4. In strategic sectors, there will be bare minimum presence of the public sector enterprises. The remaining CPSEs in the strategic sector will be privatized or merged or subsidiarized with other CPSEs or closed.

5. In non-strategic sectors, CPSEs will be privatised, otherwise shall be closed.

According to NITI Aayog, "The government should continue to exit central public sector enterprises (CPSEs) that are not strategic in nature. Inefficient CPSEs surviving on government support distort entire sectors as they operate without any real budget constraints. The government's exit will attract private investment and contribute to the exchequer, enabling higher public investment. For larger CPSEs, the goal should be to create widely-held companies by offloading stake to the public to create entities where no single promoter has control. This will both improve management efficiency and allow government to monetize its holdings with substantial contribution to public finances". [3]

Similarly, *Economic Survey, 2020-21*, observed, "The proposed privatization of public sector enterprises in non-strategic sectors recognizes the need for efficient allocation and use of resources. All these reforms are intended to bolster the productive capacity of the economy, and create wealth and jobs especially at the bottom of the pyramid. This would, in turn, lead to inclusive growth and sustained demand generation in the economy. The policy package ensures that the regulatory environment is conducive to ease of doing business with simpler, transparent and time-bound procedures for doing business.

Most of these reforms have long been recommended for enhancing the efficiency and achieving economies of scale in various sectors". [4]

In dismantling the public sector, India has adopted a gradualist approach. The public sector in India continues to be an important component of the Indian industry even after liberalisation unlike the experience in many other countries which went in for wholesale privatisation. Gradual implementation of privatisation programme has some advantages, e.g. it avoids disturbances in the economy and adverse effects on production. Rapid privatisation can lead to corruption as a result of the haphazard sale of public sector undertakings.

Government's withdrawal from non-core sectors is indicated on considerations of long-term efficient use of capital, growing financial unviability and the compulsions for these PSUs to operate in an increasingly competitive and market-oriented environment. A large number of PSEs in these sectors is either marginally profitable or loss making.

Disinvestment of a part of Government equity in public sector enterprises (PSEs) is a major policy initiative in India to carry out economic reforms. The purpose of disinvestment exercise is to improve the performance of PSEs as also to increase their public accountability by broad basing their management and ownership. Moreover, the merit of privatisation is seen in terms of improvement in efficiency and reduction in the budgetary burden of state-owned enterprises.

Private business enterprises are the principal engines of industrialisation in India.

Government is no longer promoting public sector enterprises in industry. Its principal role in industry today is to enable and regulate the activity of business enterprises in the private sector to ensure that they may profit and grow, and meet societal needs too. However, Government has been inducing private enterprises to pay more attention to societal concerns of inclusion and environmental sustainability.

Disinvestment as a strategy should also aim at wide dispersal of Government shareholding in the domestic market and broad-based ownership in the process. This of course, will be subject to limitations of the capital market in its capacity to absorb the proposed disinvestment and the capital requirements of private sector from the same market. Above all, it will be important to protect the interests of affected labour by devising suitable schemes either for retraining and redeployment or voluntary retirement with adequate compensation.

Endnotes

1. Government of India, Planning Commission, *Eighth Five Year Plan* (1992-97), Volume I, p. 16.
2. Government of India, *Industrial Policy Statement,* 1991, Para 31.
3. NITI Aayog, *Strategy for New India @ 75*, November 2018, p. 9.
4. Government of India, Ministry of Finance, *Economic Survey, 2020-21*, Volume II, p. 38.

22

Micro, Small and Medium Enterprises (MSMEs)

The role of micro, small and medium enterprises (MSMEs) in the economic and social development of the country is well known. It is the nursery for entrepreneurship, often driven by the individual creativity and innovation, with a significant contribution in the country's gross domestic product (GDP), manufacturing output, exports and employment generation.

In view of the MSME sector's role in the economic and social development of the country, the government has emphasized on its growth and development. It has taken various measures/initiatives from time to time which have facilitated the sector's ubiquitous growth.

22.1 Advantages of MSMEs

MSMEs have been recognised as engines of economic growth worldwide. In India, MSMEs manufacture products ranging from handloom sarees, carpets, soaps, pickles, *papads* to machine parts for large industries. Not only do MSMEs generate the highest employment per capita investment, they also go a long way in checking rural urban migration by providing villagers and people living in isolated areas with a sustainable source of employment. Among the MSMEs in India, the dispersed food products sector generates maximum employment. MSMEs often act as ancillary industries for the large scale industries providing them with raw materials, vital components and backward linkages.

Ever since the announcement of the Industrial Policy Resolution of 1948, small-scale industries have occupied a prominent place in the overall strategy of industrial development in India. Successive Five Year Plans allocated increasing resources for the development of small industries. In view of the abundance of labour, scarcity of capital, and rural nature of the economy, the preference for small industries is natural. The main arguments in favour of small industries are the following.

22.1.1 High Employment Potential: As development in a country takes place, the share of agriculture in providing employment and in GDP decreases. Small-scale industries provide maximum employment next only to the agricultural sector. Small industries are generally labour-intensive and therefore promise wider employment possibilities for the ever increasing population of India. They are also suitable as a supplementary source of employment for the Indian farmers who remain out of work during lean period of agricultural season. Small industries offer promising opportunities to educated unemployed in the urban areas to become self-employed gainfully.

The dispersed, unorganized and often household-based micro and small enterprises are capital-saving, labour-intensive and environment-friendly. In India, they are the largest source of employment after agriculture and are found in both rural as well as urban areas.

In view of the decline in agriculture's contribution to GDP and the near constant proportion of workers dependent on it, there is need for rapid generation of off-farm employment. There is need for diversification within agriculture (to sericulture, horticulture, pisciculture) to expand the scope for off-farm rural livelihoods. The real potential for employment generation however rests with the MSE sector which comprises weavers, artisans, and people engaged in food processing, hawkers, vendors, carpenters.

22.1.2 Widely Dispersed Entrepreneurial Base: On the eve of Independence in 1947, industries in India were located at certain selected places and were managed by a few communities like Parsis, Marwaris, and Chettiars. The Directive Principles of Indian Constitution prohibit the concentration of economic power in few hands. Small industries ensure widest possible participation by different regions and different classes in the industrial growth of the country. These industries can be set up easily in any part of the country with modest skills and resources.

22.1.3 Relatively Low Capital Investment: As is well-known, India is a capital scarce country. One chief criticism of the pattern of industrial development has been the undue emphasis on capital-intensive large-scale industries. It is probably due to this wrong policy that the industrial sector has not been able to generate sufficient employment for the massive work force. Small industries require low capital investment and that too in indigenously produced machines, tools, and implements.

MSMEs are often driven by individual creativity. A major strength of the sector is its potential for greater innovation both in terms of products and processes. An inherent strength of the sector is that these enterprises can be set up with very small amounts of investments and have the locational flexibility to be located anywhere in the country. They are amenable to ancilliarisation and thus have natural linkages with large enterprises.

22.1.4 Regional Balanced Development: Balanced development of all the regions of the country has been an accepted objective of national economic policy. Many districts of the country, particularly in tribal and hilly areas have remained industrially undeveloped/underdeveloped as compared to certain other regions of the country. It may not be feasible to set up modern large-scale industries in backward areas. Therefore, these areas can be developed through a network of cottage and small industries.

22.1.5 Export Potential: MSMEs dominate in exports of sports goods, readymade garments, woollen garments and knitwear, plastic products, processed food and leather products. It is interesting to note that handicrafts have emerged as a leading revenue-earning item in India's exports. There is tremendous potential to expand the quantum of exports by small enterprises which produce handcrafted and hence eco-friendly items. Further, while small firms are unable to take advantage of economies of scale, they are ideal for meeting small orders from bulk exporters of ready-made garments, home furnishings etc.

22.2 Micro, Small and Medium Enterprises Development (MSMED) Act, 2006

22.2.1 Background: Prior to the enactment of this Act, small industries in India comprised tiny, cottage, traditional, village and modern small enterprises. These enterprises were fragmented across various Ministries/Departments of the Government of India for the purpose of development schemes and concessions. Sectors like handloom, power loom, handicrafts, khadi, coir, suffered greater neglect than other manufacturing and service-based enterprises.

In order to correct these discrepancies and neglect, MSMED Act was enacted on June 16, 2006 which became operational from October 2, 2006. This Act provides the first-ever legal framework recognising the concept of *enterprise* (comprising both manufacturing and service entities), and defining the three tiers of these enterprises, namely micro, small and medium.

22.2.2 Classification and Definitions of MSMEs: There is no globally accepted definition of MSMEs. Different countries use different criteria, most of which are based on investment ceiling and number of people employed. In India, the MSMED Act 2006 defines MSMEs. Thus, from July 1, 2020, the classification is as under:

1. An enterprise is defined as *micro* where the investment in plant and machinery or equipment does not exceed ₹ 1 crore and turnover does not exceed ₹ 5 crore.
2. An enterprise is defined as *small* where the investment in plant and machinery or equipment does not exceed ₹ 10 crore and turnover does not exceed ₹ 50 crore.
3. An enterprise is defined as *medium* where the investment in plant and machinery or equipment does not exceed ₹ 50 crore and turnover does not exceed ₹ 250 crore (Table 22.1).

22.2.3 Main Provisions of the MSMED Act, 2006: This legislation was enacted for facilitating promotion and development and enhancing the competitiveness of micro, small and medium enterprises.

1. The Act defines *enterprise* instead of *industry* to give due recognition to the service sector.
2. It provides statutory basis (legally enforceable) to procurement preference policies of Central and State Governments for goods and services provided by micro and small enterprises.
3. It strengthens the legal provisions to check delayed payments to micro and small enterprises.
4. It makes provision for ensuring timely and smooth flow of credit to MSMEs.
5. All schemes and programmes of assistance to be notified under the Act.
6. The Act provides for a statutory National Board for Micro, Small and Medium Enterprises to advise Central Government on matters under the Act.

22.2.4 Implementation of MSMED Act, 2006: MSMED Act, 2006 came into being on October 2, 2006. Subsequently, both the Central and State Governments have taken effective steps towards implementation of the Act. While the Central Government has framed a number of rules and issued notifications in respect of the Act, different State Governments have also issued notifications under the Act.

22.2.5 National Board for Micro, Small and Medium Enterprises (NBMSMEs): NBMSMEs was established by the Government under the MSMED Act, 2006 and Rules made thereunder. It examines the factors affecting promotion and development of MSMEs and reviews policies and programmes, from time to time, relating to these enterprises and makes recommendations to the Government in formulating the policies for the growth of MSMEs. Meetings of NBMSMEs are held regularly and various issues relating to development of MSMEs are discussed and remedial measures are undertaken in consultation with the concerned departments/agencies.

Table 22.1: Criteria for Classification of Micro, Small and Medium Enterprises under Micro, Small and Medium Enterprises Development Act, 2006

	Investment in plant and machinery or equipment	Turnover
Micro	Does not exceed ₹ 1 crore	Does not exceed ₹ 5 crore
Small	Does not exceed ₹ 10 crore	Does not exceed ₹ 50 crore
Medium	Does not exceed ₹ 50 crore	Does not exceed ₹ 250 crore

Source: Government of India, Ministry of Micro, Small and Medium Enterprises, Notification No. S.O. 1702 (E) dated June 1, 2020.

22.3 Ministry of Micro, Small and Medium Enterprises (MoMSMEs)

On May 9, 2007, subsequent to an amendment of the Government of India (Allocation of Business) Rules, 1961, the Ministry of Small Scale Industries and the Ministry of Agro and Rural Industries were merged to form the Ministry of Micro, Small and Medium Enterprises (MoMSMEs). This Ministry now designs policies and promotes/facilitates programmes, projects and schemes and monitors their implementation with a view to assisting MSMEs and help them scale up. The Ministry runs various schemes aimed at financial assistance, technology assistance and upgradation, infrastructure development, skill development and training, enhancing competitiveness and market assistance of MSMEs.

22.3.1 Functions: The major functions of MoMSMEs are as under:

1. Advising the Government in policy formulation for the promotion and development of MSMEs.
2. Providing techno-economic and managerial consultancy, common facilities and extension services to the MSMEs.
3. Making available facilities for technology upgradation, modernisation, quality improvement and infrastructure.
4. Developing human resources through training and skill upgradation.
5. Providing economic information services.
6. Maintaining a close liaison with the Central Ministries, Planning Commission, State Governments, financial institutions and other organisations concerned with the development of MSMEs.
7. Evolving and coordinating policies and programmes for development of the sector as ancillaries to large industries.
8. Inculcating of entrepreneurial culture amongst the youth.
9. Facilitating credit flow to MSMEs.

10. Promoting MSMEs through cluster-based approach.
11. Providing marketing support to MSMEs.

MoMSMEs has a wide network of institutes and training centres to discharge above-mentioned functions.

22.4 Problems of MSMEs

In spite of having the potential and inherent capabilities to grow, MSMEs in India have been facing a number of problems like sub-optimal scale of operations, technological obsolescence, supply chain inefficiencies, increasing domestic and global competition, funds shortage, change in manufacturing strategies and turbulent and uncertain market scenario.

MSMEs, though important, suffer from a number of constraints and weaknesses which have resulted in their retarded growth. Inadequate working capital, shortage of trained personnel, obsolete technology and lack of information to access markets and foreign business opportunities, are the major barriers to the growth of MSMEs in India.

A predominant number of enterprises is in the unorganized sector, often located in non-conforming urban zones. While the country has a large pool of human resources, this sector continues to face shortage of skilled manpower due to lack of paying capacity and poor managerial capabilities.

22.4.1 Credit Constraints: Scarcity of finance is a major obstacle in the development of MSMEs. The capital base of the small entrepreneur is usually weak and often he has to procure credit at a high rate of interest. Securing bank credits, difficulties in documentations for bank loans and lack of collateral security are bigger problems in India than in the majority of the other developing countries in Asia.

In most cases, capital comes from savings and loans from friends and relatives rather than through banking system. This problem is particularly acute for the village industries as well as the lower end of micro industries. Same is the case with traditional sector where payments are made by traders only after the stock is sold. Thus money is held up, further impoverishing the workers.

22.4.2 Inadequate and Irregular Supply of Raw Materials: MSMEs generally depend on local sources of raw material. They have to purchase raw material in small quantities and often on credit. Apparently, they cannot compete with large-scale industries in the procurement of raw material. In many cases the raw material is an imported item. Quite often, small industries have to pay a higher price for inputs and suffer uncertainty in their procurement.

Non-availability of quality raw materials like dyes and yarn (especially for handlooms and power looms), vital inputs like power (for power looms, handicrafts, other industrial MSMEs) and proper packaging facilities continue to be major bottlenecks. Lack of credit combined with inadequate raw material often pushes weavers, artisans, entrepreneurs into the clutches of loan sharks and middlemen. Though the National Small Industries Corporation (NSIC) and State Small-scale Industries Development Corporations are providing some raw materials, their efforts are not in consonance with the requirements.

22.4.3 Lack of Infrastructural Facilities: Many MSMEs, particularly in backward areas, are still deprived of infrastructural facilities like power, transport, and communication services. This has hampered their proper and efficient working thereby retarding their development.

Maintenance of industrial estates (mainly maintenance of roads, drainage, sewage, power distribution and captive power generation, water supply, dormitories for workers, common effluent treatment plants, common facilities, security etc.) is a critical component for successful functioning of the industrial enterprises in any industrial estate/industrial area. Industrial estates are generally developed by state industrial development bodies. MSMEs are either located in industrial estates set up many decades ago or are functioning within urban areas or have come up in an unorganised manner in semi-urban or rural areas. The state of infrastructure, including power, water, roads, etc. in such areas is poor and unreliable, leading to very high transaction costs.

22.4.4 Marketing Handicaps for MSMEs: Another major problem of MSMEs is absence of marketing channels and brand building capacity. Most MSMEs do not have money to invest in market research and are unable to carry out design and technical improvements to keep up with market demands.

Advertisement is one of the main tools of marketing, through which information about the products is disseminated amongst its users. While large enterprises have sufficient resources for advertisement and publicity, MSMEs have scarcity of resources which restricts them for making publicity/advertisement of their products. This limits their ability to tap markets and attract consumers. MSMEs, especially those pertaining to traditional livelihoods are, therefore, increasingly being forced to rely on middle men, petty traders and big businesses to market their products.

Access to marketing is a major constraint for enterprises in the unorganised sector. This sector produces a large proportion of industrial output in the economy and yet the sector becomes immediately vulnerable in response to volatile, fragmented and shifting demand that is characteristic of current national and international markets.

22.4.5 Challenges of Globalisation: Historically, Indian MSMEs in the manufacturing sector have been catering more to domestic markets unlike in China where exports have been a major driver of manufacturing. For some MSMEs, this may entail the advantage of being shielded from the global cyclical pulls. However, such an approach denies the possibilities of global market opportunities. The marketing strategy of MSMEs products needs to take an integrated view of both the local and global markets.

In the post-WTO agenda, domestic markets have been opened up for imports, creating severe competition for the local industries. At the same time it has created opportunities for the small industries for exports to developed countries. To gain from this opportunity, effort must be made in pushing for greater market access in the developed countries. This would need technological upgradation to produce better quality products at cheap rates. Information dissemination about availability of recent technologies, literature on modern machinery, contact details of suppliers etc. is essential.

22.4.6 Technological Obsolescence: MSMEs sector is heterogeneous with pockets of high technology enterprises but majority of units suffering from low technology base, resulting in low productivity and poor quality of products. As a result, sustainability of a large number of MSMEs is in question in the face of competition from imported goods. Also alliances of MSMEs with domestic large companies are fragile, since the large companies can themselves build alliances with overseas suppliers.

Technology is one of the most critical elements in the growth of MSMEs. India is ranked at the top in terms of availability of science and engineering personnel. However, MSMEs in India are loosing their competitive edge in the global markets due to lack of modern technology. Due to obsolete technology, cost of manufacturing is much higher than in the other developing countries in Asia. Addressing these problems to ensure a vibrant MSMEs sector is essential for sustained and inclusive growth.

The technique of production used in many small industries like weaving and wood carving is obsolete. This has led to high production cost and output of inferior quality goods. Hence, modernisation of technology is urgently required to make small industries efficient. Technology should be the foremost factor for enhancing the global competitiveness of Indian MSMEs. Without infusion of appropriate technology, survival in the global market place would be a question mark for a large majority of MSMEs.

22.5 Micro Units Development and Refinance Agency (MUDRA)

Small enterprises are at the heart of employment generation and decentralization of economic power in India. However, facilitation from the government is required to minimise the transaction costs of technology upgradation, market penetration, and modernisation of infrastructure. The sector is suffering from quite a few impediments, which need to be addressed immediately to make small businesses a hub of entrepreneurship and innovations.

MUDRA is a non-banking financial company (NBFC) which supports development of micro enterprise sector in India. It provides refinance support to banks/micro finance institutions (MFIs) for lending to micro units under Pradhan Mantri MUDRA Yojana.

MUDRA loan is extended for a variety of purposes which help income generation and employment creation. The loans are extended mainly for the following activities:
1. Business loan for vendors, traders, shopkeepers and other service sector activities.
2. Working capital loan through MUDRA cards.
3. Equipment finance for micro units.
4. Transport vehicle loans.

Following is an illustrative list of the activities that can be covered under MUDRA loans:

22.5.1 Transport Vehicles: Purchase of transport vehicles for goods and personal transport such as auto rickshaw, small goods transport vehicle, 3-wheelers, e-rickshaw, passenger cars, taxis etc.

22.5.2 Community, Social and Personal Service Activities: Saloons, beauty parlours, gymnasium, boutiques, tailoring shops, dry cleaning, cycle and motorcycle repair shops, DTP and photocopying facilities, medicine shops, courier agents etc.

22.5.3 Food Products Sector: It includes the following:

1. Activities such as papad, achaar, jam and jelly making.
2. Agricultural produce preservation at the rural level.
3. Sweet shops, small service food stalls and day-to-day catering/canteen services.
4. Cold chain vehicles, cold storages, ice and ice cream making units.
5. Biscuits, bread and bun making units.

22.5.4 Textile Products Sector/Activity: Following are included under it:
1. Handloom, power loom, khadi, chikan work, zari and zardozi work.
2. Traditional embroidery and hand work, traditional dyeing and printing, apparel design, knitting etc.
3. Cotton ginning, computerized embroidery and stitching.
4. Non-garment products such as bags, vehicle accessories, furnishing accessories etc.

22.5.5 Business Loans for Traders and Shopkeepers: These include financial support for onward lending to individuals for running their shops, trading and business activities, service enterprises and non-farm income generating activities with beneficiary loan size of up to ₹ 10 lakh per enterprise/borrower.

22.5.6 Equipment Finance Scheme for Micro Units: It pertains to setting up micro enterprises by purchasing necessary machinery/equipments with per beneficiary loan size of up to ₹ 10 lakh.

22.5.7 Activities Allied to Agriculture: These include pisciculture, bee keeping, poultry, livestock, rearing, grading, sorting, aggregation agro industries, dairy, fisheries, agri-clinics and agribusiness centres, food and agro-processing etc. (excluding crop loans, and loans for land improvement such as canal, irrigation and wells).

To sum up, while the growth of the MSMEs in recent years is quite impressive, there is need for further unshackling of the sector to derive its full growth potential. In this regard, providing a congenial regulatory framework and removal of the entry barriers are two pivotal issues. While the MSMED Act, 2006 has addressed the overall regulatory issues related to the MSME sector at Government of India level, the State level regulatory scenario is quite diverse with some of the States having highly supportive policies for the promotion of the sector while others are lagging behind.

23

Industrial Finance

Strategy of economic development of any country invariably consists of efficient utilisation of resources available at its disposal with paramount emphasis on proper utilisation of scarce productive resources. Most developing countries, including India, face the problem of paucity of capital, while having ample quantities of natural and human resources. Hence, emphasis has to be placed on effective utilisation of capital to accelerate the rate of growth and improve the efficiency of the productive system.

23.1 Need for Industrial Finance

Modern system of industrial production is very complex requiring huge investments, both in terms of material and human resources. It may be beyond the capacity of an individual to arrange on his own all the resources required to undertake production. Modern corporations or joint stock companies are the answer to these requirements.

Financial needs of an enterprise may be classified into two categories: (a) fixed capital and (b) working capital. Modern industry is capital-intensive by nature and its fixed capital includes land and buildings, plant and machinery, and tools and implements. The requirement of finance to purchase fixed capital is essentially long-term in nature. The working capital, short-term in nature, is required to purchase raw materials and meet day-to-day administrative and other such expenses.

Efficient utilisation of capital requires the establishment of sound and consistent management policies, covering both fixed as well as working capital. However, greater importance has generally been attached to the allocation and utilisation of fixed capital. The allocation and effective management of working capital appears to have been relatively neglected.

Management of working capital, which encompasses the short-term investment and financing decisions of the firm, affects profitability as well as liquidity of the enterprise. Excessive working capital leads to unremunerative use of scarce funds while inadequate working capital interrupts the smooth run of business activity. Hence, both the situations impair profitability. Sound working capital management, by optimising the use of funds, enhances profitability. It improves liquidity by focusing attention on flow of funds through proper management of cash, receivables, inventories and short-term sources of funds. While efficient working capital management can do much to ensure the success of a business, its inefficient management can lead not only to loss of profits but also to ultimate downfall of what otherwise might be considered as a promising concern.

23.2 Sources of Industrial Finance

There are various sources of finance for a modern industrial unit. These sources are of two types: (a) internal sources and (b) external sources. Internal sources include paid-up capital in the form of share subscriptions, ploughing back of profits, and reserves. The external sources include debenture issue, public deposits, loans from commercial banks and other specialised institutions, and foreign commercial borrowings. A brief description of the internal and external sources of finance available to an industrial unit is as follows:

23.2.1 Internal Sources: These include the following:

A. Shares: Industrial undertakings are generally set up as joint stock companies. These companies enjoy the right to issue shares for building up fixed capital. Companies issue two types of shares, viz. preference shares and ordinary shares. However, most of the authorised capital is obtained through the issue of ordinary shares.

Ordinary shares represent ownership capital and their owners (ordinary shareholders) share the reward and risk associated with ownership of corporate enterprises. They are called ordinary shares in contrast with preference shares which carry certain prior rights with regard to income and redemption.

B. Ploughing Back of Profits: All the profits earned by a company may not be distributed among the shareholders. A part of earned profits may remain undistributed and used for the development of the company.

23.2.2 External Sources: These comprise the following:

A. Debentures: A debenture is a loan to the company and a debenture holder is a creditor of the company. It is meant for those investors who are unwilling to risk their capital and feel satisfied with a regular income. Capital raised through debentures is generally used to finance improvements/extensions of the concern.

B. Public Deposits: The acceptance of public deposits by non-banking companies, and firms is regulated by the Reserve Bank of India. It is an important source of finance for reputed companies.

C. Commercial Banks: A commercial bank is a financial intermediary which accepts deposits of money from the public and lends them with a view to make profits. Lending operations of the commercial banks to the industry are governed by the guidelines issued by the Reserve Bank of India.

23.2.3 Development Finance Institutions (DFIs): Development finance institutions (DFIs) or simply financial institutions were set up in India at various points of time starting from the late 1940s to cater to the medium to long-term financing requirements of industry as the capital market in India had not developed sufficiently. After Independence in 1947, the national government adopted the path of planned economic development and launched the First Five Year Plan in 1951. This strategy of development provided the critical inducement for establishment of DFIs at both all-India and state-levels. In order to perform their role, DFIs were extended funds of the RBI and government guaranteed bonds, which constituted major sources of their funds. Funds from these sources were not only available at concessional rates, but also on a long-term basis with their maturity period ranging from 10-15 years. On the asset side, their operations were marked by near absence of competition.

A large variety of financial institutions have come into existence over the years to perform various types of financial activities. While some of them operate at all-India level, others are state level institutions. Besides providing direct loans (including rupee loans, foreign currency loans), financial institutions also extend financial assistance by way of underwriting and direct subscription and by issuing guarantees. Recently, some DFIs have started extending short-term/working capital finance, although term-lending continues to be their primary activity. DFIs in India can be categorised and sub-categorised in the following manner:

1. All-India Financial Institutions (AIFIs) which include the following:
*   All-India Development Banks.
*   Specialised institutions.
*   Investment institutions.
*   Refinance institutions.
2. State-level institutions which include the following:
*   State Financial Corporations (SFCs).
*   State Industrial Development Corporations (SIDCs).

A. All-India Financial Institutions (AIFIs): These are as under:

(a) All-India Development Banks: These banks are the main source of medium and long-term project financing. These banks promote economic development of India by: (a) providing medium and long-term finance to industry. It is provided in the form of term loans and advances and subscription to shares and debentures, (b) providing guarantees for term loans and underwriting new equity. Guarantees and underwriting by development banks create confidence among investors and thus facilitate the raising of funds by companies and (c) performing various types of promotional roles for the private entrepreneurs as, for example, identification of investment projects, and arrangement for managerial and technical advice.

Development banks are different from commercial banks in several respects. Firstly, development banks do not accept deposits from the public as commercial banks do. For example, financial resources of development banks in India come from Government of India, Reserve Bank of India and from international agencies like World Bank and its affiliate International Development Association (IDA). Secondly, they specialise in providing medium-term and long-term finance while commercial banks generally provide short-term credit. Thirdly, development banks perform promotional role for industrial development of the country whereas commercial banks provide utility and other services to their customers.

Some important institutions of this category are the following:

1. Industrial Finance Corporation of India (IFCI)
2. Industrial Development Bank of India (IDBI)
3. Industrial Credit and Investment Corporation of India Ltd. (ICICI)
4. Small Industries Development Bank of India (SIDBI)

(b) Specialised Financial Institutions: Some of the important institutions in this category are the following.

1. Export-Import Bank (EXIM Bank)

2. India Infrastructure Finance Company Limited (IIFCL)
3. Tourism Finance Corporation of India (TFCI)

(c) Investment Institutions: These have played significant roles in the mobilisation of household sector savings and their deployment in the credit and the capital markets. Major institutions in this category are the following.

1. Unit Trust of India (UTI)
2. Life Insurance Corporation of India (LIC)
3. General Insurance Corporation of India (GIC)

(d) Refinance Institutions: Two institutions in this category are noteworthy.

1. National Bank for Agriculture and Rural Development (NABARD)
2. National Housing Bank (NHB)

B. State Level Institutions: Operations of the state-level institutions are generally confined to their respective States. The two important institutions in this category are the following.

(a) State Financial Corporations (SFCs): They are set up under the State Financial Corporations Act, 1951. At present there are 18 SFCs in the country, assisting small and medium enterprises.

The mandate of the SFCs is to promote regional growth in the country through the development of SMEs by grants or loans and participation in their equity. The 18 SFCs across the country provide financial assistance by way of term loans. The lending is in the format of loans and debentures and they also operate schemes of IDBI/SIDBI in addition to extending working capital loans under the composite loan scheme. Many of the SFCs have failed to achieve these objectives and some of them are now almost defunct. Much of the failure could be attributed to the absence of managerial autonomy, professional management and a host of other problems related to the functioning of state-level public sector institutions.

(b) State Industrial Development Corporations (SIDCs): These institutions provide funds for promoting industrial development in their respective states.

23.3 External (Foreign) Commercial Borrowing (ECBs)

It is well-known that domestic companies in India borrow funds from foreign markets, i.e. external commercial borrowings (ECBs). ECBs are loans in foreign currency raised by Indian borrowers from non-resident lenders. ECBs are widely used by Indian companies to facilitate access to foreign money. Most of these loans are provided by foreign commercial banks. RBI regulates and monitors guidelines and policies regarding ECBs. Currently, the RBI cap on the lending rate of ECBs is London Inter-Bank Offered Rate (LIBOR) of 2 percent plus 4.5 percent, which means companies in India can borrow at an interest rate anywhere between 2 to 6.5 percent.

ECBs are bi-partite loan contracts denominated in foreign currency and initiated by the domestic borrowers. India's approach has been that since the external liability of the economy should not be allowed to expand excessively, the ECBs need to be allocated, to their most productive uses. This objective is sought to be achieved through a regulatory regime comprising restrictions on the quantum of loan, end use, tenor, lender credentials and cost of borrowing. The ECB framework has evolved over the years, as this regulatory regime has been revised from time to time.

ECBs provide an additional source of funds for corporates to finance the expansion of existing capacity as well as new investment, taking cognisance of interest rate differentials between domestic and international markets and the associated market risks. ECBs include commercial bank loans, buyers' credit, suppliers' credit, and commercial borrowings from the private sector window of multilateral financial institutions such as International Financial Corporation (IFC) and Asian Development Bank (ADB). An important objective of ECB policy in India has been to provide flexibility in borrowings by Indian corporates, while maintaining prudent limits for total external borrowings.

The policy on ECBs was made transparent in the 1990s. Procedures have also been streamlined to enable borrowers to improve access to international financial markets. The ECB policy favours long-term borrowings and maintains a strict control on short-term borrowings.

One of the guiding principles for ECB policy has been to encourage infrastructure financing since such facilities are crucial for the overall growth of the economy.

23.3.1 ECB Policy Review, January 2004: To enhance investment activity in the real sector, particularly in infrastructure, and to enable corporates to access resources from international markets at competitive rates, the policy related to ECBs was reviewed in January 2004. The review was undertaken in view of the need to supplant the prevailing temporary restrictions on access to ECBs with more stable, transparent and simplified procedures and policies. The review was based on the current macroeconomic situation reflecting subdued investment activity, challenges faced in external sector management, the experience gained so far in administering the ECB policy and concerns expressed by borrowers in this regard.

The liberalised framework was expected to introduce stability in ECB policy by simplifying and rationalising procedures, while minimising discretionary elements and promoting greater transparency. Key features of the revised guidelines were as under:

1. **Removal of End-use Restrictions:** ECB was allowed for corporate investments in industrial sector especially infrastructure sector. Money had to be parked abroad unless actually required. Usual restriction on ECB for investment in capital market or in the real estate, however, continued.

2. **Eligibility:** All corporates except banks, non-banking financial companies (NBFCs) and financial institutions (FIs) were made eligible ECB borrowers.

3. **Interest Rate Spreads:** ECBs with average maturity of 3-5 years were subject to a maximum spread of 200 basis points over six month LIBOR of the respective currency in which the loan was being raised or the applicable benchmark(s). ECBs with more than 5 years of average maturity were subject to a maximum spread of 350 basis points.

4. **Guarantee:** Banks, FIs and NBFCs were not able to provide guarantee/letter of comfort etc.

5. **Procedure:** All ECBs satisfying the above criteria were under the automatic route up to US$ 20 million for ECBs between 3-5 years of average maturity and up to US$ 500 million for ECBs having average maturity of more than 5 years.

All cases which fell outside the purview of the automatic route in the new liberalised ECB policy were decided by an Empowered Committee of the RBI.

ECB proceeds could be utilised for any general corporate purposes except investment in stock market and real estate due to risk of speculative bubbles associated in these sectors. In the real estate sector, the ECB proceeds could be used for the purpose of development of integrated townships. Similarly, ECBs were permitted for the purpose of first stage acquisition of shares in PSU disinvestments and in mandatory second stage offer to the public.

23.3.2 New ECB Framework, 2019: As per the old framework, which was in effect till January 15, 2019, ECBs could be raised either under the automatic route or under the approval route. The policy was premised on a three-track approach: Track I for Medium term foreign currency denominated ECB with minimum average maturity of 3/5 years; Track II for long-term foreign currency denominated ECB with minimum average maturity of 10 years; and Track III for Indian Rupee (INR) denominated ECB with minimum average maturity of 3/5 years. All the parameters of the framework viz., minimum average maturity period (MAMP), eligible borrowers, recognised lenders/investors, all-in-cost (AIC), end-use prescriptions, individual limits and currency of borrowing were formulated separately for these tracks.

The Fifth Bi-monthly Monetary Policy Statement for 2018-19 released on December 5, 2018 proposed, among others, to revise the above framework in consultation with the Government. Accordingly, a New Framework for External Commercial Borrowings (ECB) Policy was announced by the RBI in January 2019.

The new ECB framework came into effect from January 16, 2019. External borrowing norms have been simplified under two tracks: foreign currency denominated ECBs; and rupee denominated ECBs. The list of eligible borrowers has been expanded to include all entities eligible to receive FDI, registered entities engaged in microfinance activities, registered societies/ trusts/ cooperatives and non-government organisations. A rule-based dynamic limit for outstanding stock of ECBs at 6.5 percent of GDP is in place. Rupee denominated bonds or Masala bonds under the ECB route offer an opportunity to domestic firms to borrow from international markets without the need for hedging exchange rate risk. ECBs up to US $ 750 million or equivalent per financial year are permitted under the automatic route. Further, end-use restrictions relating to external commercial borrowings have also been relaxed for specific eligible borrowers for their working capital requirements, general corporate purposes and repayment of rupee loans. The mandatory hedging requirement had earlier been reduced from 100 percent to 70 percent for ECBs with minimum average maturity period between 3 and 5 years in the infrastructure space.

24

Recent Initiatives for Industrial Development

24.1 Make in India Campaign

Make in India is an initiative of the Government of India to encourage multinational, as well as domestic, companies to manufacture their products in India. It was launched by Prime Minister Narendra Modi on September 25, 2014. The objective is to make India as the top destination globally for foreign direct investment.

24.1.1 Origin and the Roadmap: On December 29, 2014, a workshop was organised by the Department of Industrial Policy and Promotion, (DIPP), Ministry of Commerce and Industry, Government of India which was attended by Prime Minister Modi, his cabinet ministers and chief secretaries of states as well as various industry leaders.

DIPP worked with a group of highly specialised agencies to build brand new infrastructure, including a dedicated help desk and a website that packed a wide array of information into a simple, sleek menu. Designed primarily for mobile screens, the site's architecture ensured that exhaustive levels of detail are neatly tucked away so as not to overwhelm the user. 25 sector brochures were also developed which included key facts and figures, policies and initiatives and sector-specific contact details, all of which was made available in print and on site.

These exercises resulted in a road map for the single largest manufacturing initiative undertaken by a nation in recent history. They also demonstrated the transformational power of public-private partnership, and have become a hallmark of the Make in India initiative. This collaborative model has also been successfully extended to include India's global partners, as evidenced by the recent in-depth interactions between India and the United States of America.

The major objective behind the initiative is to focus on job creation and skill enhancement in 25 sectors of the economy. The initiative also aims at high quality standards and minimising the impact on the environment. Hence, the slogan *zero defect, zero effect*. The slogan also aims to prevent products developed from India from being rejected by the global market. The initiative hopes to attract capital and technological investment in India.

Before the initiative was launched, foreign equity caps in various sectors had been relaxed. The application for licenses was made available online and the validity of licenses was increased to three years. Various other norms and procedures were also relaxed.

Devised to transform India into a global design and manufacturing hub, Make in India was a timely response to a critical situation: by 2013, the much-hyped emerging markets bubble had burst, and India's growth rate had fallen to its lowest level in a decade. The promise of the BRICS Nations (Brazil, Russia, India, China and South Africa) had faded, and India was tagged as one of the so-called *Fragile Five*. Global investors debated whether the world's largest democracy was a risk or an opportunity.

India's 1.2 billion citizens questioned whether India was too big to succeed or too big to fail. India was on the brink of severe economic failure.

Make in India was launched against the backdrop of this crisis, and quickly became a rallying cry for India's innumerable stakeholders and partners. It was a powerful, galvanising call to action to India's citizens and business leaders, and an invitation to potential partners and investors around the world. Make in India is much more than an inspiring slogan. It represents a comprehensive and unprecedented overhaul of out-dated processes and policies. More importantly, it represents a complete change of the Government's mindset: a shift from issuing authority to business partner.

To start a movement, a strategy is needed that inspires, empowers and enables in equal measure. Make in India needed a different kind of campaign: instead of the typical statistics-laden newspaper advertisements, this exercise required messaging that was informative, well-packaged and credible. It had to: (a) inspire confidence in India's capabilities amongst potential partners abroad, the Indian business community and citizens at large; (b) provide a framework for a vast amount of technical information on 25 industry sectors; and (c) reach out to a vast local and global audience via social media and constantly keep them updated about opportunities, reforms etc.

24.1.2 Four Pillars of Make-in-India Initiative: With the objective of making India a global hub of manufacturing, design and innovation, the Make in India initiative is based on four pillars—new processes, new infrastructure, new sectors and new mindset. The initiative is set to boost entrepreneurship, not only in manufacturing but in relevant infrastructure and service sectors as well. An interactive portal www.makeinindia.com for dissemination of information and interaction with investors has been created with the objective of generating awareness about the investment opportunities and prospects of the country, to promote India as a preferred investment destination in markets overseas and to increase Indian share of global FDI. In addition, information on 25 thrust sectors, along with details of the FDI Policy, National Manufacturing Policy, intellectual property rights and the proposed National Industrial Corridors including the Delhi Mumbai Industrial Corridor (DMIC), are available on the portal. The Department of Industrial Policy and Promotion (DIPP), in consultation with various Central Ministries, State Governments, industry leaders, and other stakeholders, has formulated a strategy for increasing the contribution of the manufacturing sector to 25 percent of the GDP by 2020.

The Government of India has set up Invest India as the national investment promotion and facilitation agency. With the objective of promoting investment in the country, a full-fledged Investment Facilitation Cell has been set-up under the Make in India initiative, primarily to support all investment queries as well as to handhold and liaise with various agencies on behalf of potential investors.

As envisaged by the National Manufacturing Policy 2011, Make in India seeks to create 100 million additional jobs in manufacturing by 2022. The government is taking a number of steps to enhance the skills of workers/unemployed in India in order to improve their employability. In order to tap the creative potential and boost entrepreneurship in India, the Start-up India and Stand-up India campaign have been launched. An innovation promotion platform called Atal Innovation Mission (AIM) and a techno-financial, incubation and facilitation programme called Self-Employment and Talent Utilization (SETU) are being implemented to encourage innovation and start-ups in India.

For supporting the financial needs of the small and medium enterprises sector and promote start-ups and entrepreneurship, the government has taken various steps through Make in India. The India Aspiration Fund has also been set up under the Small Industries Development Bank of India (SIDBI) for venture capital financing of newly set-up or expanding units in the MSME sector. SIDBI Make in India Loan for Small Enterprises (SMILE) has been launched to offer quasi-equity and term-based short-term loans to Indian SMEs with less stringent rules and regulations and a special focus on 25 thrust sectors of Make in India. Further, a Micro Units Development Refinance Agency (MUDRA) Bank has been set up to provide development and refinance to commercial banks/NBFCs/cooperative banks for loans given to micro-units. MUDRA Bank would follow a credit-plus approach by also providing financial literacy and addressing skill gaps, information gaps etc.

24.1.3 Sectors Identified: Make in India focuses on the following 25 sectors of the economy:

1. Automobiles.
2. Automobile components.
3. Aviation.
4. Biotechnology.
5. Chemicals.
6. Construction.
7. Defence manufacturing.
8. Electrical machinery.
9. Electronic systems.
10. Food processing.
11. Information technology and business process management.
12. Leather.
13. Media and entertainment.
14. Mining.
15. Oil and gas.
16. Pharmaceuticals.
17. Ports and shipping.
18. Railways.
19. Renewable energy.
20. Roads and highways.
21. Space.
22. Textiles and garments.
23. Thermal power.
24. Tourism and hospitality.
25. Wellness.

24.1.4 Progress of Make in India Campaign: In a short space of time, the obsolete and obstructive frameworks of the past have been dismantled and replaced with a transparent and user-friendly system that is helping drive investment, foster innovation, develop skills, protect intellectual property (IP) and build best-in-class manufacturing infrastructure. The most striking indicator of progress is the unprecedented opening up of key sectors—including railways, defence, insurance and medical devices—to dramatically higher levels of foreign direct investment (FDI).

Indian embassies and consulates have also been communicated to disseminate information on the potential for investment in the identified sectors. DIPP has set up a special management team to facilitate and fast track investment proposals from Japan, the team known as Japan Plus was operationalized in October 2014. Similarly Korea Plus, launched in June 2016, facilitates fast track investment proposals from South Korea and offers holistic support to Korean companies wishing to enter the Indian market.

Six industrial corridors are being developed across various regions of the country. Industrial cities will also come up along these corridors.

Presently, India's credibility is stronger than ever. There is visible momentum, energy and optimism. Make in India is opening investment doors. Multiple enterprises are adopting its mantra. The world's largest democracy is well on its way to becoming the world's most powerful economy.

Make in India initiative has become a catalyst to India's booming domestic manufacturing sector. The initiative has propelled progress towards high value-added manufacturing growth and heavy investment attraction. With the help of operational and legal relaxations, effective infrastructure programmes and schemes, and focusing focus on upgrading the strength of skill sets, the Make in India initiative has facilitated the government's persistent efforts to attract investments from around the world. The initiative's aggressive efforts towards reinforcing connectivity, channelizing production methodologies, and maximizing effective investment incentives have put India on a path to excellence. Make in India is contributing to nurture the country's economic and industrial transformation, and for steering the country towards an environment conducive to domestic and global manufacturing and investment.

24.2 Start-up India Initiative

Prime Minister Narendra Modi in his Independence Day address had announced a Start-up India initiative in which each of the 1.25 lakh bank branches would provide funding support to at least one *dalit* or *adivasi* entrepreneur and at least one woman entrepreneur.

Launched on January 16, 2016, Start-up India is a flagship initiative of the Government of India, intended to build a strong eco-system for nurturing innovation and Start-ups in the country that will drive sustainable economic growth and generate large scale employment opportunities. The Government through this initiative aims to empower Start-ups to grow through innovation and design.

24.2.1 Meaning of a Start-up: Start-up means an entity, incorporated or registered in India not prior to 5 years, with annual turnover not exceeding ₹ 25 crore in any preceding financial year, working towards innovation, development, deployment or commercialization of new products, processes or services driven by technology or intellectual property.

- Provided that such entity is not formed by splitting up, or reconstruction, of a business already in existence.
- Provided also that an entity shall cease to be a Start-up if its turnover for the previous financial years has exceeded ₹ 25 crore or it has completed 5 years from the date of incorporation/registration.
- Provided further that a Start-up shall be eligible for tax benefits only after it has obtained certification from the Inter-Ministerial Board, setup for such purpose.

24.2.2 Start-up India: Features: In order to meet the objectives of the initiative, Government of India announced this Action Plan that addresses all aspects of the Start-up ecosystem. With this Action Plan the Government hopes to accelerate spreading of the Start-up movement:

1. From digital/technology sector to a wide array of sectors including agriculture, manufacturing, social sector, healthcare, education, etc.
2. From existing tier 1 cities to tier 2 and tier 3 cities including semi-urban and rural areas.

The Action Plan is divided across the following areas:

1. Simplification and handholding.
2. Funding support and incentives.
3. Industry-academia partnership and incubation.

24.2.3 Simplification and Handholding:

A. Compliance Regime Based on Self-certification: The objective is to reduce the regulatory burden on start-ups thereby allowing them to focus on their core business and keep compliance cost low. Regulatory formalities requiring compliance with various labour and environment laws are time consuming and difficult in nature. Often, new and small firms are unaware of nuances of the issues and can be subjected to intrusive action by regulatory agencies. In order to make compliance for start-ups friendly and flexible, simplifications are required in the regulatory regime.

Accordingly, the process of conducting inspections shall be made more meaningful and simple. Start-ups shall be allowed to self-certify compliance (through the Start-up mobile app) with 9 labour and environment laws. In case of the labour laws, no inspections will be conducted for a period of 3 years. Start-ups may be inspected on receipt of credible and verifiable complaint of violation, filed in writing and approved by at least one level senior to the inspecting officer.

In case of environment laws, start-ups which fall under the *white category* (as defined by the Central Pollution Control Board (CPCB) would be able to self-certify compliance and only random checks would be carried out in such cases.

(a) Labour Laws:

1. Building and Other Constructions Workers' (Regulation of Employment and

Conditions of Service) Act, 1996.

2. Inter-State Migrant Workmen (Regulation of Employment and Conditions of Service) Act, 1979.
3. Payment of Gratuity Act, 1972.
4. Contract Labour (Regulation and Abolition) Act, 1970.
5. Employees' Provident Funds and Miscellaneous Provisions Act, 1952.
6. Employees' State Insurance Act, 1948.

(b) Environment Laws:

1. Water (Prevention and Control of Pollution) Act, 1974.
2. Water (Prevention and Control of Pollution) Cess (Amendment) Act, 2003.
3. Air (Prevention and Control of Pollution) Act, 1981.

B. Start-up India HUB: The purpose is to create a single point of contact for the entire Start-up ecosystem and enable knowledge exchange and access to funding. Young Indians today have the conviction to venture out on their own and a conducive ecosystem lets them watch their ideas come to life. In today's environment we have more start-ups and entrepreneurs than ever before and the movement is at the cusp of a revolution. However, many Start-ups do not reach their full potential due to limited guidance and access.

The Government of India has taken various measures to improve the ease of doing business and is also building an exciting and enabling environment for these start-ups, with the launch of the "Start-up India" movement.

The "Start-up India Hub" will be a key stakeholder in this vibrant ecosystem and will:

1. Work in a hub and spoke model and collaborate with Central and State governments, Indian and foreign VCs, angel networks, banks, incubators, legal partners, consultants, universities and R&D institutions.
2. Assist start-ups through their lifecycle with specific focus on important aspects like obtaining financing, feasibility testing, business structuring advisory, enhancement of marketing skills, technology commercialization and management evaluation.
3. Organize mentorship programs in collaboration with government organizations, incubation centres, educational institutions and private organizations who aspire to foster innovation.

To all young Indians who have the courage to enter an environment of risk, the Start-up India Hub will be their friend, mentor and guide to hold their hand and walk with them through this journey.

C. Rolling-out of Mobile App and Portal: The objective is to serve as the single platform for start-ups for interacting with Government and regulatory institutions for all business needs and information exchange among various stakeholders. In order to commence operations, start-ups require registration with relevant regulatory authorities. Delays or lack of clarity in registration process may lead to delays in establishment and operations of start-ups, thereby reducing the ability of the business to get bank loans, employ workers and generate incomes. Enabling registration process in an easy and timely manner can reduce this burden significantly.

Besides, start-ups often suffer from the uncertainty regarding the exact regulatory requirements to set up its operations. In order to ensure that such information is readily available, it is intended that a checklist of required licenses covering labour licensing, environmental clearances etc. be made available. Currently, the start-up ecosystem in India also lacks formal platform(s) for start-ups to connect and collaborate with other ecosystem partners.

Towards these efforts, the Government shall introduce a mobile app to provide on-the-go accessibility for:

1. Registering start-ups with relevant agencies of the Government. A simple form shall be made available for the same. The mobile app shall have backend integration with Ministry of Corporate Affairs and Registrar of Firms for seamless information exchange and processing of the registration application.
2. Tracking the status of the registration application and anytime downloading of the registration certificate. A digital version of the final registration certificate shall be made available for downloading through the mobile app.
3. Filing for compliances and obtaining information on various clearances/ approvals/registrations required.
4. Collaborating with various start-up ecosystem partners. The app shall provide a collaborative platform with a national network of stakeholders (including venture funds, incubators, academia, mentors etc.) of the start-up ecosystem to have discussions towards enhancing and bolstering the ecosystem.
5. Applying for various schemes being undertaken under the Start-up India Action Plan.

The app shall be made available from April 1, 2016 on all leading mobile/smart devices' platforms. The start-up portal shall have similar functionalities (being offered through the mobile app) using a richer web-based user interface.

D. Legal Support and Fast-tracking Patent Examination at Lower Costs: The objective is to promote awareness and adoption of IPRs by start-ups and facilitate them in protecting and commercializing the IPRs by providing access to high quality intellectual property services and resources, including fast-track examination of patent applications and rebate in fees. Intellectual property rights (IPRs) are emerging as a strategic business tool for any business organization to enhance industrial competitiveness. Start-ups with limited resources and manpower, can sustain in this highly competitive world only through continuous growth and development oriented innovations; for this, it is equally crucial that they protect their IPRs. The scheme for Start-up Intellectual Property Protection (SIPP) shall facilitate filing of patents, trademarks and designs by innovative start-ups. Various measures being taken in this regard include the following:

1. **Fast-tracking of Start-up Patent Applications:** The valuation of any innovation goes up immensely, once it gets the protective cover of a patent. To this end, the patent application of start-ups shall be fast-tracked for examination and disposal, so that they can realize the value of their IPRs at the earliest possible.
2. **Panel of Facilitators to Assist in Filing of IP Applications:** For effective implementation of the scheme, a panel of "facilitators" shall be empanelled by the

Controller General of Patents, Designs and Trademarks (CGPDTM), who shall also regulate their conduct and functions. Facilitators will be responsible for providing general advisory on different IPRs as also information on protecting and promoting IPRs in other countries. They shall also provide assistance in filing and disposal of the IP applications related to patents, trademarks and designs under relevant Acts, including appearing on behalf of Start-ups at hearings and contesting opposition, if any, by other parties, till final disposal of the IPR application.

3. **Government to Bear Facilitation cost:** Under this scheme, the Central Government shall bear the entire fees of the facilitators for any number of patents, trademarks or designs that a start-up may file, and the start-ups shall bear the cost of only the statutory fees payable.

4. **Rebate on Filing of Application:** Start-ups shall be provided an 80 percent rebate in filing of patents vis-à-vis other companies. This will help them pare costs in the crucial formative years.

The scheme is being launched initially on a pilot basis for 1 year; based on the experience gained, further steps shall be taken.

E. Relaxed Norms of Public Procurement for Start-ups: It is meant to provide an equal platform to start-ups (in the manufacturing sector) vis-à-vis the experienced entrepreneurs/companies in public procurement. Typically, whenever a tender is floated by a Government entity or by a PSU, very often the eligibility condition specifies either "prior experience" or "prior turnover". Such a stipulation prohibits/impedes start-ups from participating in such tenders.

At present, effective April 1, 2015, Central Government, State Government and PSUs have to mandatorily procure at least 20 percent from the micro, small and medium enterprises (MSMEs).

In order to promote start-ups, Government shall exempt start-ups (in the manufacturing sector) from the criteria of "prior experience/turnover" without any relaxation in quality standards or technical parameters. The start-ups will also have to demonstrate requisite capability to execute the project as per the requirements and should have their own manufacturing facility in India.

F. Faster Exit for Start-ups: Given the innovative nature of start-ups, a significant percentage fail to succeed. In the event of a business failure, it is critical to reallocate capital and resources to more productive avenues and accordingly a swift and simple process has been proposed for start-ups to wind-up operations. This will promote entrepreneurs to experiment with new and innovative ideas, without having the fear of facing a complex and long-drawn exit process where their capital remain interminably stuck.

The Insolvency and Bankruptcy Bill, 2015 (IBB), tabled in the Lok Sabha in December 2015 has provisions for the fast track and/or voluntary closure of businesses.

In terms of the IBB, start-ups with simple debt structures or those meeting such criteria as may be specified may be wound up within a period of 90 days from making of an application for winding up on a fast track basis. In such instances, an insolvency professional shall be appointed for the start-up, who shall be in charge of the company (the promoters and management shall no longer run the company) for liquidating its assets and paying its creditors within six months of such appointment. On appointment of the insolvency professional, the liquidator shall be responsible for the swift closure of the business, sale of assets and repayment of creditors in accordance with the distribution waterfall set out in the IBB. This process will respect the concept of limited liability.

24.2.4 Funding Support and Incentives:

A. Providing Funding Support through a Fund of Funds with a Corpus of ₹ 10,000 crore: One of key challenges faced by start-ups in India has been access to finance. Often start-ups, due to lack of collaterals or existing cash flows, fail to justify the loans. Besides, the high risk nature of start-ups wherein a significant percentage fails to take-off, hampers their investment attractiveness.

In order to provide funding support to start-ups, Government will set up a fund with an initial corpus of ₹ 2,500 crore and a total corpus of ₹ 10,000 crore over a period 4 years (i.e. ₹ 2,500 crore per year). The Fund will be in the nature of Fund of Funds, which means that it will not invest directly into start-ups, but shall participate in the capital of SEBI registered Venture Funds.

Key features of the Fund of Funds are highlighted below:

1. The Fund of Funds shall be managed by a Board with private professionals drawn from industry bodies, academia, and successful start-ups.
2. Life Insurance Corporation (LIC) shall be a co-investor in the Fund of Funds.
3. The Fund of Funds shall contribute to a maximum of 50 percent of the stated daughter fund size. In order to be able to receive the contribution, the daughter fund should have already raised the balance 50 percent or more of the stated fund size as the case maybe. The Fund of Funds shall have representation on the governance structure/board of the venture fund based on the contribution made.
4. The Fund shall ensure support to a broad mix of sectors such as manufacturing, agriculture, health, education, etc.

B. Credit Guarantee Fund for Start-ups: In order to overcome traditional Indian stigma associated with failure of start-up enterprises in general and to encourage experimentation among start-up entrepreneurs through disruptive business models, credit guarantee comfort would help flow of venture debt from the formal banking system.

Debt funding to start-ups is also perceived as high risk area and to encourage banks and other lenders to provide venture debts to start-ups, credit guarantee mechanism through National Credit Guarantee Trust Company (NCGTC)/SIDBI is being envisaged with a budgetary Corpus of ₹ 500 crore per year for the next four years.

C. Tax Exemption on Capital Gains: Due to their high risk nature, start-ups are not able to attract investment in their initial stage. It is therefore important that suitable incentives are provided to investors for investing in the start-up ecosystem. With this objective, exemption shall be given to persons who have capital gains during the year, if they have invested such capital gains in the Fund of Funds recognized by the Government. This will augment the funds available to various VCs for investment in start-ups.

In addition, existing capital gain tax exemption for investment in newly formed manufacturing MSMEs by individuals shall be extended to all start-ups. Currently, such an entity needs to purchase "new assets" with the capital gain received to avail such an exemption. Investment in 'computer or computer software' (as used in core business activity) shall also be considered as purchase of 'new assets' in order to promote technology driven start-ups.

D. Tax Exemption to Start-ups for 3 years: Innovation is the essence of every start-up. Young minds kindle new ideas every day to think beyond conventional strategies of the existing corporate world.

During the initial years, budding entrepreneurs struggle to evaluate the feasibility of their business idea. Significant capital investment is made in embracing ever-changing technology, fighting rising competition and navigating through the unique challenges arising from their venture. Also, there are limited alternative sources of finance available to the small and growing entrepreneurs, leading to constrained cash funds.

With a view to stimulate the development of start-ups in India and provide them a competitive platform, it is imperative that the profits of start-up initiatives are exempted from income-tax for a period of 3 years. This fiscal exemption shall facilitate growth of business and meet the working capital requirements during the initial years of operations. The exemption shall be available subject to non-distribution of dividend by the start-up.

E. Tax Exemption on Investments above Fair Market Value: Under The Income Tax Act, 1961, where a start-up (company) receives any consideration for issue of shares which exceeds the fair market value (FMV) of such shares, such excess consideration is taxable in the hands of recipient as income from other sources.

In the context of start-ups, where the idea is at a conceptualization or development stage, it is often difficult to determine the FMV of such shares. In majority of the cases, FMV is also significantly lower than the value at which the capital investment is made. This results into the tax being levied under Section 56(2)(viib) of the Act.

Currently, investment by venture capital funds in start-ups is exempted from operations of this provision. The same shall be extended to investment made by incubators in the start-ups.

24.3 Stand-up India Scheme

Scheduled castes (SCs) and scheduled tribes (STs) entrepreneurs are beginning to show great promise in starting and running successful business enterprises. The Prime Minister had given a call for promoting entrepreneurship among SCs/STs to become job providers rather than job seekers.

In the above context, the Finance Minister in his Budget Speech for the year 2016-17 remarked, "We are celebrating the 125th Birth Anniversary of Dr. B.R. Ambedkar. This must become the Year of Economic Empowerment for SC/ST entrepreneurs. We have extensively interacted with the Dalit India Chamber of Commerce and Industry on building an entrepreneurship ecosystem. It is proposed to constitute a National Scheduled Caste and Scheduled Tribe Hub in the MSME Ministry in partnership with industry associations. This Hub will provide professional support to scheduled caste and scheduled tribe entrepreneurs to fulfil the obligations under the Central Government procurement policy 2012, adopt global best practices and leverage the Stand-Up India initiative". [1]

24.3.1 Main Features of Stand-up India Scheme: The Start-up India and Stand-up India initiatives were announced by Prime Minister Narendra Modi in his address to the nation from the ramparts of Red Fort on August 15, 2015. Thereafter, the Union Cabinet approved the Stand up India Scheme in January 2016. Government of India launched the Stand-up India scheme on April 5, 2016.

The scheme facilitates bank loans between ₹ 10 lakh and ₹ 1 crore to at least one scheduled caste (SC)/scheduled tribe (ST) borrower and at least one woman borrower per bank branch for setting up greenfield enterprises. This enterprise may be in manufacturing, services or the trading sector. The scheme which is being implemented through all scheduled commercial banks is to benefit at least 2.5 lakh borrowers. The scheme is operational and the loan is being extended through scheduled commercial banks across the country.

Stand-up India scheme caters to promoting entrepreneurship amongst women, SCs and STs categories, i.e. those sections of the population facing significant hurdles due to lack of advice/mentorship as well as inadequate and delayed credit. The scheme intends to leverage the institutional credit structure to reach out to these underserved sectors of the population in starting greenfield enterprises. It caters to both ready and trainee borrowers.

Some of the features of this scheme are as under:

1. The Stand up India scheme is anchored by Department of Financial Services (DFS), Ministry of Finance to encourage greenfield enterprises by scheduled castes (SCs)/scheduled tribes (STs) and women entrepreneurs.

2. The scheme is intended to facilitate at least two such projects per bank branch, on an average, one for each category of entrepreneur.

3. The expected date of reaching the target of at least 2.5 lakh approvals is 36 months from the launch of the scheme.

4. The scheme provides for refinance window through Small Industries Development Bank of India (SIDBI) with an initial amount of ₹ 10,000 crore.

5. The scheme provides for creation of a credit guarantee mechanism through the National Credit Guarantee Trustee Company (NCGTC).

6. The scheme provides for handholding support for borrowers both at the pre-loan stage and during operations. This would include increasing their familiarity with factoring services, registration with online platforms and e-market places as well as sessions on best practices and problem solving.

7. The scheme focuses on handholding support for both SCs/STs and women borrowers.

8. The scheme's overall intent is to leverage the institutional credit structure to reach out to these under-served sectors of the population by facilitating bank loans repayable up to 7 years and between ₹ 10 lakh to ₹ 100 lakh for greenfield enterprises in the non-farm sector set up by such SCs, STs and women borrowers.

9. The loan under the scheme would be appropriately secured and backed by a credit guarantee through a credit guarantee scheme for which Department of Financial Services would be the settler and National Credit Guarantee Trustee Company Ltd. (NCGTC) would be the operating agency.

10. Margin money of the composite loan under the scheme would be up to 25 percent. Convergence with state schemes is expected to reduce the actual requirement of margin money for a number of borrowers. Over a period of time, it is proposed that a credit history of the borrower be built-up through credit bureaus.

Upto March 23, 2021, ₹ 25,586 crore had been sanctioned in 1,14,322 accounts—women (93,000), SCs (16,258) and STs (4,970).

Endnote

1. Government of India, Ministry of Finance, *Speech of the Finance Minister, 2016-17*, para 57.

25

Ease of Doing Business in India

In the development strategy adopted after Independence in 1947, India paid little attention to improve business environment. As a consequence, entrepreneurs struggled to do business in the face of restrictive policies and regulations that were designed to choke rather than enable business. Myriad rules and regulations inhibited business growth and held back India from achieving its potential. Economic reforms initiated in 1991 marked a clear change in direction as successive governments started paying attention to difficulties faced by businesses. Although the situation has improved considerably in recent years yet India remains a tough place to do business as per benchmarks of developed countries.

25.1 Why is it Difficult to Do Business in India?

As a large, labour-abundant economy, one would expect India to have a comparative advantage in large-scale, labour-intensive manufacturing. Yet, India has not done well in this sector. Instead, successful sectors in India have been either capital- or skilled labour-intensive and most prominently include auto, auto parts, two wheelers, automobiles, engineering goods, petroleum refining, pharmaceuticals and software. Labour-intensive products such as apparel, footwear, food processing, furniture and various other light manufactures have not flourished in India. Analysts have often pointed to regulatory burden, rigid labour laws and deficient infrastructure as possible reasons for this puzzle.

In India's federal set up, business regulations are enacted and implemented by all three tiers of governance—central, state and municipalities. The huge labyrinth of business regulations across the country has raised the compliance burden to such levels of deterrence that existing businesses are reluctant to expand while starts-ups are few and far between. At the municipality level, construction permits take long time to materialize. Challenges faced in getting utility connections, such as electricity and water at the State Government level, are formidable. Environmental clearances are equally testing at both the State and the Central level and so are the statutes and inspections under labour legislations. In view of regulatory hurdles and red tape, India was traditionally seen as a country not friendly for domestic and foreign investors.

Although licensing controls and discretionary approvals have been greatly reduced yet there are many remnants of the control regime that need drastic overhaul. Quantitative controls, where they exist, should give way to fiscal measures and increased reliance on competitive markets subject to appropriate, transparent and effective regulations. The burden of multiple inspections by government agencies must be removed and tax regimes rationalized.

25.2 World Bank's Doing Business Report

Doing Business Report is a flagship annual publication of the World Bank. It looks at domestic small and medium-sized companies and measures the regulations applying to them through their life cycle. Doing business captures several important dimensions of the regulatory environment as it applies to local firms. The purpose of *Doing Business Report* is to provide objective data for use by governments in designing sound business regulatory policies and to encourage research on the important dimensions of the regulatory environment for firms.

The first *Doing Business Report*, published in 2003, covered 5 indicators and 133 economies. The 2020 Report provided quantitative indicators covering 12 areas of business environment in 190 economies. Only 10 indicators out of 12 were used in the 2020 Report.

The 12 indicators with brief explanations are as under:

1. **Starting a Business:** Procedures, time, cost and paid-in minimum capital to start a limited liability company.
2. **Employing Workers:** The employing workers indicator set measures regulation in the areas of hiring, working hours, and redundancy.
3. **Dealing with Construction Permits:** Procedures, time and cost to complete all formalities to build a warehouse and the quality control and safety mechanisms in the construction permitting system.
4. **Getting Electricity:** Procedures, time and cost to get connected to the electrical grid, the reliability of the electricity supply and the transparency of tariffs.
5. **Registering Property:** Procedures, time and cost to transfer a property and the quality of the land administration system.
6. **Getting Credit**: Movable collateral laws and credit information systems.
7. **Protecting Minority Investors:** Minority shareholders' rights in related-party transactions and in corporate governance.
8. **Paying Taxes**: Payments, time and total tax rate for a firm to comply with all tax regulations as well as post-filing processes.
9. **Trading Across Borders:** Time and cost to export the product of comparative advantage and import auto parts.
10. **Contracting with the Government:** The contracting with the government indicators capture the time and procedures involved in a standardized public procurement for road resurfacing.
11. **Enforcing Contracts:** Time and cost to resolve a commercial dispute and the quality of judicial processes.
12. **Resolving Insolvency**: Time, cost, outcome and recovery rate for a commercial insolvency and the strength of the legal framework for insolvency.

The World Bank—which popularised the exercise of ranking countries according to the ease of doing business—gathers and analyses comprehensive quantitative data to compare business regulation environments across economies and over time, *Doing Business Report*: (a) encourages economies to compete towards more efficient regulations, (b) offers measurable benchmarks for reforms and (c) serves as a resource for academics, journalists, private sector researchers and others interested in the business climate of each economy.

In addition, *Doing Business Report* offers detailed sub-national reports, which exhaustively cover business regulations and reforms in different cities and regions within a country. These reports: (a) provide data on the ease of doing business, (b) rank each location and (c) recommend reforms to improve performance in each of the indicator areas. Selected cities can compare their business regulations with other cities in the economy or region and with the 190 economies ranked by the World Bank.

Doing Business Report relies on four main sources of information: the relevant laws and regulations, Doing Business respondents, the governments of the economies covered and World Bank Group regional staff. Responses are sought from experts, chartered accountants, lawyers and other professionals. [1]

Doing Business data are widely used by governments, researchers, international organizations and think tanks to guide policies, conduct research and develop new indexes.

25.3 Highlights of Doing Business Report, 2020

Doing Business, 2020, was the 17th in a series of annual studies investigating the regulations that enhance business activity and those that constrain it. Doing Business presented quantitative indicators on business regulations and the protection of property rights that can be compared across 190 economies—from Afghanistan to Zimbabwe—and over time.

Regulations affecting 10 areas of the life of a business were covered: starting a business, dealing with construction permits, getting electricity, registering property, getting credit, protecting minority investors, paying taxes, trading across borders, enforcing contracts, and resolving insolvency.

1. Data in Doing Business 2020 were as of May 1, 2019.
2. The indicators were used to analyze economic outcomes and identify what reforms of business regulation had worked, where and why.
3. The study showed that developing economies were catching up with developed economies in ease of doing business.
4. Worldwide, 115 economies made it easier to do business.
5. The economies with the most notable improvement in doing business were Saudi Arabia, Jordan, Togo, Bahrain, Tajikistan, Pakistan, Kuwait, China, India, and Nigeria.
6. Only two African economies rank in the top 50 on the ease of doing business;
7. Research demonstrated a causal relationship between economic freedom and gross domestic product (GDP) growth.

Table 25.1 depicts ease of doing business rankings of top ten countries of the world plus those of China, India and Pakistan.

China improved its ranking from 90 in 2015 to 31 in 2020, a leap of 59 spots. India improved its ranking from 142 in 2015 to 63 in 2020, a jump of 79 spots. Pakistan is way behind both China and India in terms of ease of doing business (Table 25.2).

25.4 Doing Business Ranking of India in Recent Years

As per the World Bank's Doing Business Report, 2015, India ranked 142 among 189 countries in terms of ease of doing business. India ranked even below Pakistan which occupied 128th rank and much below China which occupied 90th rank. With the exception of two parameters (*getting credit* and *protecting minority investors*), India did not feature in the top 100 in the remaining parameters. In *dealing with construction permits* and *enforcing contracts* parameters, India ranked in the bottom 10 economies as per the ranking.

Table 25.1: Ease of Doing Business Rankings, 2020
Top Ten Countries of the World plus China, India and Pakistan

Country	Ease of doing business rank*	Score (out of 100)**
New Zealand	1 (1)	86.8 (86.59)
Singapore	2 (2)	86.2 (85.24)
Hong Kong	3 (4)	85.3 (84.22)
Denmark	4 (3)	85.3 (84.64)
South Korea	5 (5)	84.0 (84.14)
USA	6 (8)	84.0 (82.75)
Georgia	7 (6)	83.7 (83.28)
UK	8 (9)	83.5 (82.65)
Norway	9 (7)	82.6 (82.95)
Sweden	10 (***)	82.0 (***)
China	**31 (46)**	**77.9 (73.64)**
India	**63 (77)**	**71.0 (67.23)**
Pakistan	**108 (136)**	**61.0 (55.31)**

*Figures in parentheses indicate ranking in 2019.
**Figures in parentheses indicate score in 2019.
***Not in top ten in 2019.
Note: A high *ease of doing business* ranking means the regulatory environment is more conducive to the starting and operation of a local firm.
Source: World Bank, *Doing Business*, 2019 and 2020.

Table 25.2: Ease of Doing Business Ranks of China, India and
Pakistan in Recent Years

Country	2015	2017	2018	2019	2020
China	90	78	78	46	31
India	142	130	100	77	63
Pakistan	128	142	147	136	108

Source: World Bank, *Doing Business Report* (various years).

India's overall ranking and the individual rankings in various parameters clearly showed that India was in urgent need of reforms to unlock the huge economic potential of the country. However, the reforms needed to be initiated at various levels across Centre, State and local governments. Bold and necessary reforms in various areas were needed to herald an era of high value investments, infrastructure growth, job creation, skill development and economic prosperity. As a result of reforms at various levels, India has come up well to occupy 63rd rank in the 2020 Report.

India was ranked at 130 in the 2017 Report.

2018 report was the 15th in a series of annual reports investigating the regulations that enhance business activity and those which constrain it. India was ranked at 100th position. India made a very significant jump, improving its rank from 130th in 2017 to 100th in 2018. This improvement of 30 ranks to break into the top 100 reflected Government's reform measures on a wide range of indicators.

India saw an improvement in the following six out of ten indicators:

1. Dealing with construction permits.
2. Getting credit.
3. Protecting minority investors.
4. Paying taxes.
5. Enforcing contracts.
6. Resolving insolvency.

India improved in the above areas on the back of administrative reforms in taxation and passage of the Insolvency and Bankruptcy Code (IBC), 2016. These improvements in rankings were a result of various reform measures undertaken by the Government including structural and deep-seated reforms. It is noteworthy that these were exactly the areas where India had traditionally done very poorly.

This had prompted the Government to initiate a slew of business-friendly institutional reforms including Make-in-India, simplification of tax procedures, bankruptcy laws and so on. All of these led to the big jump in India's ranking.

In the 2019 report, India was placed at 77 in World Bank's Doing Business Report 2019, making it the highest-ranked South Asian country.

In the 2020 report, India moved from 77th to 63rd position. This jump of 14 ranks was primarily driven by significant improvements in 7 out of 10 factors on which ease of doing business was measured. The 2020 Doing Business Report observed as under:

1. **Starting a Business:** India made starting a business easier by abolishing filing fees for the SPICe company incorporation form, electronic memorandum of association, and articles of association. This reform applies to both Delhi and Mumbai.
2. **Dealing with Construction Permits:** India (Delhi) streamlined the process, reduced the time and cost of obtaining construction permits, and improved building quality control by strengthening professional certification requirements. India (Mumbai) streamlined the process of obtaining a building permit and made it faster and less expensive to get a construction permit.
3. **Trading Across Borders**: India made trading across borders easier by enabling post-clearance audits, integrating trade stakeholders in a single electronic platform,

upgrading port infrastructures, and enhancing the electronic submission of documents. This reform applies to both Delhi and Mumbai.

4. **Resolving Insolvency**: India made resolving insolvency easier by promoting reorganization proceedings in practice. India also made resolving insolvency more difficult by not allowing dissenting creditors to receive as much under reorganization as they would receive in liquidation. This reform applies to both Delhi and Mumbai.

Thus, the country has performed remarkably well by jumping 79 places since 2015. The improved ranking has enhanced India's global image as a promising investment destination.

25.5 High, Moderate and Low Rank Indicators of India

Prime Minister Narendra Modi vowed to break into the top 50 by 2020 when he took over in 2014. Though the ranking in 2020 came very close to the target but it failed to achieve it. To improve its position, India should look at areas where it needs to change. Since there are 10 parameters in the rankings, and all parameters have equal weightage, it is easy to pick the ones where India does not fair well.

25.5.1 India's High Rank Indicators: These are as under:

1. Dealing with construction permits.
2. Getting electricity.
3. Getting credit.
4. Protecting minority investors.

25.5.2 India's Moderate Rank Indicators: These are the following:

1. Trading across borders.
2. Resolving insolvency.

25.5.3 India's Low Rank Indicators: These are as under:

1. Starting a business.
2. Registering property.
3. Paying taxes.
4. Enforcing contracts.

India continues to lag on the indicator of enforcing contracts. The importance of an effective, efficient and expeditious contract enforcement regime to economic growth and development cannot be overstated. A clear and certain legislative and executive regime backed by an efficient judiciary that fairly and punctually protects property rights, preserves sanctity of contracts, and enforces the rights and liabilities of parties is a prerequisite for business and commerce.

In connection with contract enforcement, the *Economic Survey, 2017-18* observed, "The Government has taken a number of actions to expedite and improve the contract enforcement regime. For example, the Government: scrapped over 1,000 redundant legislations; rationalized tribunals; amended The Arbitration and Conciliation Act, 2015; passed The Commercial Courts, Commercial Division and Commercial Appellate Division of High Courts Act, 2015; reduced intra-government litigation; and expanded the Lok Adalat Programme to reduce the burden on the judiciary. The government has also advanced a prospective legislative regime to ensure legal consistency, reducing chaos due to unpredictable changes in regulations. The judiciary has simultaneously expanded the seminal National Judicial Data Grid (NJDG) and is close to ensuring that every High Court of the country is digitized". [2]

25.6 Recent Measures to Improve Business Environment in India

The present Central Government led by Prime Minister Narendra Modi has made ease of doing business—especially for small and medium enterprises—a clear area of focus. Likewise, State Governments are also taking business facilitation measures to attract investment and enterprise to their respective States. This competitive federalism—which taps into the competitive instincts of the States—offers a powerful framework within which India can reform its business environment. Therefore, reforms at the state level are as crucial as reforms by the Central Government. This is especially true in the context of numerous clearances/filings which small and medium enterprises must obtain/comply with to start and run businesses.

State Governments have initiated significant procedural and policy reforms to promote foreign investment and encourage domestic private participation in the development of their respective States. While the incentive package varies from State to State depending upon their investment priorities, some common features are discernible. These include development of industrial estates, removing artificial barriers within States, decentralisation of decision-making, time-bound clearance of projects, investment subsidy, and power tariff concessions.

If states are to effectively compete and trigger a virtuous cycle of economic activity, they need to know whether enterprises are successfully taking advantage of the changes they are making to improve the environment. They also need to better understand the relationship of the business environment to growth and job creation.

Recent measures to promote and facilitate business initiatives have included the following:

1. Companies (Amendment) Act, 2015 has been passed to remove requirements of minimum paid-up capital and common seal for companies.
2. An investor facilitation cell has been created under Invest India to guide, assist and handhold investors during the entire life-cycle of the business.
3. The process of applying for environment and forest clearances has been made online through the Ministry of Environment, Forests and Climate Change portals.
4. Registration with the Employees Provident Fund Organization (EPFO) and Employees State Insurance Corporation (ESIC) has been automated and ESIC registration number is being provided on a real-time basis.
5. A unified portal for registration of units for labour identification number (LIN), reporting of inspection, submission of returns and grievance redressal has been launched by the Ministry of Labour and Employment.
6. The Insolvency and Bankruptcy Code (IBC), 2016 was passed in May 2016. Since then, the entire mechanism for the Corporate Insolvency Resolution Process (CIRP) has been put in place. A number of rules and regulations have been notified to create

the institutions and professionals necessary for the process to work. A large number of cases have entered the insolvency process.

7. India introduced a comprehensive Goods and Services Tax (GST) on July 1, 2017. Prior to the introduction of GST, the indirect tax system of India suffered from various disabilities. There was a burden of *tax-on-tax* in the pre-GST system of Central excise duty and the sales tax (later VAT) system of the States. GST is a tax on goods and services with comprehensive and continuous chain of set-off benefits up to the retailer level. It is essentially a tax only on value addition at each stage, and a supplier at each stage is permitted to set-off, through a tax credit mechanism, the GST paid on the purchase of goods and services.

To sum up, in recent years, Central and State Governments have embarked upon a transformational journey of improving India's business climate. A multitude of reforms have been unveiled to improve business environment. Resultantly, India is being viewed by global investors as the economic power house of the future.

Regulatory reforms are but a stepping stone towards greater investment. The private sector in India faces many challenges, and the regulatory burden is just one of them. Infrastructure and finance related challenges can be as severe as regulatory burdens in discouraging investment. More complex reforms may need to be undertaken to bring about a paradigm shift in investment.

To ensure that the private sector is aware of the reforms that have happened, Central and State Governments should undertake communications campaigns to inform businesses about their reforms. Proactive communication can be instrumental not only in generating awareness, but also in increasing usage and uptake of the reformed services. Awareness and increased usage will also allow businesses to test the effectiveness of the measures and incentivize them to report on problems.

Endnotes

1. Similarly, in India, the Department of Industrial Policy and Promotion (DIPP), Ministry of Commerce and Industry, Government of India bases its ranking of states on the responses of State Governments on whether or not they have implemented the DIPP-recommended best practices in different areas. The approach taken by the World Bank largely tells the story from the viewpoint of experts who closely follow the developments in business environment and that by DIPP from the viewpoint of the implementing agencies.

2. Government of India, *Economic Survey, 2017-18*, Volume I, p. 132.

Bibliography

Bibliography

Ahluwalia, I.J. (1985), *Industrial Growth in India: Stagnation in the Mid-Sixties*, Oxford University Press, New Delhi.

Barthwal, R.R. (1992), *Industrial Economics: An Introductory Textbook*, Wiley Eastern Limited, New Delhi.

Barthwal, R.R. (2010), *Industrial Economics*, Wiley Eastern Limited, New Delhi.

Brotherson, W., Eades, K., Harris, R. and Higgins, R. (2014), "Company Valuation in Mergers and Acquisitions: How is Discounted Cash Flow Applied by Leading Practitioners?", *Journal of Applied Finance*, Vol. 24, No. 2.

Brown, C.V. and Jackson, P.M. (1983), *Public Sector Economics*, Martin Robertson and Co. Ltd., Oxford.

Cherunilam, F. (1994), *Industrial Economics: Indian Perspective*, Himalaya Publishing House, Mumbai.

Clarke, Roger (1985), *Industrial Economics*, Oxford: Basil Blackwell.

Desai, B. (1999), *Industrial Economy of India*, Himalaya Publishing House, Mumbai.

Divine, P.J. and Jones, R.M. (1976), *An Introduction to Industrial Economics*, George Allen and Unwin Limited, London.

Genesca, G.E. and Grifell, T.E. (1992), "Profits and Total Factor Productivity: A Comparative Analysis", *The International Journal of Management Science*, Vol. 20, No. 5/6, pp. 553-568.

Government of India, *Economic Survey* (various years).

——*Industrial Policy Statement, 1991.*

Hay, D. and Morris, D.J. (1979), *Industrial Economics: Theory and Evidence*, Oxford University Press, New Delhi.

Kendrick, J.W. (1984), *Improving Company Productivity,* The Johns Hopkins University Press.

Kohli, U. (2012), *Productivity: National vs. Domestic,* Sydney, Australia: EMG Workshop, University of New South Wales, November 21-23, 2012.

Lee, N., Jones, R.M., and Tyson, W.J. (1985), *An Introduction to Industrial Economics*, Allen and Unwin, London.

Nasir, Tyabji (2000), *Industrialisation and Innovation: The Indian Experience*, Sage Publications, New Delhi.

Nayar, Meenakshi (1985), "Effectiveness of Industrial Relations System at the Enterprise Level", *Indian Journal of Industrial Relations*, Vol. 21, No. 1, July.

OECD (2008), *Compendium of Productivity Indicators.*

Reddy, K.S., Nangia, V.K., and Agrawal, R. (2013), "Indian Economic Policy Reforms, Bank Mergers, and Lawful Proposals: The Ex-ante and Ex-post Look-up", *Journal of Policy Modeling,* Vol. 35, No. 4, pp. 601-622.

Reddy, K.S., Nangia, V.K., and Agrawal, R. (2014), "The 2007-2008 Global Financial

Crisis and Cross-border Mergers and Acquisitions: A 26-nation Exploratory Study", *Global Journal of Emerging Market Economies*, Vol. 6, No. 3, pp. 257-281.

Reserve Bank of India, *Report on Currency and Finance* (various years).

Smith, D.M. (1981), *Industrial Location: An Economic and Geographical Analysis*, John Wiley, New York.

Sodhi, J.S. (1994), "Emerging Trends in Industrial Relations and Human Resource Management in Indian Industry", *Indian Journal of Industrial Relations*, Vol. 30, No. 1, July.

United Nations Conference on Trade and Development (2000), *World Investment Report 2000: Cross-border Mergers and Acquisitions and Development* (Overview), New York and Geneva.

World Bank (1994), "Infrastructure for Development", *World Development Report*.

Yamazawa, Ippei (2000), *Developing Economies in the Twenty-First Century: The Challenge of Globalisation*, Institute of Developing Economies, Japan.

Index

Index